THE BOOK OF
# PORTLAND
*Gibraltar of Wessex*

RODNEY LEGG

HALSGROVE

First published in Great Britain in 2006

British Library Cataloguing-in-Publication Data.
A CIP record for this title is available from the British Library.


ISBN 1 84114 497 5
ISBN 978 1 84114 497 9


HALSGROVE

Halsgrove House
Lower Moor Way
Tiverton, Devon EX16 6SS
Tel: 01884 243242
Fax: 01884 243325
email: sales@halsgrove.com
website: www.halsgrove.com

Frontispiece photograph: *Leslie Ward's artwork for his family's greetings card from Portland in 1950.*

Printed and bound in Great Britain by CPI Bath Press, Bath.

# CONTENTS

*Portland's beating the bounds ceremony at the Bound Stone on the Chesil Beach, maintained the ancient tradition in 1960.*

# Introduction

Visually, to quote Thomas Hardy, Portland is the 'Gibraltar of Wessex'. Grandeur is a word that applies, as do austere, industrial and treeless. Grey is its underlying colour, across 3,000 acres of offshore Dorset, in shades that often harmonise sea, ships, sky and stone. The contrast is with the soft greens of the adjacent coast and hinterland. They have always done things differently on Portland, ranging from marriage and inheritance customs to taboo words. It can still feel like another country.

Until 1839, when the first bridge was built, the Isle and Royal Manor stood apart from England both physically and psychologically. Outsiders, however, were the catalyst to charting its destiny. Mainlanders – dubbed 'kimberlins' as an epithet of disapproval by insular islanders – discovered and exploited its stone, which supplanted all others in the land on being chosen by Sir Christopher Wren for rebuilding St Paul's Cathedral after the Great Fire of London.

Even on the map, Portland looks different, as it dangles from the Dorset coast 'like a breast of mutton'. This wonderful Victorian analogy remains apt, as Portland sheep are the island's speciality rare breed. Hardy's description in *The Well-Beloved* is of the island being 'connected to the mainland by a long, thin neck of pebbles.' This is a 'singular peninsula... carved by Time out of single stone... that stretches out like the head of a bird into the English Channel.'

Centuries of isolation – notable only for shipwrecks and lighthouses – were followed by institutionalisation on a scale unprecedented for Dorset. Henry VIII's Portland Castle was overshadowed by the vast Verne Citadel. Four square miles of deep water were enclosed by huge breakwaters and turned into the Royal Navy's principal 'Harbour of Refuge'. Admiralty workers were supplied by another branch of the State, sentenced through the courts to hard labour and housed in a prison on the top of the island at The Grove.

Britain's main fleet mobilised in Portland Harbour for what became the First World War, and lines of battleships secretly slipped from their moorings on 29 July 1914. Winston Churchill, the First Lord of the Admiralty, ordered them to steam that night for the safety of Scapa Flow. Portland features at both the start and finish of the First World War. Edwin Lutyens chose Portland stone for the Cenotaph as the national memorial in Whitehall and it was also selected for the graves of the fallen.

In the next war, despite being mortally wounded, Jack Mantle continued firing his pom-pom gun at the Luftwaffe on 4 July 1940, to posthumously win the Royal Navy's first Victoria Cross from an action in territorial waters. The so-called Slapton Sands disaster, in which 700 Americans were killed by German E-boats, in fact happened off Portland Bill. Then, on D-Day, Portland Harbour was the main springboard for the American landings on Omaha Beach. Nowhere in Dorset has had such an action-packed past.

'On the word of a Portland man,' is the oath of the island. The expression signifies a gritty integrity which grips the island to the present day. For its memorial, as with that to Sir Christopher Wren, look around you, and not just in south Dorset but across London, too. St Paul's Cathedral is as much a monument to Portland as it is to England's premier architect.

Opposite page: *Air reconnaissance of Portland from 10,000 feet, by Mike Sewed in a Royal Navy helicopter, summer 1987. The image clearly shows the effect on the sea of a south-westerly wind.*

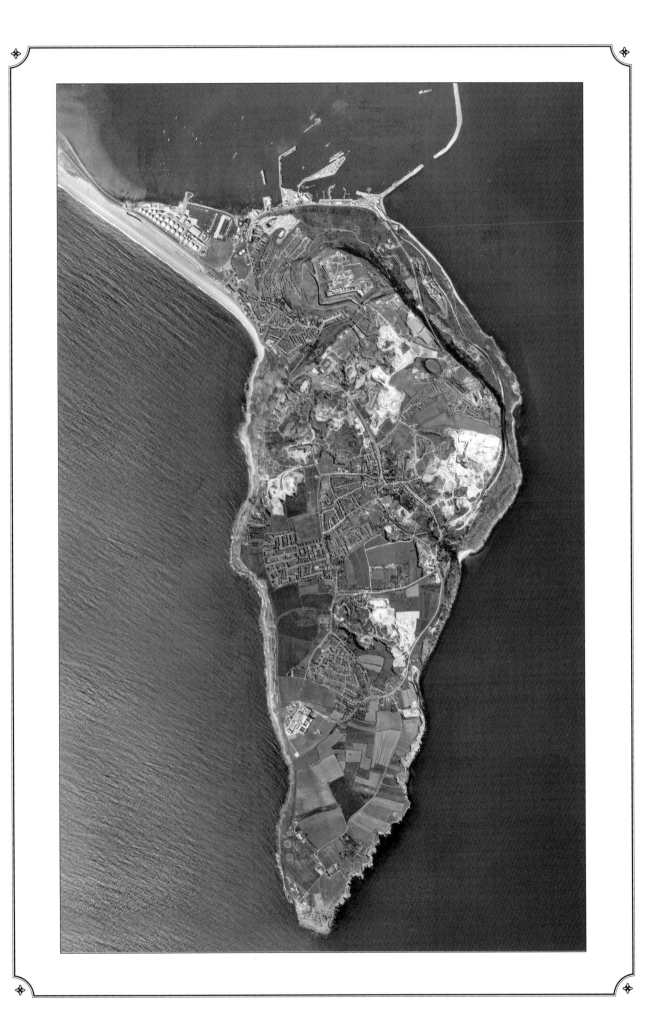

## Maps

*George Herbert Lilley's map of Portland in 1892.*

Below: *John Hutchins's map of Portland in 1710.*

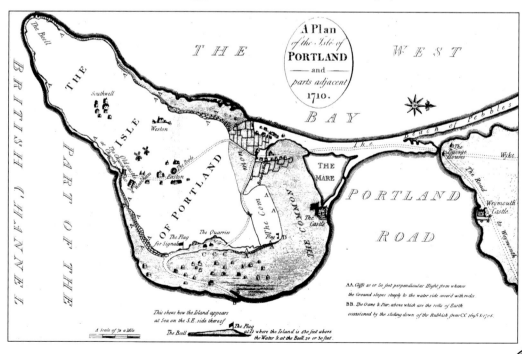

# ❖ CHAPTER 1 ❖

# *Geology*

At the heart of Dorset's Jurassic coast, its white limestone comprising the compressed shells and mud from warm-water seas, Portland, although it has its giant ammonites, lacked the conditions to preserve the sort of dinosaur remains for which Lyme Regis and Charmouth are famous. On the other hand, quarrying on Portland has revealed their landscape, with notable specimens of fossilised tree-trunks and palm-like cycad stumps. Some, from the Victorian collection of the governor of Her Majesty's Convict Prison in The Grove, have since been dispersed, via the offices of the Bath & Portland Stone Co., to Portland Museum and Portland Heights Hotel. Here, overlooking the Chesil Beach, a fossil tree stands beside the car park and links the island to its view, which embraces most of England's only geological World Heritage Site.

John Smeaton, the builder of the second Eddystone Lighthouse, realised that the Chesil Beach was of recent date in geological terms but found it 'very difficult to account for its first formation or its continued existence'. There was, he observed, a similar and still more extensive ridge bounding the Frische Haf, on the coast of Prussia.

The chalk of the rounded downs of the Dorset coast, hundreds of feet above present sea levels, are formed from the compressed remains from warm seas of plankton as they were lifted into the sky as a result of a mid-Tertiary collision of the Earth's tectonic plates when Africa rammed into Europe about 23 million years ago. This impact resulted in the mountain range which reaches from the Pyrenees to the Alps, with lesser folding and faulting as far north as 'lowland' England. Unlike in nearby Purbeck, the Portland limestones were lifted in the direction of the main pressure – pointing due south – though comparisons are complicated by the tendency of the underlying geology of southern England to subside as it gradually moves eastwards. Lesser landform details are the recent icing on this much bigger cake, showing that it is nothing new for the sea to rise and fall as glaciers melt or freeze. Climatic change has always been with us.

The western raised beach at Portland Bill, a 210,000-year-old geological rarity, is visible at its best on the southern seaward side of the Ministry of Defence site, where it is crossed by a security fence. This is a consolidated ancient beach, once at sea level but now forming a platform 30 feet above the highest tides. Marine shells date it to the cold-sea late Pleistocene period. Slightly lower, and more recent

at 125,000-years-old, the eastern raised beach at Portland Bill also shows signs of freeze–thaw sequences.

Its under-layer, about five feet thick, comprises a mixture of pebbles, stones, gravel, shells and sand, which has been fused together into a calcareous mass by constant weathering. This is covered by a wind-deposited stratum of orange sandy silt, about six feet in depth. Above this comes a deep brown solifluction deposit, two feet in thickness, which was formed during the last major glacial period, the Devensian, less than 100,000 years ago.

Dorset's great ridge of 100,000,000 tonnes of shingle extends from West Bay, Bridport, to Chesil Cove, Portland. Formerly it started further west, from Golden Cap at Seatown, but suffered from a combination of erosion and commercial exploitation of aggregates. As it approaches Portland, the Chesil Beach grows both in height and content size. It resulted from 'the late quaternary marine transgression', to quote Eric Bird's *Geology and Scenery of Dorset*, and thereby preserved the inshore beds of the brackish tidal lagoon known as The Fleet from what would have been catastrophic erosion by the open sea.

This wonder of the geological world is a classic tombolo – being a spit joined to land at both ends – eight miles long from Abbotsbury to Chiswell. Landward, sandwiched between the beach and a second shore, is The Fleet. Southwards, at the end of the shingle isthmus, is Portland. Denys Brunsden and Andrew Gourie describe the Chesil Beach in their *Geographical Association Guide to Dorset*:

*It is remarkable for its size, its regular crest line, its beautifully even curve, its lack of lateral edges, its oft-quoted grading of pebble sizes. As a result, it is the most written about of all landforms in Britain.*

The pea gravel at the West Bay end is of the sort you find in fish tanks. By the time the beach reaches Portland, in 18 miles, it is composed of oval pebbles the size of saucers (called 'cobbles'). This phenomenon of the graduation of material into size by the action of water is called elutriation and can be replicated in a laboratory.

The beach rises in stature as it goes, from an almost flat start at Bridport to 25 feet at Abbotsbury, and 35–40 feet at Portland. It came into existence about 80,000 years ago, at a time of low sea levels caused by the Ice Age, during the period known as the Devensian glacial, which 'locked' water into glaciers. The seaboard shingle, compared with its position today, was then a couple of miles into the Channel. Storm surges continue to push it inland, though at a rate that is cartographically immeasurable.

It seems that the fact that Portland is an island must be the clue to its survival, its having acted as a huge natural groyne. The materials were from a raised beach at Portland and the gravels of an extinct river that ran along the course of the present Fleet. These shingles were rendered available to wave-action after the sea had broken through and captured the valley of The Fleet. The movement of the sea proceeded to grade the materials into a sequence of general eastward growth, with the result that local fishermen landing in fog know their location to the nearest mile. The beach mainly comprises flint and chert, with quartzites, a little local limestone and odd stones from deposits as far west as Cornwall. These last stones could only have been acquired when the beach was further out to sea.

Towards Portland the crest-line of the beach can sometimes be moulded by a storm into ridges and gullies, but these are temporary features. Seepage, washing out pebbles from the base, and rolling of shingle from the crest, is causing the Chesil Beach to continue its slow advance towards the mainland – lessening the width of The Fleet lagoon – at a rate of a yard or so per century.

The shorter-term man-made threat has been shingle extraction. Scientific evidence shows that the Chesil Beach is a finite resource; it is not being replenished by some shingle-making process out at sea. Exploitation of the Chesil Beach at the historic rate of 27,000 tonnes a year – maintained until the 1970s – would have seen it all removed in 3,000 years, with the onset of coastal flooding much nearer our time.

This is not an environment for human survival. In the age of sail, countless ships were driven by the south-westerlies, unbroken from the Atlantic, into the angle of the pebble bank and Portland, which became known as Deadman's Bay. Before the use of rocket-fired lines there was no escape from the swirling shingle. Even on a normal day there is an undertow that exhausts swimmers. Above the water, climbing up and down can be painfully difficult.

Some masochists, such as the publisher and wartime Colditz prisoner Roland Gant, have walked nine miles along the beach from Abbotsbury to prove Portland is not quite an island. If you want to do likewise, allow a full eight-hour walking day. It is going to be too wild for comfort if south-westerly winds of force eight and upwards are forecast for sea area Portland, and bitterly slow against a cold easterly in winter. A force 11 hurricane from the south-west, coinciding with a particularly high tide, causes waves to break over the top of the bank, so listen to the shipping forecast on Radio 4 before setting off.

And also respect the rights of the little tern! It is listed in schedule one of the Wildlife and Countryside Act 1981, which makes it an offence 'if any person intentionally disturbs' the bird 'while it is building a nest or is in or near a nest cottoning eggs or young'. Strangways Estates agent E.W.S. Green outlined the restraints when I published details of public access some years ago:

*I would like to take the opportunity of pointing out that the Chesil Beach is closed during the nesting season – 1 May to 31 August. Both Strangways Estates and the Crown Commissioners, the owners of the bank, welcome visitors outside the nesting season but be grateful for your assistance in publicising the controls exercised in this important sea-bird nesting area.*

Two more facts for you. Firstly, 'chesil' is the Anglo-Saxon word for pebble, and secondly the answer to a question. What colour is the Chesil Beach if the pebbles are washed away? Blue is the answer, or dark bluish-grey, to be precise. Not that anyone in the twentieth century has been able to vouch for this from personal experience, but in early Victorian times it was a known fact. The underlying geology is a ridge of shale.

One of the most remarkable Chesil Beach phenomena took place in 1841, when a ground swell 'laid bare for miles' the stratum of Kimmeridge clay beneath the pebbles. A strong north-easterly wind had swept the shingle from the clay and the stones were not pushed back until the next regular sequence of strong south-westerlies. Beachcombing, to recover the losses of ancient wrecks, thrived, and people found antique rings, seals, ingots of base and precious metals, and silver and gold coins. Roman coins were 'most numerous', especially those of the Christian period third-bronze issue of Emperor Constantine. There was a similar harvest in November 1853, when it was estimated that more than 4,000,000 tons of shingle had been swept into the sea during storms.

On land, evidence is still being found of caves and their occupants during the permafrost that covered southern England during the last Ice Age. A pair of spectacular finds were of a Pleistocene mammoth and horse, from Inmosthay Quarry, in 1926. Most of the bones fell apart but a 7-foot tusk from the arctic elephant was removed on behalf of the Natural History Museum in South Kensington.

The fine-grained white oolite that is known as Portland stone can be seen much more readily on the streets of London than in Dorset generally. Typified by the stone currently produced at Independent Quarry, it comprises more than 95 per cent calcium carbonate and is one of the cleanest and most consistent of British building stones. The Portland beds are from 45 to 70 metres deep and were laid down in the warm and shallow Upper Jurassic seas of 175 million years ago.

Because these Portland limestones are porous, the entire plateau is dry, without a single stream, but the rainwater has to go somewhere. Some becomes trapped in the underlying Kimmeridge clay and, as a result, the communities at both ends of the island cluster around their wells. Tophill, however, had no access to underground water.

## Geology

*Fossil tree trunk* (far left) *at Fortuneswell in 1878, which owner Miss D. Parsons subsequently donated to Dorset County Museum.*

*Ammonite and fossil tree* (left) *beside a stone returned from St Paul's Cathedral – for copying replacements – at the offices of Bath & Portland Stone Firms Ltd in 1962.*

*The Chesil Beach, seen from dragon's teeth anti-tank defences at Abbotsbury* (lower right) *links Portland* (background) *with the mainland.*

# Geology

*Pebbles of the geological raised bed on top of the rocks at Portland Bill.*

*Present-day fossil tree, on top of the island beside the Portland Heights Hotel.*

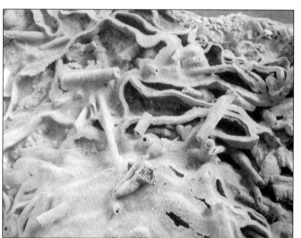

Above, centre: *A catastrophic event at the end of the last Ice Age caused the collapse of a cave near Easton, leaving these stalactites crushed in cave-base calcite.*
Above: *Hannah Sofaer showing the scale of a fern-like cycad tree stump at Independent Quarry, Easton, in 2001.*
Left: *Independent Quarry manager Mark Godden explaining the significance of the geology.*

# ❖ CHAPTER 2 ❖

# *Prehistoric and Roman*

The discovery of a Mesolithic mace head on the Lawnsheds beside Cave Hole, near Portland Bill, by Alex Cotton in 1965, was followed by more than two decades of excavations by Susann Palmer in fields towards the Bird Observatory and the nearby road at Culver Well. Thousands of smaller worked flints were found, with evidence of occupation areas with middens, pavements, shelters and walls dating from 6,000BC to Neolithic transition with the first farmers of 4,500BC. The most important discovery was the chance find of a painted pebble apparently showing a running matchstick figure in the act of throwing a spear. In terms of the quantity of finds and the extent of its occupied areas, Portland is comparable to Hengistbury Head at Bournemouth.

Nowhere in books and reports on Dorset archaeology have I found mention of the impressive megalithic monuments that survived on Portland until the 1870s. A stone circle stood on the central northern plateau of Tophill between Priory Corner and Easton, on ground not yet disturbed by quarrying. From contemporary descriptions it appears to have been similar to the Bronze-Age circles of sarsen stones on the downland between Dorchester and Bridport, and not unlike the numerous prehistoric stone circles of Dartmoor. Clara King Warry, writing in 1920, recalled the Easton circle:

*More than half a century ago, when the ground opposite the Saw Mill Tavern on the western side of Easton Lane was all but intact, several yards inland from the high road was a group of large stones, some few erect, and the remainder lying in disorder on the ground. These possessed an attraction for me impossible to analyse, and I could rarely pass them without lingering a few moments.*

Two or three of these stones were still standing, but most were recumbent. Other stones lay about Portland fields before the quarries were opened. Many must have been uncovered or moved by agricultural operations but some of the arrangements do not sound natural. A second stone circle is said to have stood near the Saw Mill Tavern, on the east side of Easton Lane, 'not far away' from the first.

The most persistent of the stories of Portland's lost megalithic monuments, before the convict prison was built, concern the region around The Grove, which featured in island mythology for supposed Druidic associations. At such an exposed spot on treeless Portland, The Grove, it is claimed, was a setting of ancient stones. 'The Druids put them there,' said one islander. 'I've been told they were heathen temples, and that there were human sacrifices.'

The Grove, having such a suitable Druidic name, was the perfect place for legends, and one of the stones was preserved by the builders of the prison in 1848 but, as it was moved, the archaeological context was destroyed. In fact, the Bronze Age of Stonehenge and its Wessex Culture predated the Celts and their Druid priests by more than 1,000 years. No detailed description survives of what actually stood at The Grove. It seems to have been a circle that was combined with a stone row in a similar arrangement to those found on Dartmoor.

Portland's largest megalith was a tall standing stone which gave its name to Longstone Ope in the bay below. These accounts, though somewhat sketchy, fit in well with what we now know of Bronze-Age monuments, with the coastal connection explaining why an isolated group of such structures should appear on Portland. Field names on old tithe and enclosure maps give further clues to their locations.

Before the building of Verne Citadel on Verne Hill, with Victorian war-works which included the ditch, ramparts and raking batteries of an underground fort, a cairn of stones stood on what was then open common land covered with grass. It stood at what was given as 499 feet above sea level on old maps (formerly the highest point on the island), beside the stone-walled ruins of a small medieval house and garden, and was surrounded by the ramparts of an Iron-Age hill-fort. To the south-west, King Barrow was another lost prehistoric monument, being a cairn on the top of the island between the High Angle Battery and Portland Heights Hotel, which was destroyed by what became King Barrow Quarry.

The hill-fort on Verne Hill comprised the double ditches and ramparts of an Iron-Age hill-fort. These entrenchments may not have been on any great scale, but size would not have been all-important in such a perfect strategic position, where sheer rock-faces and unclimbable slopes could have served as defences on two of the four sides. Facing the level south-eastern approaches, however, the fort certainly had double ramparts. These were recorded by the antiquary John Aubrey in his *Monumenta Britannica*, compiled in the 1680s, though only with a single sentence: 'In the Isle of Portland is a double-worked camp, i.e. British.'

Dorset's historian, John Hutchins, called the work 'Danish' and claimed that a trench from it extended 'to every accessible part of the island', but he was corrected by Dr Herbert Lilley, who wrote in 1883: 'This entrenchment is ancient British and is only seen on Verne Hill.'

Dating from about 400BC to the Roman invasion of AD43, Portland's hill-fort was totally destroyed in 1860, when its commanding position was chosen for the building of Verne Citadel. Thomas Hardy named Portland the 'Isle of Slingers' in his novel *The Well-Beloved*. This was an Iron-Age reference, inspired by the fact that Chesil Beach pebbles were used by prehistoric man as slingstones, caches of such ammunition having being found at Maiden Castle hill-fort near Dorchester.

The living link between prehistoric and modern Portland is its own breed of sheep. In all probability these tiny animals are the direct descendants of those that grazed southern England in Iron-Age and Roman times.

Between 1880 and 1884, during quarrying at King Barrow and Withies Croft to the east of the road from Verne Yeates to Easton, a series of underground beehive-shaped stone chambers were discovered. More than a dozen were recorded on this central plateau at about 400 feet above sea level. All seem to have been circular and corbelled, about nine feet in diameter and eight feet high, with a manhole at the top, 18 inches in diameter and capped with a stone. One pair were touching and another pair were placed one on top of the other. The structures were empty, with no indication of having been intended as graves, and casual finds such as a rotary quern, schist grind-stone, hammer-stones, slingstone pebbles, pieces of Kimmeridge shale, cockle and limpet shells, a spindle-whorl and an unidentified bronze coin indicated an Iron-Age or Roman date.

Their most likely purpose was as grain stores. Carbonised spelt wheat was found in quantity in one, together with smaller amounts of hulled barley and oats. More chambers was found in 1885 and 1886, these being in the vicinity of cist-type stone graves, with potsherds which were again vaguely dated to the Iron Age or Roman period. Another couple of beehive chambers were found at Coombefield Quarry, at about 200 feet above sea level towards the centre of the island at Easton, in 1897/98. This time, however, detailed dating was carried out on sherds of Iron-Age 'B' and 'C' type pottery, from about 200 BC.

Portland's main cluster of Roman antiquities was found in and around the Admiralty Quarries as these were being opened for the building of the Inner Breakwater in 1851. The area, close to the convict prison in The Grove, contained nearly 200 graves, mostly being roughly built stone cists, together with two Portland stone two-piece sarcophagi comprising diagonally tooled rectangular coffins and ridged roof-shaped lids. Associated coins dated from the reign of Caligula (AD37–41) through to Julian (355–363).

The coins of Caligula, and perhaps those of Hadrian (117–38), seem to have been found with military metalwork, including a javelin-head and shield bosses, and indicate that the island may have been garrisoned. More evidence of Roman occupation came from Inmosthay Quarry in 1896 with the discovery of 11 third-century radiate coins. Pottery found in the vicinity of The Grove ranged from Dorset-made coarse-ware cooking pots through to imported de luxe Samian dishes.

Road-making in 1950 at Sweet Hill, 400 yards south-west of Avalanche Road, Southwell, revealed a fine Portland stone sarcophagus, seven feet long and two feet wide with a ridged roof a foot high, and one or two stone cists. The lid had been recently lifted and the contents disturbed, but hobnails remained, and third and fourth-century Roman pottery were found nearby, together with traces of a wooden coffin. More Roman finds came in about 1960 from allotments beside Avalanche Road which were said to be associated with a circular earthwork or embankment. Vindilia has been claimed as the Roman name for Portland, on the flimsiest of evidence, but it would have had one, if only because seamen would have needed a name to avoid confusion with Vectis Insula, which was the Isle of Wight.

*Roman sarcophagus in the grounds of Portland Museum.*

# ❖ CHAPTER 3 ❖

# *Saxon and Norman*

In the time of Ethelwulf as ruler of the West Saxon kingdom, *The Anglo-Saxon Chronicle* entry for 840 records the following incursions by Norse raiders along the coast of Hampshire and Dorset:

*In this year Ealdorman Wulfheard fought at Southampton against the crews of 33 ships, and made a great slaughter there and had the victory; and Wulfheard died that year. And the same year the Ealdorman Aethelhelm with the people of Dorset fought against the Danish army at Portland, and for a long time he put enemy to flight; and [then] the Danes had possession of the battlefield and killed the ealdorman and his companions with him.*

Portland's mention opens the entry for England in *The Anglo-Saxon Chronicle* for 892. This was during the reign of Ethelred – the so-called 'Unready' – in a year of harassment from the east along both great coasts of Christian Europe.

Along the Mediterranean it was a Saracen assault on southern Italy, and in the north-west both Norse raiders and the grim reaper were at large on sea and land:

*In this year three ships of the Vikings arrived in Dorset and ravaged in Portland. That same year London was burnt down. And in the same year the two ealdormen died, Aethelmaer of Hampshire and Edwin of Sussex, and Aethelmaer's body is buried in the New Minster at Winchester and Edwin's in the monastery of Abingdon. That same year two abbesses in Dorset died, Herelufu of Shaftesbury and Wulfwyn of Wareham.*

*The Anglo-Saxon Chronicle* also records natural calamities, notably that which devastated coastal communities 'on Michaelmas eve' in 1014 – on 28 September – when 'the great tide of the sea flooded widely over this country, coming up higher than it had ever done before, and submerging many villages and a countless number of people'.

Earl Godwine, from Bruges, 'hoisted his sail' and those of his fleet during a triangular power struggle which also featured outlawed Earl Swein and Earl Harold from across the water in Ireland. In the process, retreating with remaining loyalists from Sandwich, Godwine ravaged the Isle of Wight until:

*... the people paid them as much as they imposed upon them, and then they went westward until they came to*

*Portland and landed there, and did whatever damage they could.*

Perpetuating a system of Anglo-Saxon land tenure, gavelkind continued to be practised by insular Portlanders long into the second Christian millennium. It provided for equal division of inheritances and enshrined the right of the youngest son to inherit the tenancy to the family homestead. There was an advantage for such distributions and divisions of freeholds and other property interests to be maintained on Portland. Land in itself held little agricultural potential. Quarrying, on the other hand, became the lottery that sustained island life, and everyone wanted their share.

Portland was listed first and foremost among the Dorset holdings of King William the Conqueror in the Domesday survey of 1086. His Saxon predecessor, Edward the Confessor, had held 'the island called Portland ' during his reign. There were five ploughs, operated by three slaves, in the king's in-hand lordship. Other land on the island was tenanted by a villager and 90 smallholders with 23 plough, three cobs (strong, short-legged horses), 14 cattle, 27 pigs and 900 sheep.

Portland has but one land boundary, with the parish of Chickerell, and it was established on a bleak windswept section of Chesil Beach pebbles at the point where the East Fleet lagoon begins to widen, two miles north-west of its Small Mouth entrance. Stones were placed to demarcate the line. Such boundaries, both private and public, used to be taken very seriously, as is shown by this commination against sinners which was included in the sixteenth-century Prayer Book: 'Cursed is he that removeth away the mark of his neighbour's land.'

As much as anywhere in southern England, Portland preserves the threads of its Saxon and medieval land tenure customs and rights, through to the present day. Central to these is the Court Leet. This body enforced the performance of dues and practices of the Royal Manor of Portland, including control of its commonable lands. Though owned by the Crown, these shared assets were managed as a communal resource, being effectively vested in the care of the Court Leet. It meets twice a year and comprises 24 jurymen and a foreman who are elected by the tenants and rights holders of properties on the manor.

One of the traditions which survived from the time of the Domesday Book through to its statutory

## Small Mouth

*Small Mouth and its ferry as they looked for centuries, painted from Wyke Regis, by John Upham in 1807.*

*Nineteenth-century print of pre-harbour shallows beside Portland Roads anchorage* (left) *with Castletown in the background* (centre left) *and Fortuneswell to the south-west* (right).

## Small Mouth

*Ferry Bridge and its public house* (right) *in 1980, seen from the harbour shore.*

*The girders of the second Ferry Bridge, which linked Portland to the mainland from 1896 until the 1980s.*

## Small Mouth

*Portland from the Ferry Bridge, looking through Small Mouth estuary.*

*Small Mouth and Ferry Bridge* (centre left), *in the view a wartime gunner had of Portland, from a pillbox at Wyke Regis in 1998.*

# Small Mouth

*Small Mouth as seen from a Royal Navy helicopter above Portland Harbour, in 1974, with the embankment* (foreground) *being that of the recently removed railway.*

abolition in Victorian times was the use of a reeve staff to record the manorial plots and the payment of rents. This was an annual quit-rent, for generations set at 3d. per acre, collected by an official of the court who was known as the Reeve. He was appointed at the Michaelmas Court in September and would be the tenant who paid the highest amount of recoverable rent but had not held the office before. No person could be appointed twice.

The total amount the Court Leet is obliged to pay to the sovereign is £14.14s.3d. This was never increased with inflation. From it, however, the sum of £1 is retained towards payment for the services of the Gerefa, or Reeve. These token figures remained, figuratively, set in stone, but rents climbed slightly higher than the dues, to the extent of reaching the dizzy height of £15.5s.8d. in 1875.

The historic pole of authority and record issued to the Gerefa was the reeve staff. William White is the earliest known Reeve, from 1700, but the office and its use of poles dates back to Anglo-Saxon times. Most of the surviving old staffs are in deal, but pine

and mahogany were also used, and they vary in length up to 12 feet, with sides that are 1.5 inches square. The symbols used on these to notch up the parish rates, and the signs used for hamlets and payments, date back a millennium:

O = Southwell
x inside O = Southwell
/x/ = Weston
W = Easton
V = Chiswell
whole notch = one shilling
half notch = sixpence
full scratch = penny
half scratch = half-penny
quarter scratch = farthing
dots or cuts = separate individual sums

The Michaelmas Court is traditionally held in Weston and was followed by a seasonal dinner of broccoli and artichokes. This was held at The Lugger, which had the distinction of being the first building on Portland with glass windows. Then the meeting-place moved to the nearby George Inn. Reeve staffs are displayed at Portland Museum in Wakeham, but the most precious, cast in silver from the ducat treasure recovered from a Spanish galleon shipwrecked on the island, 'was presented to Queen Victoria as Lady of the Manor.'

The open medieval strip-fields of Portland Manor survive across the southern tip of the island, around Southwell, and are known as Lawnsheds. Equally ancient is the lerret, Portland's own form of rowing-boat, which is pointed at both ends for quick changes of direction into the fierce breakers off the Chesil Beach. Portlanders were unwilling to put to sea without a pebble with a natural hole – 'a lucky stone' – being attached by twine to the stern-post. The superstition was general among the Chesil communities westwards to Abbotsbury and Burton Bradstock.

For centuries the news of the sighting of an offshore mackerel shoal approaching Chiswell from Lyme Bay, would bring out fishermen in their lerrets. Working in tandem, these would round up shoals of countless thousands of fish with seine-nets, and then draw them inshore to land on the pebbles of Chesil Beach. The whole community abandoned normal work and joined in a co-operative effort.

Poised on precipices above Church Ope Cove, balanced on an outcrop east of Castle Lodges, Rufus Castle is also known as Bow and Arrow Castle. The squat roofless tower, built on the floor plan of an irregular pentagon, dates from the fifteenth century, but the building takes its name from William II – nicknamed King Rufus on account of his red hair – who reigned from 1087 until being shot with an arrow by his 'own men' while hunting in the New Forest on 2 August 1100. William, who was unmarried, was succeeded by his younger brother, Henry I. It is reasonable to assume that there was an earlier castle on the site, built by this William Rufus, as the first of which we have a record was captured by Robert, Earl of Gloucester, in 1142, and held by him against King Stephen on behalf of Empress Maud.

Henry I granted the royal manor of Portland to the monks of Winchester, leaving marks and memories on the landscape such as Priory Corner, and it did not revert to the Crown for three centuries.

It is from this time, at the earliest, that Portland's taboo word must date, as coney or coneys were not mentioned by name, nor is their successor. Rabbits are bunnies or long-ears and their meat is 'underground mutton'. The species was not introduced to Britain until the twelfth century, and was then a valuable commodity for both meat and fur, with islands and promontories being favourite places for farmed colonies to minimise the chance of the animals escaping. It was, and is, regarded as unlucky to come across a rabbit whilst going to work on a boat or in a stone mine. Kingsley Palmer examined the superstition in *Oral Folk Tales of Wessex* in 1973:

*There is a story that the rabbits could cause a great deal of damage with their burrows, thus rendering the quarries unsafe, and had been the cause of more than one fatal accident. While this may be partly true, the rabbit may have had some significance in pagan lore that is still partly remembered.*

The latter suggestion is nonsense, however, as the rabbit was not found in Britain until its introduction by the Normans. Beliefs of ill-omen may have transferred to it from hares, which were sacred to the Celts, but they are ground-living and hardly a hazard to quarrymen.

Stone has entered our story though initially it was taken from the cliffs rather than being dug from the plateau. Portland stone has four obvious virtues to commend it. Firstly, it is white and marble-like. Secondly it cuts beautifully. Thirdly, it forms large blocks. Fourthly it is robust. These attributes make it ideal for grand buildings. Moisture trapped inside the 'living rock' allows its cutting and carving with relative ease. Then the finished surface gradually hardens 'like the crust of a cheese' and withstands long-term exposure by eroding evenly.

# ✦ CHAPTER 4 ✦

# *Stone and Castles*

Exeter Cathedral was consuming considerable quantities of Portland stone in 1303–04. This was principally for the carving of claves, or keys on bosses, and for pinnacles and cappings to battlements in the north tower. More general use included string courses and ashlar façades. Entries in ecclesiastical fabric rolls show that the stone was shipped to Exeter – probably being loaded on the medieval King's Pier on the north-east side of the island – at the cost of 10s. 'For carriage of a barge load of stones from Portland'. That was probably for a consignment of random rubble. An itemised payment of £4.16s.8d. was 'For 18 large stones brought at Portland for bosses together with 80 bases and capitals and their transport by sea.'

The rector at this time, being the first recorded at the Parish Church of St Andrew, which was '50 steps of stone' down from Rufus Castle, was John Golde of Wareham. He was appointed in 1302 and remained on Portland until his death in 1324.

One of the earliest mentions of Portland piracy dates from 1311, when a ship with 'wine laden was boarded and her cables cut, so that she drove ashore on the island where the wine was carried off by her transgressors.'

A vessel sailing up-Channel in 1322:

*... laden with cloth, linen, iron and wax for conveyance to Sutton [Southampton] was attacked by Portlanders and people of Waymere [Weymouth], who took away the goods and scuttled the ship.*

Sometime during the 51-year reign of Edward III, apparently after he assumed the title 'King of France' in January 1340, French or Genoese raiders landed in Church Ope Cove and torched St Andrew's Parish Church, perhaps in frustration that they were unable to capture nearby Rufus Castle. The island's medieval church incorporated Anglo-Saxon or Norman masonry. Ruins remain of the replacement building.

'The King's stone from Portland' was shipped to 'London River' for the building of the Royal Palace of Westminster in 1347. Shipments followed, in 1349 and 1350, for both the Tower of London and nearby London Bridge. Stone from Portland, however, was much less fashionable than its Dorset competition, polished into a marble-like finish, from the Isle of Purbeck.

In 1366 the ship *La Michel*, en route from London on its passage home to Aquitaine, was wrecked on the Chesil Beach, being 'driven ashore by the violence of the sea' and had 'her goods carried off by Dorset malefactors'.

Portland's 'year of the French' was 1416, when an invasion from across the Channel did 'great damage'. Portland's medieval archery ranges, the Butts, were beside the Battery above Red Pools, stretching inland for 400 yards to the road at Harpland, north-east of the later Lower Lighthouse.

Rufus Castle was rebuilt by Richard, Duke of York, between 1432 and 1460. Although it dated from the age of arrows – and is still alternatively known as Bow and Arrow Castle – the rebuilding brought it into the gunpowder age of the later Middle Ages, with a series of five splayed internal embrasures at first-floor level. These are 'under segmental rear arches, with circular gun-ports', to quote the Royal Commission on Historical Monuments. The polygonal walls form the core of what for the past two centuries has been an ivy-clad romantic ruin, enhanced as such by the building of a nineteenth-century bridge and gateway.

The story of the Portland cock dates from the Middle Ages. This was a fabulous maritime creature, recorded a century later by the chronicler Raphael Holinshed (died 1590), and then repeated by county historian John Hutchins:

*In November 1457, in Portland, was seen a cock coming out of the sea having a great crest on its head, a great red beard, and legs half a yard long. He stood on the water and crowed three times, and every time turned about and beckoned with his head, north, south, and west. He was in colour like a pheasant, and when he had crowed he vanished.*

The cock is strongly associated with Romano-Celtic culture, and was the subject of some charming little enamelled brooches and a phallic Hamstone carving from Dorset, not that I am seriously suggesting a lingering folk memory in this case. Such stories could well have started after the figurehead from a ship was seen floating after a wreck, emerging from the waves or disappearing in fog, at a time when most of the island population was drunk on shipwrecked spirits.

Portlanders still talk of the 'mackerel cock', the Manx shearwater, which was given its local name because its appearance often heralded the arrival of a south-westerly gale which might also drive shoals of fish up-Channel. The otherwise inexplicable

## Castles

Portland's earliest medieval buildings are the ruins of St Andrew's Church (foreground) and the keep of Rufus Castle (top) which is also known as Bow and Arrow Castle.

Northern nineteenth-century gateway inset in the late-fifteenth-century surviving walls of Rufus Castle.

Rufus Castle (centre), in a watercolour by John Upham, in about 1820, with the new Pennsylvania Castle behind it (top right).

## Castles

*Rufus Castle* (top right) *and Church Ope Cove* (left) *drawn as an archetypal medieval ruin by J.M.W. Turner for his* Tour round the South Coast of England *in 1849.*

*Rufus Castle and Pennsylvania Castle, both clad in creepers, photographed from the north in 1890.*

wave-top comings and goings of these auspicious seabirds led to a belief that they hid on the island during the day and went to sea to feed at dusk and dawn.

Rebuilt twice since it was gutted by French raiders in the fourteenth-century, the island's Parish Church was dedicated to St Andrew – the saint with the sword – in 1475. The county historian John Hutchins referred to this as a 'dedication', but it may well have been a re-dedication, though some ancient churches have no known dedication, and others were changed during the Middle Ages as new martyrs such as Thomas Becket of Canterbury Cathedral came into vogue. Hutchins described St Andrew's Church as 'a large, ancient, and rude fabric' with 'a bold very low and tiled' chancel 'which seemed to have been built at different times'. The tower, 'plain and moderately high', was detached from the nave, being 'near a yard' away, 'but had no bell in it'.

For the first time since the Norman Conquest, during the reign of King Henry VIII in 1538, European alliances gave rise to fears that England faced a real threat of invasion. Divide and rule, the historic imperative of English diplomacy, was no longer working as rivalry turned to reconciliation between Emperor Charles V of Spain and Francis I, King of France. Henry approved a master-plan for building a string of fortifications around the Welsh and English coasts that faced the continent, from Milford Haven to Hull. The new concept was for pairs of blockhouses, facing each other, to protect with cannon fire the approaches to vulnerable anchorages and strategic ports. In Dorset and Hampshire, the list included new works at Portland Castle and Sandsfoot Castle on either side of the Portland and Weymouth anchorages, Studland Castle and Branksea Castle to defend Poole Harbour, and Hurst Castle and Yarmouth Castle at the mouth of the Solent. Their building would take eight years, and cost a fortune in money and materials, much if not most of both coming from the suppression of the monasteries.

Portland Castle, which is unique as Dorset's only intact medieval castle, is a typical low-level, solid stone fort with walls of a massive thickness to withstand cannon fire in the new age of gunpowder. Built in 1540, it is a typical average blockhouse, though for the ultimate design – triangular because it had to face the sea in three directions – Hurst Castle, near Lymington, followed in 1541 and took three years to complete. It had 24 gun-ports. Thomas Bertie, no stranger to Portland and its stone, appears to have been the master mason. Both Portland Castle and Hurst Castle continued to play an active part in coastal defence during every European conflict from the sixteenth century through to the twentieth century, including the Second World War, despite having become ancient monuments by 1933.

Henry VIII's record-keeper, John Leland, visited Portland in 1540 and found the isle 'very bleak'.

Then, as now, the only trees on the island were in the glen above Church Ope Cove, though historically they were elms, now replaced by salt-tolerant sycamores. 'There be very few or utterly no trees on the site, saving the elms about the church,' Leland wrote. His description of just one street of houses near the church refers to Wakeham (old St Andrew's) rather than Fortuneswell (new St John's). There the major northern hamlet was at Chiswell (alternatively known as Chesil or Chesilton) rather than up the slope around 'Fortunes Well'.

The new Portland Castle, defending the Portland Roads anchorage, gave its name to nearby Castletown. It was strategically placed on the water's edge beside the former Mere – then a marsh – at the isthmus of pebbles joining the island to the mainland. Sandsfoot Castle, its partner on the Weymouth shore, has lost its gun-platform over a crumbling cliff.

Portland Castle was commissioned as the 'Portland Bulwark' and manned by a captain and four gunners, who were supported by two porters. A window there is inscribed in gold letters:

*God save King Henry the Eighth and Prince Edward begotten of Queen Jane Maladi Marie that goodly virgin, and the Lady Elizabeth so towardeth with the King's honourable counsellors.*

Elizabeth I granted the office of Lieutenant of the Isle and Captain of the Castle to Charles Arundel. One of Portland's best late-Tudor houses is Providence Place at No. 51 Weston Road, beside narrow Gypsy Lane which led into the medieval strip fields of Verlands Lawnsheds from Weston Green. Providence Place, a thatched one-and-a-half storeys with huge attic rooms, was originally half of a double pair, with a matching left-hand section which continued at the gable-end.

Portland's Armada-period warning beacon gave its name to the later Beacon Quarry, where Pulpit Rock has been left standing proud as the island's south-western seamark. It dates from about 1875 but the beacon was not only fired in alarm and anger but overlooked an actual engagement between the fleets of Elizabeth of England and Philip II of Spain. Here the beacon chain turned the corner from the last of the Lyme Bay flares – on the great cliff at Thorncombe Beacon and above Abbotsbury – to signal their warning to St Alban's Head in the Purbeck quarry-lands. From there on, via Lytchett Minster and St Catherine's Hill, above Christchurch, the pivotal point on the network was on the Isle of Wight. There the watchers could pass the alert directly inland, to Southampton, Winchester and London, as well as to Portsmouth and the Sussex coast.

The Spanish Armada reached Portland Bill on Tuesday, 23 July 1588. Offshore, it might have been a decisive action, but turned into a lacklustre affair which achieved nothing apart from enabling the

# Castles

Above: *Pennsylvania Castle, named for the Penn family and their American associations, was built in mock-Gothic style in 1800.*

Left: *Beach huts and flights of steps, below Rufus Castle, in a view from the cliffs to the south in 1975.*

## Castles

*Portland Castle, engraved from Portland Roads by John Upham in 1825, also showing the ramparts of an Iron Age hill-fort on the Verne skyline* (top left).

Above: *Ruins of the back parts of Sandsfoot Castle* (left) *at Weymouth facing its contemporary on Portland* (centre) *across Portland Roads in a photograph from the 1890s.*

Right: *Tudor cannon, on a replica carriage, at Portland Castle.*

Spanish to move into mid-Channel and therefore a day's sailing time closer to their Dutch interim destination. In the process they had not lost any more ships. On the other hand, had the Spanish taken advantage of the day's opportunities, it could have yielded positive gains.

Don Hugo de Moncada had wanted to exploit the calm conditions of the Monday night in order to move his oar-powered galleasses into an attack on the English flagship. Galleasses were light but powerfully gunned, highly manoeuvrable craft that were a cross between a galley and a galleon. The English flagship was the *Ark*. Built by Sir Walter Raleigh and sold to Queen Elizabeth I, it carried the flag of her Lieutenant-General and Commander-in-Chief of the Navy, the Lord High Admiral of England, 52-year-old Charles Howard, Baron Howard of Effingham.

Moncada's proposed initiative was blocked by his Commander-in-Chief, Admiral of the Ocean, 38-year-old Alonso Perez de Guzman, 7th Duke of Medina-Sidonia. Despite a complete lack of nautical experience he had been placed in overall charge of the 'Invincible Armada' that was undertaking this 'Enterprise of England'. Sidonia's ethics were those of the nobleman, rooted in medieval chivalry and based on a rule that like could fight only with like. An honourable contest therefore required that only Sidonia himself could engage Howard's *Ark*. Moncada was therefore refused permission to attack.

The initiative passed from the Spanish to the English. In an off-shore north-easterly breeze at 05.00 hours, the rash but gallant Martin Frobisher, 55-year-old veteran of the searches for the Canadian Northwest Passage, took the *Triumph* and five other ships directly towards Portland Bill. They headed eastwards through the tricky inshore waters between the Spanish ships and the rocky tip of the Portland peninsula. Frobisher judged the wind perfectly as the line of warships slipped from Lyme Bay into the outer waters of Weymouth Bay, between Portland Bill and St Alban's Head. No one could have faulted Frobisher's seamanship but his tactics were questionable – he had chosen to box himself into a corner.

Howard therefore hesitated about following. He was too cautious to risk placing the *Ark* between the enemy and the rocks and held back his cluster of vessels. The Armada's rearguard, led by de Leyva Oquendo and Bertendona, closed in to attempt boardings as Sidonia himself swung towards the action. Howard also appeared to be closing for a fight as he led his line of England's biggest ships towards the *San Martin*. They came to within 100–200 yards, according to accounts from both sides. Purser Pedro Calderon's published *Relacion* of the action is that San Martin withstood considerable fire:

*The enemy shot at the Duke at least 500 cannon-balls,*

*some of which struck the hull and others his rigging, carrying away his flagstaff and one of the stays of the mainmast.*

Fifty Spanish sailors were killed. That pounding, however, was not critical. Neither was that which the *San Martin* inflicted upon Howard's ships, even though Calderon claimed she 'fired over 80 shots from one side only and inflicted great damage.' Calderon conceded, however, that the engagement was essentially a failure as, although the Spanish were constantly 'trying to come up with them', they never closed sufficiently with the English vessels. There was also a missing element of luck as the Spaniard's heavier 50-pound cannon balls failed to smash the *Ark*'s rigging.

Meanwhile, off Portland, Frobisher's division of the English fleet was potentially isolated. Sir Francis Drake saw its quandary and was in no mood to take the *Revenge* inshore to join them. Frobisher, on the other hand, was never to be underestimated. He set about showing that the galleasses could not take on standard-sized warships in a straight fight. His great galleon – the *Triumph* was just about the biggest ship out of either England or Spain – smashed its way out of trouble.

Instead of approaching the galleasses at close quarters to try and hole their hulls, Frobisher used his massive fire-power to rake their rowing decks. This immobilised both the oarsmen and their oars. Moncada's captains had to revert to using their sails and thereby lost the manoeuvring advantage of the galleasses. None of the cornered English vessels was lost as the Spaniards took a mauling from an attack which they were now forced to abandon.

By noon the wind had strengthened and backed to the south-west. It carried with it, fast up-Channel, 50 English vessels spearheaded by Drake in the *Revenge*. Howard regained the initiative and made another attack on the *San Martin*. Drake again targeted the rearguard commander, Juan Martinez de Recalde, but he could count on his other vessels for support. The Armada was able to return to its formations and use the south-west wind to take it on past St Alban's Head and towards the Isle of Wight.

It is easier to disentangle these individual actions than to explain the venture as a whole. This first great clash of western empires came about because of a schism in Christendom. Spanish-led southern Europe was taking on Protestant northern Europe. In world terms it was Spain, not England, which was the superpower, for Philip II ruled over the first empire upon which the sun never set. It covered much of the Americas and since 1580 had incorporated Portugal's possessions, there and in West Africa, Ceylon and the East Indies. Its nearer reaches included Sardinia, Milan, Naples and Sicily. The key to the Armada escapade was that beyond the English Channel lay the Spanish Netherlands, a tenuous

## Castles

*Aerial view from the harbour of Portland Castle – Henry VIII's blockhouse at Castletown – which is the only intact medieval fortress in Dorset.*

*William Penn's jewellery cabinet, the special treasure of Pennsylvania Castle, as shown to visitor Edwin Dodshon in 1921.*

union of Holland, Belgium and Luxembourg.

There was no natural animosity between the English and the Spanish, bar competitive strains of trade with the New World. England's hereditary enemy was France. War with the French had been, and would be again, the national game for half the millennium.

The Spanish tussle was a direct result of religious interference in politics and began when an Englishman, Cardinal Allen, persuaded the Pope to excommunicate Elizabeth I in 1570 and declare her to be 'deprived of her pretended title of the kingdom'.

As a plan the Armada contained the seeds of failure by demanding double jeopardy. Firstly, the fleet of 130 ships, with 10,000 sailors and 19,000 soldiers, was not heading for England but making a Channel dash past England to the Netherlands. There it was tasked to link up with the Duke of Parma's army, with its 30,000 infantry and 4,000 cavalry being decanted into barges, and escort them to England.

Here a second problem was being ignored. Such an extended operation relied upon the weather co-operating for far longer than could be predicted and, indeed, required, against the odds, for the winds to permit two totally different fleet movements in opposite directions.

Having taken the weather for granted, the Spanish showed a similar blindness towards the English. Spanish expectations were that religion would outweigh both prudence and patriotism. Madrid believed that once the Armada came into sight, England would be thrown into civil war, with a spontaneous uprising among the Catholic 35 per cent of the population. In the event there is no evidence that a single Catholic family took up arms against their Queen.

At most, as on Portland, the people stood and stared as the show passed by, to the sight and sound of gunpowder. History is full of arguable 'what ifs', but the success of the Spanish Armada is not one of them. Even with centuries of hindsight it remains an untenable scenario. 'Keep then the sea, that is the wall of England,' wrote Richard Hakluyt (1552–1616). Portlanders had been among the first to shout for joy at the news 'The Navy's here'.

*Inside views of Portland Castle, with displays from its past, dominated by the large-as-life appearance of its creator, King Henry VIII.*

## Farming

Above: *One of the earliest Dorset photographs, of Portland haystacks on staddlestones, taken by Major John Warry in 1855.*

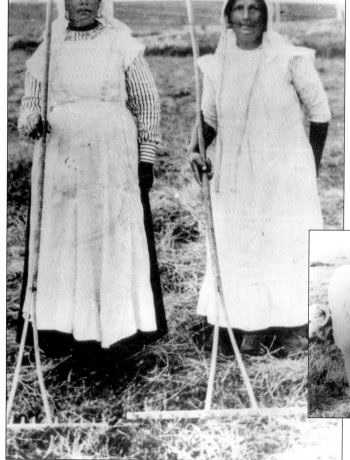

Left: *Portland haymakers Mrs Carter and Mrs Otter on medieval Lawnsheds stripfields in 1914.*

Above: *Portland sheep are the island's own rare breed.*

## Farming

Above: *Angel Mill* (left) *and South Mill, at Easton, were photographed by Rodney Legg in 1967.*

Left: *Angel Mill* (centre skyline), *towering over a graveyard of old cars in a disused quarry beside Park Road.*

# Farming

Left: *Remains of shaft and sail resting across the top of Angel Mill.*

Right: *South Mill, beside Cotton Fields, to the east of Green Hill.*

# ✦ CHAPTER 5 ✦

# *Seventeenth Century*

Between 1603 and 1623, in the reign of King James I, the extraction and use of Portland stone resumed on a capital scale. It was used for 're-edificing' the Banqueting House in Whitehall and for other private and public buildings, including the pre-fire St Paul's Cathedral. The rebuilt Banqueting House, the creation of architect Inigo Jones (1573–1652), achieved lasting distinction as the building where King Charles I was beheaded in 1649.

For this and other projects in Whitehall between 1619 and 1622, a new pier was constructed on Portland's eastern shore at a cost of £700. Other London-bound deliveries during the 1620s were for the Duke of Richmond's house in Holborn, and York House, which was being built for the Duke of Buckingham.

In 1623 the 'old trencher' outside the walls of Portland Castle was 'thrown down' and levelled as being obsolete, though at the same time 'the moat' directly beside the walls was designated for clearance and repair.

Water power was freely available across most of mainland Dorset and windmills were consequently relatively uncommon in the county, though a number of Windmill Hills carry their memory. Such mills are much more plentiful in the drier, eastern parts of England. Significantly, the only two historic Dorset examples to survive are on the dry and windswept top of Portland, on the edge of a quarry at Easton. They date from the early-seventeenth century and were recorded on maps of 1626 and 1710.

Strips of open fields run southward from the mills and cross a shallow valley. The open field in which they stand is called Haylands and was formerly known as Droopfield. The mills were traditionally operated by the Pearce family. The sails last turned corn to grist (pronounced in Portland with a long 'i') at the turn of the twentieth century, when some old people remembered there was a stone-race beside one of the mills. A carriage ran to trim the sails by increasing wind resistance. The foundations of the mills were deep – with mortared pebbles – to keep out rats. The following notes were made by Rodney Legg, on site, in 1967:

*South Mill, on south side of Cotton Fields. Height about 21 feet. Door opening 2ft. 3in. wide by 4ft. high. Internal diameter of the circular tower is 13ft. at ground level. There are four openings in the wall about 5ft. above the floor and these are about 1ft. 6in. wide by a*

*foot high. The wall, at the door, is 2ft. 5in. thick. The lower part of the mill was converted to a pill-box during the Second World War.*

*Angel Mill, east of Green Hill. Height about 18 feet. There are two door openings; the north-west is 2ft. 4in. wide and 5ft. in. high and the south-east is 2ft. 6in. wide by 4ft. high. This mill, unlike the first, is open at the top and has internal widths of 12 feet (east to west) and 11 feet (north to south). The thickness of the wall at one door ranges from 2ft. 2in. to 2ft. 6in. Remains of the sail timbers rest on the top of the mill and the shaft which once worked the mill comes to within four feet of the ground. This central spindle is over two feet thick. Both these buildings are tower-mills and their condition is deteriorating.*

Portland, Maine, originally called Falmouth, was founded by West Country seamen in 1632. That year, back home, a sailing vessel:

*... laden with cloth, linen, iron... for conveyance to Sutton [Southampton], was attacked by Portlanders and the people of Weymere [Weymouth], who took away the goods and scuttled the ship.*

Portland stonecrop was identified as such in the early-seventeenth century by the Royalist botanist Colonel Thomas Johnson (died 1644), who revised and expanded *The Herball... gathered by John Gerarde* in 1633:

*There is a plant called* Sedium Portlandicum, *or Portland Stonecrop, of the English Island called Portland, lying on the South Coast, having goodly branches and a rough rind. The leaves imitate* Laureola *(Laurel). It grows among the Tithymales (spurges;* Euphorbia *species) but is thicker, shorter, more fat and tender. The stalk is of a woody substance like* Laureola.

Johnson goes on to say that Portland stonecrop is also reminiscent of *Crassula*, *Sempervivum* and Tithymales, and concludes somewhat uncertainly that 'it shall be less prejudicial to the truth to account it as a shrub degenerating from both kinds.' Botanists have continued to debate the point, with the favourite for its specific name being *Sedum praeltum* 'Cristatum', though *Sedum reflexum* 'Monstrosum Cristatum' and *Aeonium arboreum* 'Cristatum' also have their supporters.

Peter Mundy, a Cornishman, visited Portland in July 1635 and recorded that stone was being cut for the repair of St Paul's Cathedral, which was the biggest building in Europe:

*I went to the hewers of stone, which was carried for the reparation of St Paul's Church in London. There were about 200 workmen, some hewing out of the cliffs aloft, some squaring, some carrying down, others loading. Some stones that were ready squared and formed, of 9, 10 and 11 tons weight, as they said, some of the them ready squared aloft and sent down in carts made of purpose.*

Mundy also observed that there were 'great oyster shells' in a stone-bed on Portland – in what is the first recorded note on the island's fossils – and showed an accurate insight into how they came to be there:

*On the Cleaves, two or three fathom above full sea-mark, are scores of great oyster shells; not as others growing or sticking fast to the rock, but incorporated into the same. The reason may be that those places in former times were under water, ouse, or mud, where those shellfishes did breed and feed.*

Avice's Cottage, a rare example of island thatch at Wakeham on the corner with Church Ope Road, was built by Bartholomew Mitchell and has a 1640 datestone.

Beached 'in the West Bay of Portland Island', the schooner *Golden Grape*, heading up-Channel from Cadiz to Dover, was laden with more than 2,000 barrels of raisins. 400 jars of oil, 12 butts of 'sherry sacks', 240 pieces of silk and many bags of gold and silver Spanish coins. Seven 'men and boys' drowned and, apart from goods salvaged personally by surviving members of the crew, 'the people of the country' carried away the rest 'by force and violence'.

The interesting detail to this contemporary account of the wreck of the *Golden Grape* is that it gives the location as the 'New Works' in The Narrows at the southern end of the East Fleet, which was an ambitious but failed seventeenth-century scheme aimed at draining the lagoon behind the Chesil Beach. In the four days during which the ship-wreck was breaking-up 'many hundreds of persons worked to get all they could', and 400 of them were later apprehended or examined by the authorities in an attempt at recovering the loot.

Portland Castle was one of the first fortresses to be garrisoned for Parliament on the outbreak of Civil War in 1642, though it changed hands several times. It held ordnance and prisoners and became the intact veteran of several sieges. Lord Carnarvon used two small parties of Royalist cavalry to trick the occupants into thinking half were Parliamentarians. One group (dressed as Cavaliers) chased the other (dressed as Roundheads). The gates were opened to

them on 9 August 1643 and from then on Portland Castle was held for the king.

When Colonel William Ashburnham, the Royalist governor of Weymouth, was ousted from the town on 15 June 1644, he retreated to Portland Castle and reinforced its garrison ahead of the arrival of the Earl of Essex with substantial Parliamentary forces, supported by their fleet. Ashburnham was relieved and replaced in the autumn by fellow Royalists Sir Thomas Wentworth and Sir Bernard Astley, who arrived from Blandford on 12 October 1644. Sir Walter Hastings was then appointed Governor of Portland Castle. The garrison of pikemen and musketeers now had little to do apart from sit and wait as the island was effectively left behind by the war. It continued to be held by the losing Royalist side for the remainder of the conflict. The Parliamentary Army did not receive its surrender until 4 April 1646.

Defeat came with dignity, being negotiated by Captain William Batten, Vice-Admiral and Commissioner-in-Chief of King Charles's Navy, and Colonel Thomas Sidney Gollop, Governor of the Castle and Isle of Portland. They and their officers and soldiers were free to:

*… march away with all their horses, not surmounting the number 15, full arms, match alight, bullet in mouth, colours displayed, drums beating, and bag and baggage to Oxford.*

Future bishop Humphrey Henchman (1592–1675) was rector of Portland until the Civil War between King Charles I and Parliament in 1643. His Parsonage House at Wakeham, together with an extensive library, was destroyed by Parliamentarians and he withdrew to live in the Close at Salisbury, from where he maintained a secret correspondence with Royalist leaders. The building remained a ruin and was never rebuilt.

Henchman's greatest service to the monarchy was to the ill-fated king's son, when he was largely responsible for the successful last leg of Charles II's escape from England after the Battle of Worcester in 1651. Having looked after the defeated monarch at Hele House, near Salisbury, he escorted him:

*… on foot to Clarendon Park Corner where he took horse with Colonel Philip and proceeded to Hambledon, in Hampshire, and thence to Brighthelmstone, where a barque had been provided to carry him to France.*

Henchman's rewards, after the Restoration in 1660, included his appointment as Bishop of Salisbury and then to the see of London as Lord High Almoner in 1663. He died wealthy in 1675 and left £767 towards the rebuilding of St Paul's Cathedral, which had been gutted in the Great Fire of 1666.

The Battle of Portland took place on 18 February

# History

*Unfinished Palladian mansion, known as the Old House, at Maidenwell, seen in 1975 when it was a play-place for the children of Chiswell and Fortuneswell.*

Left: *Court Leet officer and his reeve staff, as used for centuries to record rents and rights across Portland's common grazing lands.*

*Parsonage House at Wakeham, left as a ruin by Parliamentary forces during the Civil War, engraved by Samuel Hooper in 1784.*

1653 in an engagement that continued until dusk. Admiral Robert Blake (1599–1657) had intercepted a Dutch fleet of 73 warships, commanded by Maarten Harpertszoon Tromp (1597–1653), which were escorting a convoy of 300 merchantmen homewards from the Isle of Rhe. They escaped, both from Portland Bill and from a similar fight off the Isle of Wight, but at the cost of five warships sunk, four captured, and the loss of 40 merchantmen. A total of 1,500 Dutchmen were killed or wounded and 700 taken prisoner.

Blake also lost warships off Portland, including the *Sampson*, a fourth-rate man-of-war with 26 cannon. She had been taken as a prize vessel and refitted for Royal Navy service, as was signified by the St George's Jack flying on her bow. *Sampson* was so hopelessly disabled that the crew were taken off and she was left to sink. He commander was Captain Edmund Button.

Though claimed on Blake's behalf as a 'famous victory', it was nearly a disaster for both the English and Dutch fleets. Admiral Blake narrowly escaped with his life. *Triumph*, his flagship, was heavily engaged, with the loss of her captain, Blake being severely wounded. Tromp was also fortunate to survive and escape with the bulk of his fleet.

The turning point came in the afternoon, when Vice-Admiral Sir William Penn arrived with the Blue and White squadrons of the English fleet. It was now an even battle, as Tromp turned towards the Isle of Wight – and home – via a second-stage battle off St Catherine's Point the following morning. Tromp's luck ended later in the year when he was killed by the British, led by Monck, off Texel Island.

The inscription 'C.R. 1660' on a new gateway at Portland Castle confirms that Charles II had regained a royal isle and manor along with the rest of the kingdom that went with it. It is a Restoration stone, both literally and figuratively, that underscores the end of the Republican experiment.

Cliffs south of Rufus Castle, towards Southwell, collapsed into a dramatic slant on either side of Cheyne Weare during a major landslip in 1665.

The *Victory*, described as the 'personal privateer' of Charles Stuart, 3rd Duke of Richmond (1639–72), was washed up on the Chesil Beach at Portland on 1 December 1666. She carried ten cannon.

The demand for Portland stone received a great boost as a result of the Great Fire of London in 1666. It became the material of choice for the rebuilding of St Paul's and many other of the new or replacement city churches. In November 1666 Sir John Denham (1615–69), the King's Surveyor General of Works, came to Dorset to see 'the famous freestone quarries' at Portland and approached to within a mile of them, reaching the Small Mouth ferry passage. There, however, he was 'seized with a distemper of madness' and turned back for London, where he told Charles II that he was the Holy Ghost.

Denham's deputy, the architect Christopher Wren (1632–1723), picked up the pieces on being appointed 'Surveyor-General and Principal Architect for rebuilding the whole City; the Cathedral Church of St Paul; all the Parochial Churches... with other Public Structures'. The 'new model of building in the city' called for stone and slate and outlawed half-timbering and thatch. Wren chose to rebuild London in deliberate denial of its medieval past, shunning pastiche and aiming for a grander design that reflected its older roots, in an orderly classical style inspired by the memory of what had been the capital of the Roman province of Britannia. Thomas Gilbert, a member of the London Masons' Company and the largest purveyor of Portland stone, was required to:

*... make or cause to be made a substantial and good way leading from the quarries to the pier in the said island, as he shall be directed, for the sum of £500, and to keep the same in good and sufficient repair at the rate of £40 per annum.*

Under the command of Captain George Legge, the fifth-rate warship HMS *Pembroke* collided off Portland in 1667. She carried 28 cannon and rammed a larger vessel, HMS *Fairfax*, displacing 745 tons and carrying 52 guns. *Pembroke*, sailing from Tor Bay, came off worse and sank later in the day. Another vessel was lost off Portland Bill in 1667, en route down the Channel from Dover, after having been 'obliged to run on to rocks to avoid a French sloop'. There were a further two Portland shipwrecks, in which unnamed civilian vessels were declared complete losses, in 1667/68.

Unusually, when the *John* was washed up in Chesil Cove on 10 February 1669, her 'crew and cargo were saved'. It may have been of some relevance that the manifest gave her contents as 'cloth', with the added disincentive of the unexciting word 'general'.

Charles II had granted to the Dean and Chapter of St Paul's the right to raise and remove stone from his quarries on Portland for the rebuilding of their cathedral, and placed the project under the control of 42-year-old architect Christopher Wren. The original minute survives of a committee meeting held at St Paul's Cathedral on Friday, 20 January 1698, authorising a contract with Thomas Gilbert for him 'to provide and ship off such Portland stones... as he shall from time to time be directed by the surveyor.' He was also required to:

*... make or cause to be made a substantial and good way leading from the quarries to the pier* [King's Pier] *in the said island, as he shall be directed, for the sum of £500, and to keep the same in good and sufficient repair at the rate of £40 per annum.*

Sir Christopher Wren – he was knighted in 1672 – attended the meeting, together with the Archbishop

## Stone

*Surplus stone for St Paul's Cathedral, still carrying Sir Christopher Wren's markings, found on Portland by William Attwooll.*

*Derrick and stone from Tout Quarry being loaded onto a horse-drawn sledge at Priory Corner, after the arrival of the railway* (centre right) *in 1864.*

## Stone

*The Admiralty Quarries, in the north-east of the island, in about 1902.*

Above: *Quarry section at the centre of the island, near Easton, photographed by Dixon Hewitt in 1932.*

Left: *Nicodemus Knob, left as a sea-mark, in the stark quarrylands above East Weares.*

## Stone

*At Priory Corner in the 1920s Portland stone was still being loaded onto wagons hauled by steam traction engines.*

*Vintage quarry engine found by Rodney Legg on a walk in 1990, north of the road into Southwell from Freshwater Bay.*

of Canterbury, the Bishop of London and the Dean of St Paul's.

Cathedral accounts for St Paul's, from the start of rebuilding in 1674 to Michaelmas in 1700, when the dome had still to be erected, show that a total of 50,322 tons of Portland stone was purchased, for £28,065.16s.8d. Its shipment doubled the cost, adding £28,951.2s.8d to the bill. Most of the stone came from the King's Quarry, which was to remain Crown property – later owned by the Admiralty – in the north-eastern part of the island, above its own wharf, which was King's Pier. The project also consumed nearly 26,000 tons of other stone, from elsewhere in the country, at a cost of almost £40,000, which seems to have included transport costs.

Moving the stone from the quarries to King's Pier and later to Castletown was described in an early account as being 'most distressing to the horses'. A pair of what were called 'ape horses' used to be 'made to drag behind when going downhill' in order to steady the precarious descent. Improved practice, however, was 'to have stones dragged behind in chains and on slides to stop the carriages from going too fast down the precipices'. Horses would continue to suffer in this way, however, until the building of the Merchants' Railway in 1825.

William Attwooll, writing in 1965, recorded that several of Sir Christopher Wren's surplus stones were visible on Portland into living memory. They were incised with his personal wine-glass symbol and identification numbers – such as 'Y 332' – to indicate that he approved their use. Ironically, Sir Christopher admitted that he deliberately over-ordered stone, fearing that the island supply would be exhausted, and persuaded King Charles II to prohibit its export in 1669. This restriction turned it into London's special stone. The king granted to the Dean and Chapter of St Paul's the right to raise and remove stone from Portland for the rebuilding of their cathedral.

There were oranges for Christmas on Portland in 1681. The *Angel Guardian*, heading up-Channel from Lisbon, became a complete wreck in Chesil Cove but '6,000 oranges were saved' on 16 December 1681.

By the time of the Duke of Monmouth's ill-fated Western Rebellion in the summer of 1685, which began in Holland and passed Portland Bill en route to Lyme Regis and the Battle of Sedgemoor, Portland Castle was no longer listed as a military asset. Portlanders kept their distance from the subsequent horrors of the Bloody Assize and had as their reward an event of the year that provided its own celebration. Four hogsheads of French wine were salvaged from the *Peter of St Georges* when she foundered in Chesil Cove on 1 November 1685. A hogshead of wine or spirits comprised 63 gallons (or 54 gallons in the case of ale).

Portland Castle had been relegated to something between redundant and ruinous and remained ungarrisoned when Prince William of Orange came down-Channel and turned into Lyme Bay – though this time making for Brixham in Tor Bay – to take the Stuart throne. The despotic rule of James II collapsed in the Glorious Revolution of 1688. Following the reign of William and Mary, Queen Anne authorised the restoration of Portland Castle, and the island and the military were to be inseparable for the rest of the millennium.

Portland became a personal name in national politics. The earldoms (plural) and dukedom (singular) of Portland have their complex roots in this period. Courtier and politician Richard Weston (1577–1635) was created 1st Earl of Portland by King Charles I in 1633. Sir Edward Herbert (1647–98) was the titular Earl of Portland. Then the leading co-conspirator of William and Mary during the Glorious Revolution, William Bentinck (1649–1709), was created 1st Earl of Portland of the Bentinck line for their coronation in 1690. The Bentincks were further elevated, as Dukes of Portland, in 1716.

Sir John Clayton was granted a patent to erect a lighthouse on the Bill of Portland – still its name on the map – in 1699. The permission was for a tower showing two lights. In the event, he failed to proceed with this consent and the matter was on hold until 1716. The first street at Fortuneswell (then Fortunes Well) dates from this time and ran uphill from Chiswell via Maidenwell. It is now the High Street, which has 20 surviving houses dating from 1700 or thereabouts, plus ten times more in the next two centuries, onwards and upwards to Fortuneswell and the main ascent in Verne Hill Road.

## Stone

*Tramway bridge in the middle of Tout Quarry, with a keystone reading 'J.C. Lano, 1854'.*

*Scree slope of rock and rubble, representing generations of waste from Tout Quarry, strewn down West Weares.*

## Stone

*Independent Quarry, stretching southwards to Easton, reaching its final phase in 2001.*

*Local lads sketching their quarrying heritage, from a stack of London-bound stone, at Independent Quarry in 2001.*

## Stone

*Stoneworker Jonathan Phipps pointing out a modern drystone artwork set among the boulders of disused Tout Quarry.*

Above: *Fabulous birds and beasts appear at every turn in Tout Quarry, where a derelict landscape was transformed into a living artwork during the 1990s.*

Left: *Powerful novice work – completed in just a week – typifies that which has turned Tout Quarry into Portland Sculpture Park.*

# Stone

*Quarrying tools depicted on the millennium monument of welcome at Priory Corner, with the words 'Portland – Home of Portland Stone'.*

*'The Spirit of Portland' is the main sculpture at Priory Corner, with this side representing fishing and the sea.*

*Stone on stone is the principal theme of the Priory Corner carvings.*

# ✤ CHAPTER 6 ✤

# *Eighteenth Century*

Sir Christopher Wren, who had passed through Melcombe Regis and Weymouth many times whilst visiting the Portland quarries, was elected Member of Parliament for the town on 26 November 1701. He was a local man, having been born on the Dorset–Wiltshire border at East Knoyle.

When the *Katherine*, from Brest, was shipwrecked 'near the Isle of Portland' on 27 December 1701 'the country people did not only embezzle and carry away the chestnuts, but beat up and abused the officers in the execution of their duty.'

For Sir Christopher Wren, his greatest moment of achievement came in 1710, as he watched from the ground as his son, Christopher, climbed into a bucket and was hoisted 360 feet into the sky above the dome of St Paul's Cathedral. He placed the topmost piece of Portland stone on the lantern. The main part of the building was finished, though the architect became increasingly vexed about various details which were never completed to his satisfaction.

By 1710 Church Hope Cove had the first two elements of its present name, being recorded as 'Churchhope'. It was named firstly for St Andrew's Parish Church and secondly for the 'Ope', which was the local dialect word for 'an opening in the cliffs down to the water's edge'. That was the view of Dorset parson-poet William Barnes, a student of philology, and the third name – 'Cove' – sums up its other attribute as a small, rounded bay.

The need for warning lights on the Bill of Portland was taken up by Trinity House, which obtained a patent to build a pair of lighthouses there in May 1716. A lease was granted to William Barrett and Francis Browne for £100. Work began within weeks on what was described as 'one of the most treacherous headlands of the Channel coast'.

They were authorised to build and maintain:

*... one or more convenient lighthouses with good and visible lights to be kept continually there in the night season, so as ships might the better come to their ports without peril.*

The Customs Office in London was instructed to collect dues from all ships passing the light at a rate of a half-penny per ton levied on English ships and a penny a ton from foreign vessels that put into English ports. On 29 September 1716 Charles Langridge stoked the coals to illuminate the glazed lanterns of the original Higher or Upper Lighthouse on Portland Bill.

The island suffered another large landslip in 1734. Two clusters of eighteenth-century cottages in The Straits between Easton and Wakeham include a date-stone for 'John Stevens 1734', though this has since been re-set when the building was heightened and provided with a third storey. Part of the house seems to have been occupied by quarryman William Nelson (1711–70) and his wife Jane, who had as their guest the Methodist pioneer Charles Wesley (1707–88) for the night of 4 June 1746. He preached there the following day.

The earliest collection of Portland epitaphs, dating from the seventeenth and eighteenth centuries, lies in St Andrew's churchyard, on a terrace high above Church Ope Cove. Some survive, at least in part, but many have suffered from double jeopardy through exposure and subsidence. The inscriptions, recorded in the *Portland Year Book* for 1905, included the following:

*Abel Flew (buried 25 October 1676). In life I wroath in stone, / Now life is gone and I shall be raised. / By a stone and By such a stone / as giveth living breath and saveth / The Righteous from the Second death.*

*Susannah Comben (died 22 June 1737, aged 31). My friends and lover left behind, I pray for me no longer weep. I am espoused to Christ in Heaven with God, my marriage day to keep.*

*Edward Pearce, Superintendent of His Majesty's Quarries (died 19 June 1745, aged 58). I never did a slander forge, / My neighbour's fame to wound, / Nor hearken to a false report, / By malice whispered round,*

*Abel Pearce (no date; young boy). Grieve not for me nor be sad. / The shorter time I live the fewer sins I had.*

*Andrew Stone (died 30 July 1764). Remember me as thou pass by, / As thou art now, so once was I, / and as I am now, so you must be. / Prepare yourself to follow me.*

An eighteenth-century speciality was Portland sago, or arrowroot, which was a derivative of the lily-like *Arum neglectum* that was marketed from the island. Though similar in basic appearance to common cuckoo pint, the Portland species is much lusher and grows to twice the height. By 1740 it was being widely grown and synthesised on a commercial scale, but even in its raw state it is a potent medicinal

## St Andrew's Church

*Portland burial in the landslipped churchyard above Church Ope.*

*The churchyard of St Andrew's Church.*

## St Andrew's Church

Above: *Gateway on the public path downhill from Woodbine Cottage, beside St Andrew's Church.*

Right: *The ruins of Portland's medieval Parish Church, in a view from the north-east.*

plant, being potentially poisonous, a violent purgative and a common cure for ringworm. The roots, however, are edible when ground into Portland sago, which was used as a common starch and a cosmetic, with claims that it could remove freckles.

The evangelist John Wesley (1703–91) visited Portland's Methodist community in 1746 and lodged with its founder, quarryman William Nelson, at Easton. He preached there at a house in The Straits and may also have delivered his message from the old Parish Church of St Andrew. While in Dorset, 'before preaching at Portland', he wrote a hymn that was inspired by the stone trade:

Come, O thou all-victorious Lord!
Thy power to make known;
Strike with the hammer of Thy word,
And break these hearts of stone.

*De Hoop* (Anglicised as the *Hope*), sailing from Jamaica and bound for her home port of Amsterdam, ran aground on the Chesil Beach in 'tempestuous weather' in the early hours of 16 January 1749. She carried unparalleled riches in the form of a £50,000 cargo of gold-dust, silver coins, specie and plate. Boli Cornelius and his 75 crewmen clung to the snapped mast and then crawled along it to the relative safety of the pebbles as the populace of Portland and Wyke Regis responded to the cry 'Ship ashore' and arrived in their hundreds to take control and plunder the stricken vessel. In terms of her cargo and its values then and now, she was the richest recorded wreck ever to founder on the Dorset coast.

The pillaging began 'as soon as the reflux of the sea had made the ship accessible'. The 'vast concourse' proceeded to push the crew aside and disregarded their faltering, foreign pleas: 'No wreck. The goods ours. Bring it to we and we will pay you for it.' By this they meant salvage money, but the hostile crowd grew to an estimated 4,000, who held the Chesil Beach for several days. They were organised by Augustin Elliott, a Portland labourer, who 'was the muster-master, the treasurer, and divider of the prey amongst the plundering regiment.'

They were brought to a halt by three Justices of the Peace and an armed party, which went on to carry out house-to-house searches and recover £25,000 for agents of the ship's owners. Elliott, put on trial at Dorchester on 15 July 1749, was acquitted by a sympathetic jury after a six-hour hearing. *De Hoop*'s anchor was recovered in 1985 by a West Bay fisherman and now lies beside the Anchor Inn at Seatown, near Chideock.

The *Elizabeth Johanna*, bound from Curaçao to Amsterdam, was 'beaten to pieces' on Portland on 6 July 1752. Her cargo – comprising tobacco, cocoa and coffee – was largely lost, though such impressive wording implies that some reached the islanders or was otherwise recycled into the local economy.

The last recorded burial in St Andrew's churchyard took place in 1752. The church there was already dilapidated, and was described as being in complete disrepair, with the disadvantages that it was both too small and in jeopardy from landslips. Furthermore, a pragmatic parish committee decided, this was now the wrong place for most of the island's population, so it would be:

*... imprudent for the inhabitants to put themselves in the expense of a thorough repair of the same, since it appears to us that such repairs must cost more than half the expense of building a new church.*

In 1753 St Andrew's was abandoned in favour of 'a temporary Tabernacle' in Wakeham, which remained in use for the building of the replacement St George's Church from 1754 to 1766. The Tabernacle was 'built beside Edward Cooper's house, which was apparently the last building at the bottom of Wakeham Street, on the east side'. The communion table and its plate remained in the ruinous St Andrew's – being brought back and forth as required – in order that they should be kept in a consecrated place. This led to an annual payment of a shilling, which appeared in the church accounts.

On 26 July 1754 the *Biscaye* from Bilbao, with a cargo of wool bound for Rouen, became a total loss in Chesil Cove. This stranding was up-staged on 11 December that year by the plight of the *Charming Molly*, three miles to the north-west on the most open and exposed section of Chesil Beach. She had been heading home from Bordeaux to London and 'young jeweller' Anthony Rivers attempted swimming from the dismasted wreck to the beach. He and 'a common sailor' were buried under the pebbles close to where their bodies had been found.

Work began in 1754 on Portland's second Parish Church, that of St George, at the western end of Reforne. This huge baroque building was described by Sir Nicolaus Pevsner as 'the most impressive eighteenth-century church in Dorset'. It is Georgian three times over – in style, dedication and patronage – with George applying as much to the monarch as to the saint, for King George II, as lord of the manor of Portland, not only gave the land on which it stands but also donated £500 towards its construction. This took much longer than expected and it was not consecrated by the Bishop of Bristol until 1766, although the commemorative stone below its grand, classical central dome reads: 'Thomas Gilbert of this island, architect and builder of this church, AD 1758.'

His work may be diminished as 'provincial', but this is the best example of Portland stonework that you will find on the island, though it faces close competition from churches and country houses in the county beyond. Its lines of box pews, to accommodate a congregation of 600, are overlooked by a twin pulpit and galleries that are preserved intact – a

## Cottages

*Avice's Cottage (right) at Wakeham, immortalised by Thomas Hardy and given to the island by Dr Marie Stopes, is now part of Portland Museum.*

*The 'Old Cottages' at Southwell, representing the most southerly thatch in Dorset.*

## Cottages

*The south end of the street at Wakeham, to Avice's Cottage and the wall of Pennsylvania Castle (far right), in a watercolour from the 1950s.*

*Beach-side cottages in Brandy Row at Chiswell, pictured in 1905, had remained semi-derelict since being inundated by the Great Storm of 1824.*

## Cottages

*Cottages in Chiswell Square and Big Ope in the 1930s.*

Above: *Joe Stone, who used Ranters' Lodge (left) and the Dead House (right) as a boat store for two decades after the Second World War.*

Left: *Washing-day glimpse of life in Big Ope.*

perfect time warp. The surrounding churchyard preserves the best collection of Georgian and Victorian memorials and monuments in Dorset.

Behind the survival of the pews, against the odds, lies a story that is uniquely Portland. Gavelkind, the ancient system of shared property inheritance distinguished by equal division amongst heirs, was perpetuated by Portlanders. It had a purpose, in sharing and preserving interests in land that potentially held a high future value if quarrying took place. However, in the case of less lucrative assets – such as seating arrangement in a church – it caused ownerships to become hopelessly subdivided and entangled. The building, by custom, also played a part in bestowing authority on the practice of gavelkind on the island, in that the vendor or person transferring property would sign the documentation at the Parish Church in the presence of two witnesses. Failure through gavelkind to 'modernise' the seating caused this church to be declared redundant and replaced in 1917.

The Royal Navy returned to Portland Roads to re-group after having destroyed Louis XIV's war-works and shipping at Cherbourg on 7 August 1758. From 1678, the Marquis of Vauban, France's great military engineer, had been responsible for the construction of the fortifications, which were the strongest on either side of the Channel.

Tout Quarry dates from about 1755. John Smeaton, builder of the second Eddystone Lighthouse after the first was washed away, visited this and other Portland workings in 1759. Mr Roper, his guide, told Smeaton of a local love custom which ensured compatibility by not allowing marriage until the girl was pregnant. Similarities existed with a current American practice of bundling, but it was known in Dorset as 'Portland custom'.

Smeaton admired the strength and healthy looks of the Portland men and asked Roper where 'they could possible pick up such a set of stout hardy fellows'. He was told they were all island-born, bred into a culture of hard labour, as a result of which they 'are very early in a condition to marry and provide for a family'. Intermarriage was customary, with islanders 'very rarely going to the mainland to seek a wife' and 'it had been the custom of the isle, from time immemorial that they never marry till the woman is pregnant.'

Failure to conceive would end the liaison, with no stigma attached to either party, but pregnancy would cement the relationship and lead to immediate marriage. Mr Roper said that, prior to his arrival on the island, 'there was but one child on record of the parish register, that had been born a bastard, in the compass of 150 years.'

Native islanders were considered married after they had gone through a bizarre communal courting ritual of jumping over a long-handled quarry shovel. Substantiation of this has been claimed from a study

of marriage registers for Portland. These reach back to 1591 but for several years there are no entries for people with the three commonest Portland names – Pearce, Comben and Stone. Instead, there are many names of non-Portlanders, coming from as far away as Yorkshire. These 'kimberlins' do not seem to have married Portland girls, which is not surprising as the island had a tradition of being a self-sufficient community that rarely absorbed outsiders.

The inference is that these couples were runaway marriages. Portland could only be reached by ferry from Wyke Regis, though that may not have been the main attraction. Legally, by custom rather than any written rules, Portland functioned almost as a separate state – in a similar way to the Channel Islands today – and mainland Dorset had little control over its affairs.

A contemporary account of the Passage Boat chain-ferry across Small Mouth to the Chesil Beach describes it as being powered by a horse plodding around a capstan. The operating wire was in a circuit, running through the water and attached to the boat, the return length being on pulleys and in mid-air. A platform or barge could be substituted to carry a carriage and its horses across the waterway

The quarries were busy in 1760 and New Pier was constructed beneath East Weares. It turned out, however, to be a pier too far, in terms of the exposed position and landward inaccessibility. As a result, it soon became known as Folly Pier, and was consigned to history.

One of the notable buildings on the top of the island, No. 28 Easton Street, which stands on the east side beside the entrance to Loves Croft, carries an inscription on the first-floor fireplace, where columns and mouldings proclaim opulence and style: '1760 – William Pearce and Rebecca his wife builded this house.'

The New Inn, on the west side of Easton Street, also dates from the eighteenth century. Palmers Croft lies behind.

On 19 August 1763, a 'tidal wave' hit Portland's fishing hamlet of Chiswell, when the sea suddenly rose by ten feet 'and then retired instantly'. This was what we would now call a tsunami. Its cause was almost certainly an oceanic earthquake rather than the weather and something similar happened in 1979.

The dedication of St George's Church, in 1766, was celebrated in another marker of the new Georgian age, the adjacent George Inn at the west end of Reforne. This has a datestone for 1765, when an original building from about 1700 was extended upwards to give lofty ceilings. A window from the earlier period has chamfered stone mullions. King George II is commemorated on a plaque for giving £500 towards the project, but when it came to the subsequent appeal for repairs – also recorded in stone – his successor, George III, donated precisely nothing ('£00').

## St George's Church

*The south side of St George's Church.*

*The former Parish Church of St George at Reforne from the north.*

## St George's Church

*Gravestone architecture matching that of the church in grand style, in a study by Colin Graham, from 1975.*

Left: *'This church of Portland was founded in the year of the Lord 1754, and consecrated 1766 at the expense of the inhabitants. Benefactors – His late Majesty King George the Second gave £500, George Pitt and Humphrey Sturt Esquires, Knights of the Shire, £40 and to a Charity School per annum £30. John and Richard Tucker, Esquires, £100. King George the Third gave towards the repairs of this church – £0.00.'*

Right: *Cylinder mechanism of the barrel-organ in St George's Church.*

Quarrymen at Portland were complaining in 1766 that they had little work and were finding resistance to a shilling a ton increase in the price of stone. They were faced with inflation in the costs of working tools and in the carting and carriage of the stone that were a third more than historic prices.

William Nelson (1711–70), a pioneer island Methodist, is buried in St George's churchyard. The memorial to its builder, Thomas Gilbert (1706–76), is in the chancel and records that he was 'of this island, Gentleman, Architect and Master Builder of this Church.' His memory is also perpetuated on a plate beside the classical doorway of a prim and neat guest-house at the top end of Fortuneswell.

John Hutchins's county history of 1774 gives both the ancient and modern names for Portland Bill, by describing it as 'Beale Point (vulgarity called the Bill)'.

Wild asparagus was first recorded as a Portland plant in 1782 though, given its bitter taste, it is unlikely to have been a local delicacy. This is a maritime species, which will recur in our story, though unfortunately never in the densities found at Asparagus Ravine at Cadgwith or Asparagus Island in Kynance Cove, to mention two places where it continues to flourish in Cornwall.

Captain John Hope Bowers, commander of the sloop HMS *Orestes*, was commemorated in 1783 by a brass plate in the chancel floor of St George's Church.

The Lower Light at Portland Bill was reconstructed in 1789 with a tower 63 feet high. The historic King's Pier, embarkation point for Portland stone into Weymouth Bay from between Middle Drum and Lower Drum on the north-eastern shore, was destroyed by storm-force seas in February 1792. It was replaced by the New Pier, a short distance to the north, near Lower Drum.

When pastor Robert Carr Brackenbury (1752–1818), from Raithby Hall, Lincolnshire, visited mainland Dorset in 1791, he heard rumours of witchcraft being practised across the water and was told: 'The island of Portland is all darkness; you must go there.'

As a result, he made it his personal mission to counter such 'devilry and disbelief', at 'his sole expense'. In 1792–93 he built a Methodist chapel towards the top end of the main street in Fortuneswell, and made his home in Wakeham. The chapel was replaced in 1903 by the Brackenbury Memorial Church.

In March 1793, a French brigantine was captured as a prize by the frigate HMS *Crescent* whilst carrying salt from Rochelle to Rouen. She was towed into Portland Roads but dragged her anchor and was driven ashore near Portland Castle. The cargo of what became known as 'the salt wreck' was lost, but her crew was saved.

The biggest loss of shipping to take place off Dorset during a single gale took place within sight of Portland Bill on 16 November 1795, with the loss of Christian's Fleet. Rear-Admiral Sir Hugh Cloberry Christian (1747–98) had set sail from Spithead into a wind that became a hurricane. Carrying a substantial number of troops, they were tasked to sail to the West Indies, where Christian was appointed to take over as Commander-in-Chief. Disaster struck within hours, and few of the vessels reached a point in Lyme Bay between Portland and Bridport, and none went any further. Wreckage and bodies were washed up in Deadman's Bay and Chesil Cove. Just one sailor, from the *Golden Grove*, was saved.

Sir Hugh Christian was among the few fortunate ones. His flagship, the 98-gun *Prince George*, limped back into Portsmouth Harbour with her rigging smashed and in a state described as 'unseaworthy almost beyond repair'. The unlucky craft foundered or were driven ashore. A total of 1,000 men were estimated to have drowned and 200 bodies were washed up along the Chesil Beach. History repeated itself with a replacement West Indian convoy, on 29 January 1796, which also had to turn back to Spithead.

At such times, beach-side sheds for boats and nets became makeshift mortuaries, and the former fish-store behind the Cove House Inn at Chesil Cove is still known as the Dead House. Built as a net, pot and tackle store, garage-sized double doors opened directly onto the pebbles. Inside there was a 60-gallon copper, heated by regular fires of driftwood – always appearing on the beach – on which the fishermen's nets were 'barked'. This was a process in which the nets were dyed dark brown to make the sides of the net visible to the fish, in to order to direct the fish into its invisible hose. Boys were employed to sit on the beach and cut 'merks' – pieces of cork – two of which were fitted into each lobster pot.

Beach-top maintenance also included rebinding the bottoms of the pots and replacing their weights before they were dipped in boiling tar and laid out across the pebbles to dry. Each weighed 40 pounds and they tended to take a battering from Portland's sliding shingle and its hostile environmental forces. Some of the pots took hours to refurbish.

After storms and shipwrecks, bodies were dragged into the Dead House and held there, to await their inquest and burial. Thomas Hardy used the local name – Deadman's Bay – rather than its West Bay alternative from the first edition of the Ordnance Survey map in 1811, which can be so easily confused with the West Bay of Bridport Harbour. Hardy was thinking, in particular, of the bodies washed up after the destruction of Sir Hugh Christian's fleet.

The *Rodney*, a sailing barque, returning in ballast from Topsham to Sunderland, ended her final voyage in Chesil Cove on 26 September 1799. The crew were saved but the vessel was smashed to pieces.

## Fishing

*'Fish shout' – the sighting of a shoal was rapidly followed by the readying of boats and nets at Chiswell in the 1890s.*

*Hauling a seine-net ashore in Chesil Cove.*

# Fishing

*Sorting the catch.*

*Mass of mackerel on the Chesil Beach.*

## Fishing

*Edwardian fishermen John Carter* (left) *and Richard Otter posing with a giant pair of skate beside Cove House Inn.*

*The 'harbour fleet' of lerrets and rowing-boats beached along Castletown Strip in 1891.*

# Fishing

*Fishermen relaxing beside a ruined cottage at Chiswell to pose for photographer Wyndham C. Goodden in 1938.*

# Fishing

*Crab and lobster pots at Red Crane – the boat-haul derrick north-east of Portland Bill – in 1973.*

*Boats and a boardwalk, on the pebbles of Chesil Cove, with Lyme Bay as flat as a millpond in 1973.*

# CHAPTER 7

# Nineteenth Century

The mock-Gothic sham fortification of Pennsylvania Castle was designed for John Penn (1760–1834), Governor of Portland from 1805, by eminent architect John Wyatt (1746–1813) in 1800. The story is that King George III was riding across Portland with John Penn when His Majesty stopped at the spot now known as Pennsylvania and said: 'What a delightful spot for a house.' Penn answered: 'Your Majesty, it shall be built.'

This may well be apocryphal, but there is another royal connection as Princess Elizabeth, the King's daughter, carried out its opening ceremony and inscribed her name in a presentation book of etchings. It was named for the other Pennsylvania across the water, which contains Philadelphia – Penn's land of trees – which was founded by his grandfather, William Penn (1644–1718). The Pennsylvania epithet is not inappropriate on the island as it stands amid the sycamores of the island's only wood. John Penn, a poet and dramatist who was also exceedingly rich, had his main home at Stoke Poges Park, Buckinghamshire.

Though unmarried, John Penn founded a 'matrimonial society' named the Outlinian Society, which aimed to improve the life of married persons and held meetings between 1818 and 1825. He translated Virgil and also wrote his own poems, which were published in a private press at Stoke Poges. His greatest success on stage was *The Battle of Eddington*, or *British Liberty*, about King Alfred and the Danes, which was performed at Windsor, the Haymarket, Covent Garden and Sadler's Wells.

The strangest architectural feature of Pennsylvania Castle lies below its grounds, on the rocky ledges above Church Ope, and is known as Penn's Bath. Visually it is a fusion of a Roman plunge-bath and a Dorset sheep-dip, supplied by its own cliffside spring and underground reservoir, though the effect is now lost as the waterworks have failed, and only stones and ferns mark the spot.

While John Penn was building Pennsylvania Castle, Revd John Manning and his family were restoring Portland Castle, though Penn pulled rank on Manning when it came to status of governorship. Captain Charles Manning continued the occupancy of Portland Castle from 1834, and their benign occupancy secured for us what remains, basically, a Tudor fortress. Lead repairs to the roof, which saved the building in 1793, are stamped with the local names Angrish and Samway.

In the evening of the first Saturday of April, 1803, a Royal Navy press-gang of 60 marines and sailors landed on the beach beside Portland Castle, from the frigate HMS *Eagle*, anchored in Portland Roads. They proceeded to raid Chiswell village, taking away Henry Wiggot and Richard Way to join Nelson's fleet. Other young men fled uphill, onto the top of the island, and made their stand at Easton Pond in Easton Square.

Here, the captain of the press-gang grabbed a man by the collar. He resisted, pulling back, and the captain fired his pistol. This was taken as a signal for the marines to fire into the crowd and three Portlanders fell dead. They were quarrymen Richard Flann (aged 42) and Arthur Andrews (47) and middle-aged blacksmith William Lano. The latter had been watching from the door of his smithy. All three were hit in the head. Another man was wounded through the thigh, and a young woman suffered a back injury. 'Wilful murder' was the inquest verdict in what became known as the 'Easton Pond massacre'.

Invasion nerves peaked in 1804, the year before the destruction of the French fleet at Trafalgar, and Portland was central to the series of Royal Navy signal posts along the Dorset coast. Napoleon was said to have set foot in Lulworth Cove in a reconnaissance mission, though the story is probably apocryphal. On Portland there were observation posts at either end of the island, at Portland Bill and on Verne Hill, which was designated Portland North Point. Captain Steward could mobilise a total of 103 volunteer infantrymen on the island. Signal stations to the west were at Abbotsbury Castle hill-fort and Golden Cap. Coverage eastwards was to White Nothe, St Alban's Head, and Round Down at Swanage.

King George III's adoption of Weymouth as his favourite seaside resort saw the frequent arrival of warships, which anchored in Portland Roads. Visits along the coast, such as to Lulworth Cove, were escorted by such vessels as the frigate *Niger*, the 32-gun HMS *Southampton* and the 74-gun HMS *Magnificent*. The King's favourite boats were the royal yacht *Princess Augusta* and its companion ship *Sovereign*, the former being under the command of Captain Foote, who retired as Vice-Admiral Sir Edward James Foote (1767–1833). Displacing about 175 tons, *Princess Augusta* dated back to the reign of George I, and was distinctive both in sight and sound, with three masts, gilt-leather decor and eight brass 4-pound cannon. These were used for the royal salute which, in September 1804, had Revd John Skinner (1772–1839) fearing for his eardrums:

*When the salute was fired I thought they would have deafened me, as the ringing of the brass conveys a more piercing sound than the heavy report of an iron gun. We had a very pleasant sail, running down as far as Lulworth, and tacking backwards and forwards in the [Weymouth] Bay. Whenever we passed under the stern of the Sovereign our shrouds were manned, and the sailors gave three cheers in compliment to the Royal party.*

John Skinner also visited Portland and described in his Journal the barbaric method by which stone was being hauled down from the top of the island:

*... large hewn stones lie scattered in all directions; indeed the quarries worked on the island are prodigious and the mode of conveying the ponderous masses down the steep [slopes] unavoidably arrests the attention of the stranger. The blocks being placed on a strong wooden carriage with solid wheels apportionate to the weight they are to sustain, two horses are harnessed on before and one and sometimes two behind, the latter being supplied with strong breaching, in order to act as drawbacks to the carriage, and prevent it running with too great velocity down the steep.*

*Indeed the sagacity and exertions of these poor animals in this arduous employment is really astonishing; they squat down on their haunches and suffer themselves to be dragged for many yards, struggling with all their strength against the weight that forces them forward. To one unaccustomed to the sight it appears as though their limbs must inevitably be dislocated or their sinews cracked by the violence of their exertions. Indeed one compassionates these poor creatures the rather [more] as all this labour might be obviated by the simple construction of a railroad.*

Captain John Wordsworth (1772–1805), commanding the outward bound East Indiaman *Earl of Abergavenny*, was among more than 250 who drowned on the Shambles sandbank, off Portland Bill, on 5 February 1805. The disaster had been caused by a pilot's error. A contemporary painting shows the doomed vessel approaching a mass of angry white-water as a pale rising sun can be glimpsed in the overcast sky behind her sails.

The commander's brother, the poet William Wordsworth (1770–1850), was deeply distressed by his death and made many references to it in his verses. He attempted a commemorative poem but was too distressed to conclude it, though he did produce elegiac verses referring to his last parting with John, near Grisedale in the Lake District. 'The Happy Warrior', though inspired by the death of Lord Nelson later in the year, incorporates aspects

of John's character. The body was washed up and lies buried at Wyke Regis.

Portland sheep were hardly a rare breed in their heyday. The paucity of the island flora, or rather its general miniaturisation caused by a combination of thin soil and exposed position on rock that juts into the English Channel, no doubt accounts for their smallness and average weight of only 70 pounds. This in turn enhances the taste, yielding a fine-flavoured mutton, but their coats are minimal, with short, soft wool. Their other distinguishing characteristics are yellowish legs and a black nose. The following description of Portland's sheep was compiled by William Stevenson for the Board of Agriculture in 1811:

*... there is a very small breed of sheep, and there are a few of the same kind at Studland, but they are not kept generally. They are said by many to be the true Dorsetshire breed... The Dorset sheep, when compared with such as are at present kept in the Isle of Portland, will weigh three times as much; and it is not to be wondered at, as it may be observed that there are 3,000 sheep kept on the island, which contains but 2,800 acres of which 800 are waste, 400 arable, 250 meadow, which leaves 1,350 acres of pasture for the sheep, and this is very poor land, rented at 7 shillings an acre.*

The East Indiaman *Alexander*, homeward bound from Bombay to London during the war with Nepal, was driven into Chesil Cove on 27 March 1815. She was dashed to pieces towards the top of the beach in appalling conditions, with the death of some 140 men, women and children. Only seven lascars were saved. For Portlanders, however, there was a bonanza of riches to be salvaged from amongst the wreckage.

Apsley House, in the middle of the north side of Reforne, dates from the year of the Battle of Waterloo and carries an 1815 datestone.

Portlanders were reluctant to renounce their traditional belief in witchcraft, and many of them split from the Wesleyan church over the issue in 1816. The minister, Revd Francis Derry, found himself with only half a congregation after an acrimonious confrontation with those who were said to have 'The Power' – 50 were said to have admitted such beliefs: 'Almost every event was supposed to be regulated by this evil power, and every misfortune was attributed to the witch.'

The result was the making of an alternative chapel, in a loft-conversion beside the seaward end of Clements Lane at Chiswell, by witch-believing Methodists. This became known as the Conjurers' Lodge. It was founded by Charles Whittle and Robert Hinde, who led the exodus from Derry's flock. Their 'Prayer Room', immediately north-east of Cove House Inn, was reached by an external staircase. Below there was a store for fishing tackle.

The building, which is still known as Ranters' Lodge, remained in breakaway hands for a decade, until 1826.

Much Portland stone went to the capital from 1823 for the elegant designs by Sir Robert Smirke (1781–1867) to re-home the British Museum at Russell Square in Bloomsbury. The number and scale of its treasures had grown greatly since the founding collection of 69,352 artefacts and 50,000 books was acquired from the daughters of Sir Hans Sloane and housed by the Government in Montagu House. Its new Ionic façade, completed in 1847, was described as 'the most imposing in the metropolis'. Sir Robert also chose Portland stone for the east wing of Somerset House, from 1828 to 1831, and for a number of other key buildings.

The West Indiaman *Colville*, homeward bound for London, foundered in West Bay – known locally as Deadman's Bay – on 23 November 1824. The bodies of the captain, 16 of his crew and one passenger, were buried in St George's churchyard, Reforne. On 3 December 1824 the grave was reopened to receive a further washed-up body, identified as that of Hugh, Baron Fraser, Civil Commissioner of Demerara which, with Essequibo and Berbice, formed the colony of British Guiana in South America. A contemporary account, with pragmatic attention to detail, records that eight casks of wine and 15 bales of cotton were salvaged.

Waves washed over the Chesil Beach that morning, in what became known as the Great Gale, flooding coastal communities from Fleet to Chiswell. In sight of the sinking *Colville*, the 95-ton government sloop *Ebenezer* was also in difficulties, but with a very different outcome. Carrying stores for the Royal Navy en route from Plymouth to Portsmouth, she made history by becoming the first ship to sail up the English Channel without passing Portland Bill. Instead, as the sea abated, she was left high and dry on the top of the Chesil Beach. The *Ebenezer* was later tugged down from the pebbles eastwards, and successfully refloated in the calm waters of Portland Roads anchorage. Here she was pronounced to be 'safely seaworthy' and resumed her voyage.

On land, too, there were casualties, such as that reported on this concise inscription on a stone in St George's churchyard at Reforne:

*Sacred to the memory of William Hansford, aged 54 years, who was killed on the 23 November 1824 by the sea overflowing the village of Chissel [Chiswell]. His leg was broken in attempting to make his escape. Afterwards the house fell on him.*

On the Wyke Regis side of Small Mouth the Passage House was washed away and the 'old ferryman' was drowned as he went to the aid of a dragoon who was attempting to wade across the Fleet.

The patent for Portland cement was applied for by Leeds bricklayer Joseph Aspdin in 1824. It had nothing to do with Portland, apart from being the man-made substitute for its stone, of similar colour and texture. The supposed connection has since led to unlikely statements in print, such as that by G.E. Mingay in *Rural Life in Victorian England* in 1977, telling us that 'Cement works appeared around Portland Bill'.

Joseph Aspdin mixed chalk with clay and heated the mixture to produce a product which, when used with sand, was found to be impervious. It was reckoned to be as durable as that used by the Romans, though it would seem to have been a little premature for making that sort of claim. Roman cement has a decayed spongy look but is in fact rock-hard. Its magic ingredient, considered in Border folklore to be human blood, is in fact calcium silicate hydrate.

The first Portland railway was authorised as 'the Portland Railway'. Unlike Fayle's Tramway in the Purbeck clayfield and the majority of private lines already in existence, the Portland line 'cannot be effected without the Aid and Authority of Parliament' and duly received George IV's royal assent on 10 June 1825: 'An Act for making and maintaining a Railway or Tramroad in the Parish of Saint George, in the Island of Portland, in the County of Dorset.'

Its promoters were named as:

*Gabriel Tucker Steward, Richard Augustus Tucker Steward, Rebecca Steward, John Charles Tucker Steward, the Revd. Edward Tucker Steward, Robert Browne, Thomas Richardson the younger, George Frampton, Richard Lane, Hall Wake, Thomas Daniel, Benjamin Hatchard, Thomas Dike, Bartholomew Comben, George Buckham and John Searle.*

Known on the island as Freeman's Incline, this Portland railway opened in 1826 as a mineral line with a gauge of 4 feet 6 inches. Partly operated by horses, and otherwise a double track cable-worked incline with full loads descending, hauling empty wagons back to the top, it ran from the quarries at the 'Priory Lands' on Priory Corner 'to the Stone Pier near Portland Castle' at Castletown. In later years it was called the Merchants' Railway to distinguish it from the convict-operated Breakwater Railway incline on the eastern side of the island.

Freeman's Incline, which snakes around the west side of Verne Citadel, ceased operation in 1940 and is now trackless.

Well preserved parallel arms climb to the top of the island at the east end of Verne Yeates, and then skirt its northern slope together on a gradual climb to Priory Corner, above the Chesil Beach. An offshoot, from the approach to the Verne Citadel end, continues into the top of the island at King Barrow Field. Many stone sleepers survive in situ below a remarkable series of tall, neatly-arched Victorian stone bridges. But for being on Portland, with industrial relics all around, this would be a national treasure.

On 6 September 1826, His Majesty's Post Office packet vessel *Francis Freeling*, under sail from Weymouth to the Channel Islands, was allegedly 'run down by a Swedish brig' off Portland Bill. She had left Weymouth Harbour at dawn, 06.09 hours, 'and disappeared with all hands' in sight of the island after the rogue vessel crossed her path. The crew of ten and their six passengers were all drowned. A total of 30 children were 'left fatherless'.

Gold coins are still occasionally washed up on the Chesil Beach, but no longer in the quantity recorded by the *Dorset County Chronicle* of 18 December 1828:

*Many of the Portland Islanders, as well as others, will be enabled to enjoy the Christmas holidays most merrily, from the effects of the late high tide and heavy gales of wind, which have been the means of throwing up on the beach bars of gold and silver. Guineas, crowns and dollars are picked up in abundance, which have been buried in the sea for many years from the various shipwrecks; the old adage 'It is a bad wind that blows no-one good' is thus amply verified.*

History was made on 23 February 1830 with the first steamship wreck to take place on the Dorset coast. The *Meteor*, returning in fog to Weymouth from Guernsey, beached in Church Hope Cove. The time was eight o'clock in the evening and 'a large crowd descended on the wreck'. They proceeded to loot the vessel and torpedoed the islanders' reputation after an emergency in which the crew, in contrast, emerged with distinction:

*The profits arising from the sale of the wreck were divided amongst the crew for their exertions in saving the passengers' lives. Most of the luggage was carried off or destroyed by the islanders. If general attention can be called to this national disgrace, a great public good may be effected.*

Poverty and protest peaked in England in 1830 as revolution rippled across Europe. General unrest, in the form of arson attacks and rural riots fomented under the pseudonym Captain Swing, spread along the South Coast from Kent and reached Portland in December 1830. A letter delivered to John Penn, Governor of Portland and owner of Pennsylvania Castle, demanded £50. Penn published the threat and doubled the money, with the offer of £100 for the arrest of those who had written the following:

*One of us will step into the Castle and leave this letter; what we want you will not miss, you have so much more than you ever can want, much more than you deserve, while others have not the necessaries of life.*

Incomes on Portland were supplemented by involvement in the smuggling industry. More than 150 Portlanders passed through the courts, via Dorchester Prison, in the early-nineteenth century, as the great smuggling era was brought to a close by Customs and Excise officers and a gradual liberalisation in tariffs and trade. Many were caught by the Revenue cutter *Eagle*, which notched up a run of successes in the 1820s. Most of those who were caught – one presumes that many more were not – were sentenced to six months, though then, as now, this seldom represented the actual punishment, and usually only one month would be served.

Invariably, this being Portland, they tended to be quarrymen or fishermen (or both) and many of the island's traditional family names occur time and again in the *Calendar of Prisoners in Dorchester Gaol* – such as Attwooll, Bennett, Byatt, Champ, Charles, Comben, Flann, Miller, Pearce, Stone, Sweet, Way and White. Women also played their full part, in both the offences and the time-serving, the concealment of spirits and other smuggled goods being their main contribution.

Hiding holes were constructed by quarrymen beside the rocky beach at the foot of steep cliffs around Church Ope, a spot as remote and inaccessible as any on the island, despite the presence of Governor Penn in the big house above. Temporary stone hideouts were concealed in working quarries and an underground bunker was discovered in Will Stone's garden.

In August 1835, Sir George Crewe arrived from Calke Abbey, Derbyshire, with helpers and staff, and was ferried across to Portland from Wyke Regis. He had come to seek out farmer William Lowman at Easton. He wished to purchase some sheep in order to improve the blood-line of Crewe's own flock of Portland origin, which had been established by his grandfather in their great expanse of soft parkland near Burton upon Trent. The party hired a carriage and travelled uphill, through the stone quarries towards Portland Bill, as Sir George recorded in his journal:

*Farmer Lowman, as they call him, was in his harvest field. A boy volunteered to run and fetch him, and meanwhile I walked with the shepherd to look at some of the flock – nearest at hand – for having upwards of 1,000 sheep, some of them are scattered far and wide. I found them certainly not so good as my own – longer in the leg and not so well shaped.*

*The mystery of their small shape is soon unravelled, when you see them among their native hills. They are nothing more than the Dorset horned sheep starved into a smaller compass. I wonder how they live at all, at this time, as there is apparently nothing for them to eat. The shepherd told me, that for the last six weeks they had really been living upon thistles, and how indeed unless some rain came, there would be nothing to eat, of the said thistles. I never saw such a crop in my life and never until now knew it could be made useful.*

William Lowman, 'a very plain spoken civil young man' whose grandfather had apparently supplied Sir George's grandfather in 1770, agreed that he had plenty of sheep to sell. Crewe and Lowman settled upon the transfer of a flock comprising two score 'nots or polled' (hornless ewes) at £1 each, a score of three-year-old wethers (castrated rams) at £1.5s.0d. each, and a ram for £1.3s.0d. Having arranged for their delivery, the party then descended to Chiswell for lunch at the New Hotel, where the table was spread with German Westphalian ham from London, fried eggs, 'and some of the most delicious lobsters, I have tasted for many years'. The drink was bottled stout.

On leaving, the sun was hot and the cheerful travellers offered a ride to 'a decent looking islander plodding along the lane' – of the female gender – between Chiswell and the ferry passage. Having returned to the mainland, to 'the Royal but dirty Hotel' in Weymouth, they ordered the horses for their own carriage, paid the bill, and departed for Dorchester, which they reached at about seven o'clock.

As well as Portland mutton, wheatear were an island delicacy, these 'small delicious' migratory birds being netted or trapped as they made landfall 'in great numbers' each spring.

The schooner *Margaret & Ann*, carrying slate from Cardigan, was a total loss on the Chesil Beach, on 25 October 1835:

*We had on Sunday last one of the most violent gales witnessed for a long time, which blew a perfect hurricane. It is feared several vessels suffered on the coast and West Bay. The schooner* Margaret & Ann *has gone to pieces and all lost. The beach west of Portland is strewn with wreck, articles of furniture, broken pieces, parcels of goods, etc. Five bodies have been recorded on the north side, and doubtless more will wash in.*

The biggest public building in Reforne, dating from 1836, is St George's National School opposite the Police Station. This was established by the Anglican educational movement – full title the National Society for Promoting the Education of the Poor in the Principles of the Established Church – for 400 children. Average attendance soon reached 300–350 pupils. The field behind it is known as Jordan.

The schooner *Columbine*, outward bound from Gravesend to the Gambia in West Africa, was washed ashore on the Chesil Beach, opposite the Ferrybridge, on 28 November 1838. All hands were lost, together with the six 'respectable passengers'. They included newly-wed Methodist missionaries Reverend and Mrs Edward Peard, who were due to take over a mission station on Cape St Mary. Robert Fraser, a young officer, held a commission with the Royal African Corps. This became known as the 'Missionary shipwreck'.

The *Arethusa*, in sail from London to Antigua, in the West Indies, was a victim of the same gale, its remains being found washed up on the Chesil Beach, opposite the ruin of old Fleet Church, on 29 November 1838. The dead included John Gill, nephew of Revd Dacre Clemetson, chaplain at Dorchester Prison, whose family were shocked at the news given that the vessel had sailed three weeks earlier and should easily have cleared the Channel coast in that time. There was also a further cause for distress, as the *Dorset County Chronicle* reported:

*We grieve to add that whilst lying on the beach, the corpse was plundered of a valuable gold watch, priced beyond intrinsic value due to family associations. The vessel has since gone to pieces.*

In 1839 the building of the first Ferry Bridge, a timber viaduct, caused redundancy for the Passage Boat ferry. The boat was drawn from side to side by handholds on a suspended rope. Portland was now a peninsula rather than an island. Despite the building of the bridge, for the next three generations, people at Wyke Regis continued to refer to Small Mouth and its Ferry Bridge as 'down Passage'. As with the ferry, there was a toll for crossing the bridge, but this was of little consequence to most Portlanders, who seldom left the island.

Urban Portland was provided with an Anglican place of worship, in sight of the beach-side approach road, with the building in 1839–40 of St John's Church in the Street at Fortuneswell. The architect was either Edward Mondey or Charles Wallis. Constructed in Portland stone and dominated by a three-stage tower, it had sittings for 616 and cost £2,115, plus £200 for the ground. The chancel was added later, in 1876, by George Crickmay.

The schooner *Commodore*, from Exeter, was washed ashore into the Chesil Beach on 19 January 1839 and provided rich pickings, though there were arrests and a conviction. Samuel Wingate, from Portland, was fined £20 for stealing part of the cargo, with 'six months hard labour in the House of Correction' in default of payment.

Shipwrecks in 1840 included the *Saggitario* from Antwerp on the Chesil Beach and the schooner *Delight*, en route from Poole to Liverpool, on Portland Bill. The dates were 24 January and 26 October, respectively, but nothing was recorded locally of the loss of life or cargo, apart from the fact that both vessels were declared to be total losses.

The *John*, a schooner in sail from South Shields to Jersey with a cargo of coal, failed to round Portland Bill and was a total loss there on 13 January 1843. At the time a Royal Commission was looking into the effectiveness of a breakwater at Plymouth, and considered that something similar for Portland was also feasible, particularly as all the material needed for its construction could come from the island itself. The project was estimated at £500,000 which in retrospect sounds modest. Someone then thought of providing a prison complex on Portland for the specific purpose of providing cheap labour. The convicts could be bribed with the prospect of remission in their sentences and earlier release on a 'ticket of leave'.

The country's prison accommodation was already overcrowded as crime figures escalated as a result of famine and economic depression during what had become the 'Hungry Forties'. Establishments such as Pentonville were hopelessly inadequate and 2,000 men languished in hulks. Officially, the service could absorb a total of 10,900 prisoners, though only with the inclusion of facilities at Gibraltar and Bermuda as British prisons. In theory, the system demanded that men sentenced to be transported had to serve the penal part of their sentence in a British prison, before being shipped overseas. Such transportation was being resisted in the colonies, which were beginning to assert their own rights, for example by insisting that they would only accept convicts who had been given a trade. Here Portland was to have a place in the process.

The Home Secretary, Sir George Grey, complained that the Irish regarded a sentence of transportation as 'a reward rather than a punishment'. He believed in the principles of solitary confinement and regarded religious and work-related educational instruction as essential prerequisites to exile. The inclusion of Portland was seen as a practical way to provide a fresh start with a fair rate of pay – proceeds to be banked on behalf of the convicts – so that they would arrive in the colonies with an applied work ethic backed by independent means. The system was not unduly harsh, according to Sir Charles Fitz Roy, who argued that there were 'few English criminals' who would not delight in receiving 'a free passage to the gold-fields via Hobart town'. *The Times* agreed that transportation was 'a frightful inducement to the commission of crime'.

The pyramid-shaped Trinity House navigation beacon on Portland Bill was erected in 1844 to replace a 30-foot high column. While a lighthouse is used to warn distant shipping, a beacon is a danger signal for inshore craft, and to be used further out as a means of obtaining a precise fix on a chart. A beacon, in this sense, is any structure, including a landmark such as a church steeple, that can be used by navigators to check their position. Despite the 'TH 1844' date on the Portland Bill beacon, it was listed in 1861 as 'date of erection unknown' in a report on British lights and beacons. G.S. Thomson, the information officer at Trinity House in 1973, confirmed to me that it was their stone. The reason for establishing this was that I received a letter at what is now *Dorset Life* magazine asking why there was 'a memorial to Thomas Hardy at the age of four'.

It was a topical issue in 1844 because Portland had long been synonymous with shipwrecks, and to avoid that fate captains in mid-Channel headed for sanctuary in Portland Roads anchorage, between Castletown and Wyke Regis, as the prevailing wind gathered strength. Merchant seaman Joseph Red confirmed this practice for the Commission of Enquiry into Harbours of Refuge in 1844:

*I have seen some 60 to 70 vessels riding out a storm in Portland Roads, with more joining them by the hour. My experience of 30 years has borne this out in each south-westerly gale.*

Portland Harbour, promoted as a project to provide the principal Harbour of Refuge in the English Channel for the new ironclad warships of Queen Victoria's imperial-style Royal Navy, was conceived and planned by civil engineer James Meadows Rendel (1799–1856). He also built Holyhead Harbour on Anglesey – Portland's equivalent in the Irish Sea – and docks at Birkenhead and Grimsby. Work was to start at Portland in 1847.

A total of £20,000 was awarded by Lord John Russell's government to Portlanders in 1847 in what was initially considered to be a 'generous settlement' package in compensation for harbour-related loss of rights across extensive areas of common land at Verne and along the East Weares. Local enthusiasm waned, however, when Inclosure Commissioners, who regulated such allocations, insisted that only £10,000 could be shared among individuals and that the rest would have to be spent on projects to benefit the community. Of this, they decided, £4,000 had to pay for outstanding costs of the 1839-built Ferry Bridge. This was regarded as an unfair imposition because the government itself, in bringing men and materials to Portland for building the prison and the harbour breakwater, would have incurred sufficient tolls to more than cover all the debts.

Portland Prison, later known as the Borstal – after the location of the first such establishment in Kent and latterly the Young Offenders Institution – stands in The Grove on eastern cliffs overlooking Folly Pier. The gatehouse and boundary wall were built in 1848 beside Grove Road with temporary timber structures behind, though huge permanent buildings soon followed. This was the top-security gaol for category-one felons of the day. The convicts, after creating the quarrying infrastructure and its network of mineral railways, were to extract roughly hewn boulders and then produce 'knobblers', which were building blocks dressed on five sides of the cube with only one face remaining rough.

This was the third institution of a national prison service, after Millbank in 1821 and in 1842 Pentonville which, together with Portland, was the creation of Colonel Sir Joshua Jebb (1793–1863). As

## Convicts

*Jabez Balfour, Portland's convict MP, reflecting in later life.*

*Pandemonium on the scaffold at Exeter Prison as John Babbacombe Lee became 'the man they couldn't hang' and was sent to Portland instead.*

Left: *The Chief Warder of Portland Prison pictured in his office at The Grove on 7 September 1908.*

*'Portland Convict Establishment', showing the frontages facing Grove Road, in a lithograph engraved from the south-west in about 1870.*

## Convicts

*The Convict Prison in The Grove, seen from the rear, in the final stage of construction.*

*Prison warder's funeral cortège passing through Easton in 1888.*

*Detail of the bell cote and Byzantine-style roundel in the west wall of St Peter's Church, which the prisoners built for their own use to designs by Major-General Sir Edmund Du Cane of the Royal Engineers.*

*The completion in 1875 of St Peter's Church – known as the 'Convict Church' – in The Grove.*

# Convicts

*The 'Forger's Slate', a tribute to chief warder William Thomas Brooks, who died in 1881.*

## Convicts

*Sentries and Edwardian ladies beside the entrance to Portland Prison in Grove Road in 1902.*

*Convicts wearing clothes stamped with the broad arrow of government ownership as they set off from Portland Prison for work in the quarries.*

# Convicts

*Guards, convicts, worked stone and railway wagons on Portland in the 1890s.*

*Team of six convicts removing rubble in wheelbarrows* (centre) *with worked stone in trucks on the railway above* (top left).

## Convicts

*Convicts under guard as they use pickaxes and hammers in the 1890s, with war-works towards the Verne forming the skyline.*

*The vast expanse of Admiralty Quarries, looking south towards the Convict Prison (top left), during the building of breakwaters in the 1890s.*

*Armed guards and working convicts pose for the camera beneath a derrick in a corner of the Admiralty Quarries in 1890.*

Surveyor-General of Convict Prisons he envisaged these special prisons as an extension of the government's public works programme. The effort and co-operation of inmates were to be rewarded by cost-free inducements, principally the remission of up to half the length of sentences, 'for hard work and good behaviour'. He claimed the alternative of transportation 'had ceased to deter', in that of the 90,000 convicts and ex-convicts who had been transported to Australia and were still alive, an estimated 80,000 had chosen to stay there.

The first convicts reached Portland Roads on 21 November 1848, by boat in the Driver from Portsmouth, and landed at Castletown. An escort was provided by police from Weymouth and Coastguards Pepperell, Cleall, Ball and Fisher, who marched the men up Verne Hill and across King Barrow to the prison at The Grove. The reason for choosing Portland as the beneficiary of judicial sentences of hard labour was to provide manpower for quarrying stone for the building of breakwaters to enclose four miles of deep water in Portland Harbour. Other camps accommodated the 'free workmen' – navvies and artisans – who carried out most of labouring work on the breakwater itself under the auspices of the Royal Engineers.

The historical painter Charles West Cope (1811–90) stayed at Pennsylvania Castle in 1848, the year he was accepted as a full member of the Royal Academy, and painted Rufus Castle and St Andrew's Church as romantic ruins. Portland and its approaches would never look the same again. Holes were pegged out for digging on an unprecedented scale and the first stone of the Inner Breakwater was laid by Prince Albert, Queen Victoria's consort, on 25 July 1849. As one Portland man recalled in the 1920s, schoolchildren were given the day off to witness events:

*There was a large elevated platform full of grandees, and of course no place for me, but I wanted to see the so-called 'laying' and so, eluding official eyes, I got under the platform, which was many feet above my head, and sat on the rocks quite alone. When the stone was released it fell through the platform aperture, and in my full view – only a few yards off – plunged into the sea, giving me a parting douche from its slash as it disappeared beneath the water. I consider I had the most perfect view of any present of the sinking of the foundation stone.*

The inscribed stone incorporated a waterproof hollow which contained contemporary coins and newspapers. It was soon covered 'by several loads of rough rocks'. Progress might have looked slow from the mainland, but the statistics soon became impressive, with a record quantity of 25,000 tons of stone being dumped into the sea in a single week. Railway lines made this possible, as they stretched out with

the arms of the breakwater into the sea, and a permanent cage of timber scaffolding went ahead of each completed section, from which trucks with trapdoors could drop their loads vertically into the water. This method had been devised by engineer James Meadows Rendel for the deep-water Millbay Pier at Plymouth. The speed with which he could block off the force of the waves was unprecedented, though the platform at Portland looked suitably awesome.

William Flann, a 'good old Portland name', as I have been reminded, was the hero of both the island and the National Lifeboat Institution in 1849 'for saving lives from the wreck' of the sailing ship *Vibular* in 1849.

Towards the far end of the island, Southwell hamlet was growing up beside South Well and its green at the point where the clifftop east and west roads converge for the final mile to Portland Bill. A Methodist chapel was built near the ancient well, on the east side of the junction, in 1849. To the west of the junction stands the Eight Kings Inn, which is said to have been given its name by a well-travelled Victorian landlord who knew of hostelries called the Seven Kings, but none with a larger number of monarchs.

As the Inner Breakwater of Portland Harbour took shape it looked like a viaduct, having been designed to stand in 11 fathoms of water (66 feet), with a workable height above sea level. In most places, at the top, both the timber-built viaduct and the finished stone breakwater were 90 feet above the bottom of the bay. Holding this structure in place – defying the changeable waters of the English Channel – called for great logs and a screw-driving capstan. Before installation, each log was immersed in a specially constructed vat, 100 feet long, in which it was saturated, under pressure of 100ppsi in a vacuum, with creosote preservative for a couple of days. These logs were then bolted into piles and given a Mitchell-type screw head (a flat screw of just one-and-a-half thread turns) at the bottom end. At the top a cap was fixed to the pole, serrated to grip ropes, and then lowered into position and revolved, being turned until it was embedded deep in the clay below the seabed.

When each stage of the timber framework was completed – like a skeleton for the structure that followed – the railway was extended along the top and trucks began to drop their stone. Each section of the viaduct became concealed by thousands of tons of rock and remains encased to this day. This pile-driving can now be taken for granted but was vulnerable during construction, despite cross-bracing. Historian T.F. Hattersley pointed out that a storm from the wrong direction 'could uproot the structure as if it were made of matchsticks, destroying the work of months in as many minutes.'

The Inner Breakwater, with its two arms, extended 1,800 feet and consumed 5,750,000 tons of

Portland stone, sometimes at the rate of between 2,000 and 3,000 tons a day. Much was in the form of large blocks, weighing between four and six tons, and all pieces of infill were graded accorded to size, from lumps of about two hundredweight down to cobble-size pieces.

Such grading was essential to ensure even compacting. The stone was dumped and allowed to settle, and then gouged out to the level of the lowest tides, at which point it was reinforced with walls of squared granite blocks from Devon, Cornwall or the Channel Islands. Skilled engineers built the actual breakwaters but the supply of Portland stone which owed so much to slave labour – courtesy the prison system – was in the best tradition of architectural achievements across the ancient world.

The major quarrying area for stone to build the Inner Breakwater was the Admiralty Quarry to the north-west of the prison, at the top of East Weares, down which navvies (known on Portland as 'free-men' to distinguish them from convicts) constructed a slope nearly a mile in length and comprising three separate inclines known collectively as the Admiralty Incline. At the top of each of the three slopes there was a revolving drum, with steel cables, which controlled the descent of the trucks. Two parallel sets of rails were used; along one set travelled loaded stone wagons which, as they descended, pulled empty wagons back to the top along the second pair of rails. A third set of rails, near the beginning, were used as sidings and for construction work. The central incline (1 in 10 gradient) was not as severe as the upper and lower inclines (1 in 15 gradients).

Powerful screw-brakes were needed to regulate the descent of the stone-filled trucks. The cables of galvanised steel, which were tested to a breaking strain of 40 tons, were continuous and had a length of more than two miles. All loads passed over a weigh-bridge at the top which automatically recorded the weight of the wagons. Visitors were allowed to use Admiralty Incline as a footpath when convicts were not at work.

The long-running row between Portlanders and the government over the compensation for loss of their common rights was settled with a special Act of Parliament in July 1851. This enabled funds to be released to finance projects for the 'public good', such as the improvement of schools, establishing a Portland Dispensary, and providing a more reliable water supply. Much of this had become imperative because of the influx of labourers, warders and other mainlanders. It seemed to many on the island that they were having to pay for their own colonisation.

Until this time, most Portland stone was cut and carved at its destination, and the 1851 census shows that only 33 masons were actually employed on the island. They were mostly working for the Admiralty on the construction of the breakwater. More were on their way, however, as the building of Verne Citadel was already planned and commenced in 1852, with work on an unprecedented scale continuing until 1867. Its immense ditches were to double as quarries and provide stone for the breakwaters.

The schooner *Tamar*, under sail from Newcastle to her home port of Plymouth with a cargo of coal, became a total loss off Portland on 30 August 1851. On 12 January 1852, an unidentified brig was 'seen to founder under close-reefed topsail', in the Race off Portland Bill, taking her crew with her. Whilst 'working' in Chesil Cove on 16 April 1852, the galliot *Maria Johanna*, with a cargo of Cheshire salt, grounded for a time, refloated with the tide, then collided with the schooner *Triton* from Emden. The Liverpool vessel came off worst and capsized with the loss of her crew, who were drowned with the exception of 'the captain, his mate, and a boy'. The schooner *Laurel*, stranded on rocks on Portland Bill, was declared a total loss on 13 May 1852.

On 11 August 1852 a Coastguard on duty at the Higher Lighthouse on Portland Bill witnessed through a telescope the sinking of an unidentified brig to the east of the Shambles, 'having painted gun-ports, and having lost her mainmast, her foremast broken at the top.'

The smack *Horatio*, carrying bricks, wine and citrus fruit from St Peter Port, Guernsey, to Plymouth, was abandoned by her crew of four, who took to their boat in Lyme Bay during a force-9 south-westerly gale on 8 November 1852. The vessel was driven towards the Chesil Beach, where she became a total wreck, north-west of Ferry Bridge, the owners claiming £250 insurance for the boat and £30 in respect of the cargo.

The barque *Nouvelle Loire*, setting out from Le Havre for Algiers, began her voyage inauspiciously and was driven steadily north-westwards to Portland on 16 December 1852. She effectively ended her transit in Chesil Cove but was to go further, after the vessel had been literally split apart on the top of the tide, 'one part of the vessel' being beached to the west near Langton Preventive Station, Langton Herring, and the remainder washed up on the other side of Portland Bill, 'ashore at Osmington'.

The crew of the *Commodore*, en route from Hamburg to Vera Cruz, abandoned the schooner off Portland in a light north-westerly wind on 11 June 1853. The loss of the schooner *Charlotte*, at anchor in Portland Roads on 9 September 1853, had even less to do with the weather, as conditions were virtually calm. The crew took to their own boat, and divers later removed a cargo of stone, which was to have been taken from Portland to Southampton. The salvage attempt was partially successful, the hull being re-floated and taken into shallow water, but the *Charlotte* was then left to rot.

The German schooner *Neptunus*, in sail from Cardiff to Leer with a cargo of coal, foundered at Portland on 17 October 1853. This seems to have

## Shipwrecks

*Brunel's* Great Eastern, *the biggest ship in the world, put into Portland Roads with six dead after a boiler explosion in September 1859.*

*A rocket-fired lifeline (right) saved most of the passengers and crew of the émigré ship* Royal Adelaide *on the Chesil Beach in November 1872.*

Left: *Clifftop view of the paddle-steamer* Bournemouth, *wrecked on Portland Bill in August 1886.*

Above: *The* Bournemouth *on the rocks at Portland, seen from the shore to the north.*

*St Andrew's Church at Southwell, seen in about 1895, was built as a memorial to the New Zealand émigrés who lost their lives off Portland in the* Avalanche, *which sank after a collision in 1877.*

## Shipwrecks

*The anchor of the* Avalanche, *discovered in 1984 and raised from the sea, now rests beside St Andrew's Church.*

*The end of the* Patria *in Chesil Cove in October 1903.*

*The wreck of the* Resolute *on Chesil Beach.*

*The steamship* Patroclus *stranded below West Weares in September 1907.*

Above: *The freighter* Dorothea, *from Rotterdam, washed up on the Chesil Beach in February 1914.*

Left: *The French sailing ship* Madeleine Tristan, *washed up in Chesil Cove, in September 1930.*

been a windy week, as the Dartmouth smack *Two Brothers*, in ballast on a voyage to Jersey, was driven ashore on the Chesil Beach in a force-8 south-westerly gale.

Lano's Bridge, named on its keystone for quarry-master 'J.C. Lano, 1854', brought an extension from the Merchants' Railway through Tout Quarries to the south-west of Portland Heights Hotel. Lines above and below Lano's Bridge operated at two levels, the lower rails taking worked stone outwards and the upper system being used by push-and-tip wagons for dumping quarry waste from West Weares. This and other splendid little bridges, with expertly constructed arches and delicate drystone walls, were constructed where one part of the mineral tramway crossed another.

'Tout' was recorded in 1828 by William Lisle Bowles in his *Dissertation on the Celtic Deity Teutes* as being the ancient word for 'a lookout' in that 'most of the hills of the sea-coast, and through Dorsetshire, are still pronounced Teuts [*Toots*] by the common people.' Tithe, estate and military maps from the mid-nineteenth century record the contemporary names for the cliffs on each side of the top of the island.

East Weares, collectively, overlook Weymouth Bay and comprise Hellier's Weare, Durdle Weare, Sue Flew's Weare, Gilbert's Weare, Outer Weare, North Wall Weare, Penn's Weare, North Weare, St Andrew's Weare and Church Point Weare.

West Weares, above Lyme Bay, begin at Chesil Cove and incorporate Killick's Hill Weare, Flower's Weare, Pranker's Weare, Pitt's Weare, Silverwell Weare and Knight's Weare. By 1854, the entire northern summit of West Weares was being quarried from a string of workings that were merging into each other – Tout Quarry, Inmosthay Quarry, Trade Quarry and Bower's Quarry – with most of their waste being tipped over the clifftop. Thus began to form immense scree-slopes, 300 feet deep in terms of the contours, from the edge of West Cliff to the water at Clay Ope.

A much bleaker landscape, with dusty areas of grey nothingness, spread across the eastern toplands from Waycroft Quarry at Verne Yeates to the summit above the historic King's Pier at East Weares. These were King Barrow Quarry, Withies Croft Quarry, Independent Quarry and Admiralty Quarry. South of the Admiralty Incline were High Headlands Quarry, France Quarry, Broadcroft Quarry, Yeolands Quarry and Silklake Quarry.

To the south of the hilltop villages of Weston and Easton were Bottom Combe Quarry, Perryfield Quarry, Grangecroft Quarry and Suckthumb Quarry. Between Church Ope Cove and Cave Hole, above the landslipped south-eastern cliffs, lay Sheat Quarry. Inland, south of Southwell village, was Langley Hill Quarry. Finally, undermining the site of the island's Armada period signal station, Beacon Quarry was on

the southernmost tip of Portland and Dorset on the Bill of Portland.

The Wesleyan chapel at Easton dates from 1854. Victorian prison warders' homes in Alma Terrace and Alma Road, between the convict prison and The Grove, were named for the Battle of Alma. Fought against the Russians on 20 September 1854, this battle marked the turning point for the British in the Crimean War. Portland's other topographical link with the Black Sea lies below, to the north-east, in the outer bay created by the building of the Inner Breakwater. Balaclava Bay was named for the Battle of Balaclava, which included the famous Charge of the Light Brigade, on 25 October 1854. Balaclava Coastguard Station was built beside it, just outside the Inner Breakwater.

Louis H. Ruegg, in a report to the Royal Agricultural Society in 1855, mentions both Portland's own breed of sheep and the 'genuine old Dorsets' found on the island, which were traditional Dorset-horns before they were crossed with Somerset-horns:

*Portland mutton is prized as a delicacy by epicures, probably as much on account of the shortness of the supply and the diminutive size of the individual animal as for its 'shortness' in eating. It will cut up sometimes as small as 10 pounds or 12 pounds a quarter, and very fat, and is not thought at maturity until five or six years old. Indeed a butcher who kills a goodly number of these little dainties spoke to me with complacency of one particularly delicate little ewe who had attained her majority of 21 years [his emphasis] before she was brought to the slaughter. The description given of the breed by a Portland farmer is – 'small size, black nose, yellow legs, mutton fine-flavoured and short, wool fine.' The number kept in the island has somewhat diminished since the Government works have been in operation, but the estimates of it vary so materially, that it might mislead if figures were quoted.*

The average weight of a Portland fleece, given as two pounds, had 'increased since the enclosure of the commons'.

When civil engineer James Meadows Rendel died on 21 November 1856, seven years after work had started at Portland, 40-year-old John Coode took over as Engineer-in-Chief for the remainder of the first stage of the project. Rendel's final design, still on the drawing board, was a suspension bridge across St James's Park to complete the landscaping in front of Buckingham Palace.

The Belgian barque *Petroville*, carrying rice from Akyab in Burma to Dunkirk, was washed into Chesil Cove 'in a heavy gale and thick fog' on 9 December 1856. She had been at sea for 170 days with 'the crew suffering severely from scurvy and scarcity of provisions', according to the *Dorset County Chronicle*. Brave efforts were made 'in raging seas' to save the captain, the second mate, and four Asian seamen. Although he was brought ashore, the captain had been ill for months, and expired with exhaustion, as did another of the men. Three other crewmen and a boy were drowned and another sailor had already died during the voyage. The rice, however, was salvaged by a team of 70 labourers.

A lighthouse indirectly claimed a wreck when the *Amelia*, from Lyme Regis, carrying granite from Plymouth for the construction of the Needles light on the Isle of Wight, came to grief whilst attempting to round Portland Bill on 2 July 1857.

Pierre Picard of the Honfleur fishing smack *Victoire Desirée* was awarded the silver medal of the National Lifeboat Institution for his rescue of the three-man crew of the *Dart*, en route from Alderney to Lyme Regis, which capsized in the Race off Portland Bill in heavy seas on 8 March 1857. A fortnight later the barque *Hebrides*, sailing from London to Sebastapol with chemicals and medicines during the Crimean War, was washed into Church Ope Cove and stranded in 16 feet of water beneath Rufus Castle.

In Fortuneswell, the Anglican educational movement established St John's National School in 1857, with room for 500 children, though as early as 1888 the average attendance was only 320.

The Royal Navy dockyard was created beside and around the stone quays east of Castletown, in 1857, for 'running repairs' to warships on their return to Britain from service against the Russians in the Black Sea and the Baltic during the Crimean War. The man-made Harbour of Refuge at Portland was taking shape as the biggest in Europe. The project received added impetus as a result of efforts across the Channel, where Cherbourg was being turned into a great naval fortress. Its breakwaters could shelter the whole of the French Navy and the Grand Napoleon Docks were completed in 1858.

Weston was becoming Portland's new town, as it grew around the junction beside Weston Pond in the centre of the island, and took its name from the street heading northwards to Reforne. The second Weston Street went east to the grounds of Pennsylvania Castle. Just north of Weston Corner and Coopers Place, Weston widens into Weston Green, with Providence Place and Gypsy Lane to the north-west. An eighteenth-century house used to stand here in splendid isolation.

One arm of Weston's Methodists built themselves a Wesleyan chapel (near the Royal Exchange Inn) in 1858 and the fundamentalist faction of the faith answered with a rival Primitive Methodist chapel (near the Prince Alfred Inn) in 1860. Portland's Nonconformists were maintaining their long-standing tradition of disagreeing with each other. There was also increasing tension between convicts and warders in Portland Prison, sparking a mutiny in September 1858 which was 'promptly suppressed'.

In March 1858 the Liverpool barque *Matilda* was stranded on Portland Bill and became a complete loss. On 14 March 1859 the French brig *Les Cinq Soeurs* was washed ashore in a force 10 gale and was broken up on the Chesil Beach.

The first light vessel to be provided by Trinity House beside the offshore Shambles sandbank, four miles east-south-east of Portland Bill, went into position on 1 September 1859. These hazardous shoals were named for their shipwreck carnage, a 'shambles' being a medieval meat market. The sandbank extends for four miles eastwards of Portland Bill and at low tide is covered by only 14 feet of water, which becomes broken and white in a gale.

Isambard Kingdom Brunel's greatest leviathan, the 28,093-ton steamship *Great Eastern*, was built in 1858 and remained the biggest ship in the world by far for the next 41 years. Her trial trip, however, was marred by a boiler explosion which ripped through the funnel casing and wrecked the salubrious grand saloon. Six men were killed. The accident occurred off Hastings on the morning of 9 September 1859 but, despite the damage, the vessel was able to resume her voyage down-Channel. She put into Portland Roads, from where five of the bodies were taken by boat to Weymouth Harbour for burial on 14 September 1859.

The register for Melcombe Regis cemetery gives the names of those killed as Robert Adams (aged 35), John Boyne (45), Richard Edwards (38), Michael Mahon (35) and Michael McIlroy. All had been stoking the boiler concerned. The *Great Eastern* went on to Holyhead and then came back up-Channel to Southampton, where she remained for repairs and her first crossing to America, in June 1860. Six years later she carried and laid the entire transatlantic telegraph cable – 2,300 miles of wire weighing 25,000 tons – from Valentia in Ireland to Heart's Content, Newfoundland. On 28 July 1866 the following message was sent from the Isle of Wight to the White House:

*From the Queen, Osborne, to the President of the United States, Washington. The Queen congratulates the President on the successful completion of an undertaking which she hopes may serve as an additional bond of union between the United States and England.*

In 1859 geology was on the move above Chiswell, with great rumbles that shook Fortuneswell, as 30 acres of the West Cliff cracked and collapsed into West Weares undercliff. It was also noted in 1859 that Tophill was changing its shape, though this was due to the immense war-works of Verne Citadel and its adjacent quarrying.

By 1860 the fortifications on Verne Hill were already half finished by the Royal Engineers and their convict labourers when the Royal Commission on the Defence of the United Kingdom reported to

# Verne

*Spectators and Royal Naval ratings gathering beside Verne Citadel for the 'Sham Fight' to test Portland's defences on 8 December 1908.*

*Inland south-west corner of Verne Citadel from across its dry-ditch moat in 1975.*

*'VR 1881' date-stone for Victoria Regina, topping the back entrance of Verne Citadel, 'The Verne' notice refers to its current role as one of Her Majesty's Prisons.*

*Dry moat and the south side of Verne Citadel, looking eastwards, in 1997.*

Right: *Dating from 1891, the High Angle Battery emplaced a line of huge anti-ship guns, hidden in the heart of the island between East Weares and Verne Yeates.*

Prime Minister Viscount Palmerston during the Franco-Prussian War. Verne Citadel was designed by Captain Crossman of the Royal Engineers to be colossal in scale and great in area, with steep cliffs topped by low-profile walls that could have been described as impregnable as anywhere in Europe. Behind were barracks for 1,000 troops. Their accommodation was both bomb and shell-proof, beneath vaulted brickwork and a semicircle of stone arches which were covered with rock and grassed on the surface into a steep slope that dropped down to a central and level drill-ground. Everything was within the walls, from cricket pitches to the gymnasium, from tennis lawns to the hospital.

Huge 32-ton rifled muzzle-loaded cannon were emplaced in barbettes overlooking the approaches to Portland Harbour. These were for nine such fixed guns, plus ten mobile artillery pieces, operational in 1888. On the other side, set into the flat top of the island, was the High Angle Battery, with an immense dry ditch between it and Verne Citadel. This is 120 feet wide and 70 feet deep at its eastern end, and became the largest single source of stone – no less than 1,500,000 tons – for the harbour's Outer Breakwater. A winding staircase snaked underground through the solid stone interior of Verne Citadel to emerge at a door in the bottom of the ditch, which was laid out as a rifle-range.

'Makes you hold your stomach,' a Portlander remarked to me. 'A man named Verne built it all and when they finished the ditch he threw himself in.' Unfortunately for the story, this hill was named Verne in 1608, and Ferne before that, to 1321 or earlier. The Dorset dialect turned 'f' into 'v' and fowls, for instance, were vowls. Dorset's placename expert, A.D. Mills, suggested the Verne could mean 'wooded', but there is as much chance of a tree canopy having been found across this barren mountain top as there would be of establishing commercial forestry in the Falkland Islands.

On Boxing Day in 1860 the *Irene*, from Norway, in full sail with a shipment of timber bound for Bristol, attempted to take refuge in Portland Roads during a blizzard and had the distinction of being the first vessel to be wrecked by the new Harbour of Refuge. An easterly gale had gathered what were described as 'huge seas' which propelled the vessel into the outer piles of the breakwater in the course of construction and 'concealed the light at the end'. She shivered most of her timbers into pieces 'no longer round than Lucifer matches'. The crew of five were saved but the remains of the vessel and its contents were washed up along half a mile of shore between the Ferry Bridge and The Mere.

On 30 December 1860, the schooner *Norval*, in ballast from Harfleur to her home port of Plymouth, was washed ashore on the Chesil Beach near Ferry Bridge. Seven Portlanders put out in a lerret to rescue the crew, being led by William Flann and

Joseph White, who were awarded silver medals by the National Lifeboat Institution. Their companions were John Flann, David King, Henry Mitchell, George Stone and John White.

The Dundee barque *Tamora*, having sailed from London with materials for building Portland's breakwaters, was dragged along the shore as she prepared to unload in a gale on 15 January 1861. The hull was torn apart and the remains of the contents were sold at auction. On 16 March 1861 the lugger *Jeune Marie*, returning to France with a cargo of coal, became a total loss off Portland.

The national railway network had reached Weymouth as an extension of the Waterloo line via Dorchester, in 1857. The arrival of steam could be seen from Portland and it was regarded as inevitable that the 'iron horse' would come to the island. On 7 October 1861 two schemes were proposed for a further addition at a meeting in the Royal Hotel, Weymouth. Schemes for a quay tramway and for a line of 4 miles 17 chains to Portland were agreed for promotion. This latter would cross the Backwater to the north of Arthur's Bridge and terminate in Victoria Square, Portland. Only a single local steamer operator objected to the Weymouth and Portland Railway Act, which received royal assent on 30 June 1862 and promised:

*A Railway to commence in the parish of Wyke Regis, or near, the west end of the wooden bridge over the Backwater, to pass thence along Chesil Beach to the Isle of Portland, and to terminate in the said Isle at, or near, a point about 45 yards west of the Victoria Lodge Inn.*

The enabling legislation also contained powers to bring the 7ft broad-gauge Wilts, Somerset & Weymouth Railway southwards from Dorchester to the seaside as a third rail in tandem with the 4ft 8.5in. standard-gauge rails of the existing London & South Western Railway. The construction contract, including bridges and land acquisition, totalled £90,000 and was awarded to John Aird & Son of Lambeth.

The Royal Navy's training ship HMS *Britannia* came to Portland Harbour in 1862 and remained until 1865, when she moved on to Dartmouth.

Work on the Portland branch railway began in October 1862 with the spanning of the Backwater at Weymouth by a timber viaduct in a great curve of 66 spans, with an embankment across the swamp commonly known as the Marsh. The embankment was to be 700 feet in length and had to rise at one point to nearly 50 feet in height at a gradient of 1 in 58; this tricky feat of navvying was accompanied by several serious slippages. Once beyond these difficulties, blasting created the Rodwell cutting and produced further hardcore for the next length of embankment, bringing the line to a 27-span timber viaduct across The Fleet at the former Small Mouth

# Railways

*Horse-drawn wagons on the tramway section of Merchants' Railway, being loaded at Priory Corner in the 1920s with stone from Tout Quarry, looking east to the skyline profile of Verne Citadel (top left).*

*The three bridges of the Merchants' Railway, dating from 1825, carrying Verne Hill Road and New Ground, in the 1890s.*

Above: *Stone being lowered into Castletown on the cable-operated Freeman's Incline of the Merchants' Railway, in 1912, with oil-tanks above the harbour (right).*

Left: *The main descent of the 1825-built Merchants' Railway down Freeman's Incline from Verne Yeates to Castletown, in the 1880s.*

# Railways

*Stone wagons in the mineral line sidings at Castletown in the 1920s, with the viaduct* (centre right) *carrying standard-gauge track into the dockyard and below Verne Citadel* (top left) *towards Easton.*

*Industrial Castletown, beside the mineral railway, included engineering works and a steam laundry in the 1920s.*

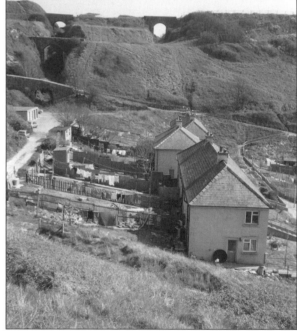

*Above: Loading stone from the Merchants' Railway, at Castletown Pier in the 1920s.*

*Right: Bridges of the Merchants' Railway, on Verne Hill and New Ground* (top) *from houses in Tillycombe Road* (centre) *in 2000.*

*Portland from Wyke Regis, on being linked to the mainland by both rail and road, in 1865.*

# Railways

*Portland Station, which opened in 1865, with a siding heading to the stone terminal at Castletown (centre) and the Inner Breakwater of Portland Harbour stretching out behind.*

*Saddle tank 30179 at Easton Station, which was the ultimate end of the line on Portland for just half a century from 1902 till closure in 1952.*

*Mix of standard-gauge and narrow-gauge wagons in the quarry loading bay at Easton from where stone for the Cenotaph started its journey to London in 1920.*

*Left: Circular site of a turntable and rail lines in the concrete along which trucks were man-handled to supply the guns of the 1891-dated High Angle Battery with cartridges and shells.*

# Railways

*British Railways 2F-class engine No. 47160 stripped to its chassis at Tradecroft in 2003.*

*Boiler and parts of No. 47160 in the process of restoration at Tradecroft.*

*Track and three engines in the railway yard at Tradecroft.*

*Stack of rails, mainline locomotive* (top left) *and saddle-tank engine* (right) *in the Tradecroft railway yard.*

*Saddle tank and 2F-class boiler in the process of restoration on Portland in Tradecroft rail yard.*

ferry crossing. Beyond, two miles of embanked track skirted the foreshore and Mere, landward from the Chesil Beach to the original Portland Station (later the Goods Depot), the line continuing for a further 34 chains to reach the Merchants' Railway at an exchange siding in Castletown.

Because the branch line to Portland was to be operated jointly by the Great Western Railway and its London & South Western Railway competitors it required mixed-gauge construction. The work was completed in 1864 but opening was delayed for a year due to reinforcements being required to the viaducts, both across Weymouth Backwater and at Small Mouth, and due to the resolution of a row between the two operating companies as to which should occupy station accommodation in Weymouth. The track was double gauged with three rails, in order to take both broad-gauge trains of the GWR and standard-gauge trains of the LSWR.

Portland Roads, in the process of being turned into Portland Harbour, received many of the principal ships-of-the-line of the Royal Navy between 15 and 17 August 1865. They were taking part in an act of cross-Channel reconciliation, visiting Cherbourg on a social basis to celebrate the peace with France after more than a century of conflict. Queen Victoria had already paid her respects, at the opening of the Grand Napoleon Docks, in August 1858.

The delayed opening of Portland's branch railway took place on 9 October 1865, passenger services beginning with a train leaving Weymouth at 7.30a.m. on 16 October. LSWR locomotive No. 154 *Nile* headed the six-coach train of four-wheeled carriages which contributed to the acceptable £26 gross takings for the day but made an inauspicious arrival – being half an hour late – at Portland Station.

Within sight of the end of the new railway line, a Coastguard crossing Portland Common in August 1865 came across 'what turned out to be 24 demijohns of the best Holland gin, each containing four gallons which had been recently smuggled in.' The contraband was taken to Custom House Quay in Weymouth.

On 22 November 1865 the French brig *Emmanuel*, sailing between Rouen and Ferrol with a cargo of oak, was washed ashore in Chesil Cove, 'at the calmest place on the beach', behind Chiswell village. The description from the *Dorset County Chronicle* is relative, however, as, although the vessel exposed her beam to the sea, there was a 'terrific surf' in which one sailor drowned as he attempted leaping towards land. Hundreds of Portlanders watched and threw ropes to save the remainder of the crew before swarming over the remains to retrieve 'loose tackle, masts, anchors and spars'. The shipwreck occurred on a Wednesday and 'she went to pieces that Friday'.

A total of 17 ships were driven on shore around Portland in mid-January 1866 during what was described as 'one of the most destructive gales which have ever visited this coast.' It is an ill wind that does no good, however, and in this case there was gold for some lucky Portlanders:

*The rough seas of last week washed upon the Chesil Beach a quantity of the gold coins which in years gone by formed a portion of the cargo of a vessel wrecked in the bay. Some of the coins are frequently found after a very rough sea.*

At 23.20 hours on 4 June 1866 the steamship *Mary Nixon* collided with an unidentified schooner off Portland. The sailing vessel sank almost immediately but the voices of her crew were heard shouting and some were said to be swimming for their lives. The *Mary Nixon* eventually lowered her boat, 13 minutes later, but this made only a cursory circuit of the spot and then the steamer departed the scene. This led to a Board of Trade inquiry, as a result of which her master's certificate was withdrawn for a year, on the grounds that he had been drunk.

The ketch *Rebecca* sank in the Race off Portland Bill with a cargo of granite on 6 June 1866. Another stone-carrying vessel, the brig *Rachel*, from Exeter, was 'run down' by a modern steamship of the London & Liverpool Steam Packet Co. on 25 June 1866. This time, unlike the collision involving the *Mary Nixon*, efforts were made to search for survivors, but only some papers were found floating off Portland Bill. Her five-man crew – the master, three seamen and a boy – had gone down with the sailing ship.

The third Portland collision that summer claimed a steamship, the 564-ton *Osprey* from West Hartlepool, en route from Liverpool to Antwerp on 10 July 1866. Steaming at 8.5 knots, she was cut in two by the 1,040-ton sloop HMS *Amazon*, which was heading in the other direction, being outward bound from Portsmouth for Halifax, Nova Scotia, with the loss of ten passengers including several women and the captain's three children. Though the *Amazon* was able to lower her boats, to save most of *Osprey*'s crew and passengers, they then had to rescue their own as Amazon also began to sink.

Having served with the Baltic Fleet during Crimean War, the third-rate 70-gun wooden battleship HMS *Boscawen* was pensioned off in 1866, and sailed to the newly-constructed Harbour of Refuge at Portland. Her new role, as a Royal Navy cadet Training Ship, was shared by HMS *Wellesley* in 1873.

Because of its isolation and military presence, Portland was designated in 1866 as the principal holding prison for members of the Fenian Brotherhood, who had taken an oath to liberate Ireland and establish a republic:

*I promise by the divine law of God to do all in my power to obey the laws of the society Fenian Brotherhood, and to free and regenerate Ireland from the yoke of England. So help me God.*

The Habeas Corpus Act had been suspended in Ireland. An estimated 350,000 Fenians in the United States included volunteers who had attacked Canada and seamen whose Irish Republican Navy, in the shape of the schooner *Friend*, captured and scuttled the British schooner *Wentworth*. 'Home Rule for Ireland' had become a live and violent issue and brought a clever and committed clientele to the island. A Roman Catholic chapel was provided for the newcomers inside the prison, but visiting Catholic priests were discouraged from having any conversations with their Irish parishioners, either pastoral or political.

Jeremiah O'Donovan Rossa was the most notorious Portland islander from 1866 until 1869. His release was brought forward as a result of a letter which had been smuggled to the national press. It told of horrific conditions in what others dubbed the 'Hotel des Convicts', and was timed to coincided with an election, across both stretches of water, in which he was the absent candidate. Fenians refused to take their seats at Westminster, where O'Donovan Rossa was the new Member of Parliament for Tipperary. Irish aspirations were never satisfied by sitting for the London legislature. On securing his freedom, O'Donovan Rossa left both Britain and Ireland to become the leader of the Irish-American lobby for Home Rule. The campaign for hearts and minds had its icons and martyrs on both sides. O'Donovan Rossa survived an assassination attempt in which he was gunned down by a young British widow on the streets of New York. It was as an old Fenian that he eventually died there, but his body was repatriated for burial at Glasnevin, where he went 'into British-occupied ground' to an oration to this effect from Patrick Pearse on 1 August 1915.

The sailing vessel *Junior* was lost in the Race off Portland Bill on 21 January 1868. A week later, on nearby Broadhope Ledge, the barque *Bank*, carrying coal, coke, rails and fire-bricks from South Shields to Cartagena, ran 'high and dry on the rocks' in dense fog. Richard and Bridget Larn, compiling the *Shipwreck Index of the British Isles* in 1995, record that the Southwell expression 'Stick to the pork, Archie' dates from this wreck. The words were shouted down from the cliff by wife Molly Archie to her husband, Samuel Archie, as he salvaged the crew's barrels of pickled pork when the vessel was breaking up. 'Never mind anything else,' she said. 'Stick to the pork!'

The captain of the German brig *Amalie*, sailing with wine, tobacco and ballast from Antwerp to St Thomas, made a mistake that proved fatal on 1 February 1869, when he mistook Portland Bill for the Needles, Isle of Wight, and turned towards Chesil Cove thinking that he was entering the Solent. Two crewmen, Joaclin Breos from Ydassen and Emier Bryott, of Hamburg, were drowned as the 'embayed' vessel was washed onto the pebble beach.

The effectiveness of this sanctuary for shipping in Portland Roads was being compromised by an adverse effect on tidal flows that was blamed on the new southern and central breakwaters. This was the cause, apparently, of the loss of the Aberystwyth schooner *Henry & Dora* while sailing from Trouville to Llanelli on 5 February 1869. She had anchored in Portland Roads during a south-westerly gale but foundered beside Fort Head, in fine weather and light wind, on attempting to go round the end of the Outer Breakwater.

An offshore gale, blowing force 10 from west-north-west, parted anchor cables and drove another Aberystwyth schooner into the same breakwater at 05.30 hours on Sunday 12 September 1869. The *Salathiel* had been prepared to take a cargo of wheat from Weymouth to Cardiff, but the crew spent Saturday night on the mainland, leaving only a boy aboard. He was drowned.

The third loss of the year beside the Outer Breakwater took place in thick fog on 4 November 1869. The master, two seamen and a boy left the Dutch schooner *Jacoba Catherina* in the ship's boat but this fouled in the rigging and capsized. They were drowned but the mate and a third seaman lashed themselves with halyards to the main topmast. Although the ship had sunk in 11 fathoms while carrying coal from South Shields to Barcelona, the pair remained just above the water until they were eventually spotted by Customs Officer John Barrett as the mist began to clear. The lucky Dutch seamen, suffering from hypothermia, were rescued by the Weymouth Watch Boat after their 13-hour ordeal.

Portland convict Josiah Detheridge was hanged at Dorchester on 12 August 1869 for the murder of a prison warder. A year later Thomas Radcliffe suffered the same fate, for a similar offence at Portland, on 15 August 1870. Convict numbers had reached 900 inmates, requiring a staff of 700. One 27-year-old prisoner who set fire to his cell was sentenced to 36 lashes of the cat-o'-nine-tails. He lost consciousness during the 'properly administered' scourging with a 52-inch whip, circled and tipped with metal barbs, and was found to be dead on removal from the restraints.

Both the original Higher or Upper Lighthouse and the nearby Lower Lighthouse were demolished and rebuilt in 1869. At the other end of the island, on outgrowing their 'Preaching Room' beside Chesil Cove, which everyone else knew as Ranters' Lodge, the Primitive Methodists moved to a purpose-built chapel. It stood on Miser's Knap and was subsequently converted into the Royal Manor Theatre.

Ornithologists recorded the winds of 1870, from 8 January onwards, after a little auk had been shot near Ferry Bridge: 'During the same month seven were seen in the Portland Roads, the wind at the time blowing a hurricane, which lasted a week.'

The Liverpool brig *Cynthia* foundered on Portland

on 19 February 1870 and was followed a week later by the sailing vessel *Julia*. In March 1870 they were joined, on Chive Rock, by the Bridport ketch *Surprise*. On top of the island, the fetid and open water of Easton Pond was eventually subjected to hygiene tests and condemned as 'unpotable', being unfit for human consumption, in 1871.

The completion of the first two stages of the building of Portland Harbour established the reputation of a Cornishman, Sir John Coode (1816–92), as an eminent civil engineer, and earned him his knighthood in 1872. As a result he also received a commission from the colonial government in South Africa to build a similar 'Harbour of Refuge' in Table Bay on the Cape of Good Hope. Coode established the science of dock and harbour engineering as an exportable field of British expertise.

The Inner Breakwater at Portland, finished in 1868 and running for 1,800 feet, was followed by a 400ft gap – the southern entrance – and then the second arm, completed in 1872, which ran for 7,500 feet. Together they totalled a mile and three-quarters and gave shelter to an area calculated at about two square miles. At the landward end of the Inner Breakwater, an inscription reads 'These are Imperial Works and Worthy Kings,' and records two commemorations:

*From this spot on the 25th of July 1849 His Royal Highness Prince Albert, consort of Queen Victoria, sunk the first stone of the breakwater. Upon the same spot, Albert Edward, Prince of Wales, on the 10th of August 1872 laid this last stone and declared the work complete.*

That statement was somewhat premature, as an extensive further stage of breakwater building followed between 1894 and 1903. It was, however, the Inner Breakwater that proved such work on this scale was feasible and, were we a nation that praised famous engineers, we would talk of Rendel and Coode in the same breath as Telford and Smeaton. The Prince of Wales, later King Edward VII, had been a frequent visitor on the royal yacht, during excursions from Osborne House in the Isle of Wight.

The cost had already escalated to £1,000,000 and would climb further as the breakwaters were provided with two forts as finishing touches. One, at the outer end of the far section, was built in granite with a wooden drawbridge separating it from the breakwater. Guarding this moat were eight 64-pound guns. One pointed along the sea-walls towards the island and the others protected the circumference. Yet this was only a light pillbox compared with the massive circular fort that was placed at the end of the second section, more than a mile out to sea. This was the most futuristic in appearance of all the Victorian forts on the South Coast.

Fort Head looks like a flying saucer, having a wide sloping surround with a dome-shaped middle. In profile it is lower and more streamlined than the forts of Spithead, which are the closest comparison. As for size, it is enormous – far larger than you would think from mainland glimpses. The walls at the sides are laminated iron sheets infilled with concrete more than 12 feet across and the dome at the top was originally open, and then closed with sheets of iron mounted upon girders.

A structure of this size had its inevitable problems. Settlement difficulties began with its initial placement, in 1868, after which contemporary accounts refer to a shuttle of boats that were involved in running repairs:

*The force of the sea is very great here and some hundreds of tons of stone are often sent across the harbour in a day to repair the breaches made by the sea in the foundations of the outer fort.*

The armament at Fort Head comprised 12.5in. rifled muzzle-loaded cannon of 38 tons apiece mounted on iron carriages and platforms which weighed 12 tons. Their field of fire met that of the Nothe Fort at Weymouth, a 'Palmerston Folly' from the 1860s built as a result of the conflict Britain was able to avoid, the Franco-Prussian War. The Nothe was 3,400 yards away to the north-west across what was still the open remainder of Portland Bay. Some, perhaps all, of these great gun-barrels lie in the water off the south-east corner where they were dumped when breech-loaded 6-inch guns superseded them towards the end of the century.

Overlooking all of this, from the top of Portland, was the fortress of Verne Citadel and coastal gun batteries on the lower slopes of the East Weares. The firepower of the latter should have totalled seven 10in. and thirteen 9in. guns, but this was never achieved because one battery could not be built due to subsidence.

New Ground, comprising the parking area and sports fields beside Yeates Road between Portland Heights Hotel and what is now Portland Prison, were cleared of rocks by convicts in 1872 and levelled to provide the defenders of Verne Citadel with a clear field of fire. Expansion to the south-east of the Admiralty Quarries, for breakwater building, left a rough lozenge-shaped rock standing 30ft high near the eastern edge of the plateau. Known as Nicodemus Knob, it might have been intended as a sea-mark, but the stone is more likely to have been cut for a boundary marker 'at the east part of the Common or Weir', Weare being the Portland name for a cliff. It seems to have taken its name from Nicodemus Knowle, a name applied in Victorian times to an outcrop on the undercliff beneath the original Portland Prison at The Grove.

Prison labour, now freed from building breakwaters, was turned in 1872 towards building a church in

The Grove for prison officers and the Army, who resented being marched across the island to St George's in Reforne. Captain Du Cane of the Royal Engineers, who retired as Sir Edmund Du Cane (1830–1903), had been Director of Convict Prisons and Military Prisons since 1863. He had designed the immense land defences of both Plymouth and Dover, and relished the chance to sketch his ideal of 'a neat little church' on Portland, in fashionable mock-Byzantine style from the twelfth century.

The convicts built St Peter's – known as the 'Convict Church' – on the inland edge of the prison complex. The prison and its prisoners were already a tourist attraction, with visitors gathering to await the sight of work gangs being led to the quarries. The new church, which was to provide for the 'moral improvement' of the prisoners, cost £2,400, which was met by public subscription. Sir Edmund Du Cane later advised and lectured on prison management and produced his thesis on *Punishment and Prevention of Crime* in 1888. Between 1851 and 1856, as a Sapper, he had superintended the work programme of convicts transported to the new 'regular penal settlement' in Western Australia.

The high-quality Portland stone masonry and carvings were the work of those convicts, and the mosaic floors were laid by Constance Kent, convicted of murdering her stepmother in 1913. Apparently she was held in Dorchester Prison and commuted to Portland by train. Ceilings were in Finnish redwood, entirely assembled in pure tongue and groove perfection, held with wooden pegs rather than nails. A remarkable finishing touch, in the bell cote, was a miniature carving of the church itself. Whatever qualities were lacking in the minds of the Victorian prisoners, their skills were inspirational.

A visitor at this time, writing in 1873, described the punishment room in the prison where floggings were administered with the birch or cat-o'-nine-tails. Such extreme forms of discipline generally resulted from attacks on prison guards or other serious acts of violence. The room reminded the visitor 'of a beautifully kept harness room' and was a surreal tribute to Queen Victoria:

*We saw the bright steel triangles to which the prisoner is tied while being flogged. The convicts had arranged the handcuffs and other instruments of coercion in symmetrical order along the wall, and had formed with them the figure of a crown and the letters V.R. in honour of Her Majesty.*

The 1,385-ton Liverpool-based émigré ship *Royal Adelaide*, outward bound from London to Sydney with 30 crew and 35 passengers, ended her voyage on Chesil Beach near Ferry Bridge. She was first spotted by Portland pilot Arthur Mazo, at 04.00 hours on 25 November 1872, fully-rigged and with her head to the east, being blown towards Portland

from two or three miles offshore, though he remarked that if he had been aboard he would have 'beaten her out' of Chesil Cove. Instead, she rolled towards the pebbles, by which time Coastguards from Wyke Regis were firing rocket lines to the vessel. A number of passengers were reluctant to use the breeches buoy life-saving apparatus and, tragically, this snapped after those who had been helping the rescue effort from the ship itself had retreated to the stern.

Five passengers and one crewman were drowned. Nonetheless, it was regarded as a miracle that any, let alone dozens, had been saved. Portlanders would receive acclamation for their 'prodigies of valour'. Meanwhile, the wreck was surrounded by a huge crowd, estimated to number 3,000, many of whom became drunk and violent as the ship broke up and disgorged a cargo of spirits and provisions. There were also ornithological casualties, many storm petrels being washed ashore, at least one surviving bird being 'knocked down by a boy with his cap'.

Three barques from South Shields, each carrying coal, foundered off Portland Bill during the February gales of 1873. They were the *No* (making for Genoa), the *Peru* (destination unknown) and the *Ulverstone* (heading for Cartagena). The latter had been in collision with the *Abraham*, which had lost its rudder in heavy seas. The Weymouth pilot cutter *Turk* picked up survivors from their ship's boats. The Plymouth smack *Alice Jane*, carrying granite from Jersey to Poole, was lost further out at sea, 12 miles south-west of Portland Bill, on 15 March.

During the summer HMS *Trafalgar* arrived in Portland Harbour as the replacement Training Ship, and was renamed HMS *Boscawen* after her predecessor. Built in 1841, she was a first-rate battleship of 4,579 tons and 70 guns, and had seen action off the Crimean peninsula with the Black Sea Fleet in 1855.

The outer wall of the Inner Breakwater of Portland Harbour claimed the Spanish brig *Caamano* on 7 November 1873. She was carrying cigars, mahogany, sugar and wine from Havana to London and was making for what should have been the safety of Portland Roads when an easterly gale completely obscured both breakwaters with the spray from great waves. As the *Caamano* 'broke and bilged' in Balaclava Bay, Coastguards fired a total of eight rocket lines into the vessel, but the terrified crew thought they were under attack – an understandable reaction as one of the missiles set fire to the rigging. Finally, however, they realised their purpose and all the seaman, plus one pig, were safely rescued by breeches buoy.

The Exeter schooner *Perseverance*, carrying 110 tons of china clay from Plymouth to Hull, foundered off Portland Bill on 8 June 1874. In challenging conditions on Portland Roads, relatively safe inside the breakwaters, some 30 vessels rode out a gale on 29 November 1874, with the single exception of the

Plymouth smack *Sultan*. Her anchors were dragged by wind and waves from the north-east, and she was battered into one of the breakwaters, while Portlanders in a lerret were smashed into the side of the sailing ship as they made a perilous attempt at rescuing two seamen. The lerret was saved by Captain Scott in the Admiralty tug HMS *Royal Alfred*, which towed the rowing-boat ashore.

An unidentified French barque was smashed to pieces in Chesil Cove on 24 January 1875. This was another occasion, the *Southern Times* reported, in which Coastguards and their rocket-fired apparatus saved the day, for the entire crew, just before 'mast after mast fell with a deafening crash and she split in two.'

It was a case of déjà vu a week later, on 30 January 1875, as the French barque *Marie Reine*, in transit with coke from Dunkirk to Senegal, was 'embayed' off Portland in a hurricane. At 05.00 hours the vessel was rolling in swell 30 yards from the beach, as the first of the Coastguard rocket-lines missed the ship. Two seamen jumped into the waves but were dragged down by the under-tow and drowned. The *Southern Times* recounts this further example of how rockets saved lives, despite further foreign confusion as to the purpose of this British innovation:

*A second rocket line landed across the ship but the crew did not understand how to rig it, and merely tied it to the vessel instead of pulling out the heavier breeches buoy cable. The equipment was eventually rigged and the rest of the crew came ashore in the cradle, including the captain who had broken his arm. The masts fell shortly after and within 30 minutes the vessel was a total wreck.*

James Jameson, a boy sailor, fell 14 feet to his death down a hatchway in HMS *Boscawen* in October 1875. An inquest was held at the Breakwater Hotel at which the jury added a rider to its verdict of 'accidental death', asking coroner, R.N. Howard, to write to the Admiralty suggesting 'a cross-bar should be placed from stanchion to stanchion around the hatch to prevent the boys from falling down.' There was also concern at the increasing casualty rate among convicts – who were being 'worked to death by forced-labour' in the words of one complainant – and questions were asked in Parliament. Deaths on Portland peaked at one prisoner per week, mostly through a combination of accident, exhaustion and disease, but one coroner's jury accused the authorities of failing to provide medical attention. The prisoner surgeon was suspended and an inquiry ordered.

Commissioners for the Ferry Bridge met in October 1875 to discuss their diminishing tolls. Before the railway bridge was constructed they totalled £900 a year. By 1873 they were averaging £500 a year, but in 1874 the receipts slumped to £360. Rather than increase the tolls, the commis-

sioners decided to reduce charges to make the bridge a more competitive option. The *Dorset County Chronicle* reported:

*Ammunition belonging to the Government is allowed to pass free of charge, also bona fide Government stores. The new tariff came into operation this week – horses and carriages that were 6d. are now 4d., carts formerly 5d. are now 3d.*

Pulpit Rock, the famous feature of Portland Bill, was created in about 1875, when quarrymen working the adjoining Beacon Quarry left a chunk of cliff standing proud from the ledges of their working floor as a sea-mark.

On the afternoon of 11 January 1876 the Norwegian brig *Nordkap*, en route from Santos to Rotterdam, 'ran down' the Jersey schooner *Annie Edwin* eight miles off Portland Bill. Between 14.30 and 15.00 hours, when the schooner sank, the brig was able to rescue her crew and took them to Plymouth. There was to be a spate of such collisions in the late-nineteenth century – some with disastrous outcomes – before the concept of shipping lanes was introduced. Describing such collisions required the same economy of language as a modern reporter reserves for road traffic accidents. Unless a moving object has impacted upon a stationary one, it is unsafe to attribute blame (such as by stating that a sailing vessel has been 'hit' by a steamship), apart from in exceptional cases where an official inquiry establishes the facts. Though only academic, in an historical context such essential rules of journalism are ignored at one's peril in this litigious age.

In a 'violent storm' on 5 March 1876, a Coastguard lookout at Blacknor watched an unidentified barque in serious difficulties far out in Lyme Bay, eight miles to the south-west. Through his telescope, he saw crew in the rigging as the vessel appeared to 'settle down' and resume a westerly course, but then he watched her founder with no boats being lowered. A week later the Ardrossan brigantine *Athlete*, carrying guano fertiliser from London to Sligo, failed to cross the Race off Portland Bill and was 'seen to founder with all her crew in the rigging', drowning six crewmen and the master's wife. One lucky boy was plucked from 'raging seas' by the *Amelian* and named as John McHaven on being landed at Bridlington on 21 March.

The Swedish barque *Ornen*, carrying guano from Peru to Leith, was 'run into' out in the Channel by another barque, said to be the *Kassa*, at 05.30 hours on 26 September 1876. From the *Ornen* 20 crewmen abandoned ship and were later picked up by the Cardiff schooner *John Morrison*, which put them in to Portland.

Shortly after dark, at 19.30 hours on 13 December 1876, the brigantine *Anemone*, outward bound in ballast from London to Morocco, was in collision with the barque *Hannah Parr*, returning to Christiana from Quebec with a cargo of deal pine-boards. The Norwegian was able to continue on her way but two of the seven crew of the *Anemone* were lost, the cook after volunteering to return to the brigantine to try and repair rigging and block holes, following which she was abandoned for the second time.

The 1,160-ton three masted Shaw Saville Line clipper *Avalanche* sank to the south-east of Portland Bill on the night of 11/12 September 1877 after colliding with the *Forest*. There were just 12 survivors, rescued at great risk by Portlanders in two boats, and a total of 106 lives were lost. Many were New Zealand émigrés, outward bound from London on the *Avalanche*, including colonists who were going back again after a holiday visiting friends and relations in 'the old country'.

It was initially thought that both vessels had sunk, but three days later reports appeared that the upturned *Forest* was visible from the Nothe and the Inner Breakwater and 'had not shifted far from the Shambles lightship'. The following week the battleship HMS *Defence*, an ironclad from the Channel Fleet, spent several days alternately shelling and then placing kegs of explosive on the wreck, with minimal effect on 'this great towering hull, rising like a rock out of the sea.'

The body of the *Avalanche*'s carpenter, J.H. Jamieson, was buried in St George's churchyard with 'five others names unknown'. Some were recovered from Chesil Cove but others were washed up miles away, such as that of Robert Dudgeon, the 29-year-old ship's cook, which lies in the old churchyard at West Lulworth. He is named 'Dundem', probably in error, on the Portland memorial plaque.

Their demise is commemorated by St Andrew's Avalanche Memorial Church, built at Southwell, at a cost of £2,000. The Bishop of Salisbury consecrated 'the most southerly church in my diocese' on 3 July 1879. The huge anchor from the *Avalanche* is set on the grass beside it. This was recovered from the sea after divers from Bingham Sub-Aqua Club, Nottinghamshire, discovered the wreck in 1984. They also brought up quantities of dinner service and other pottery carrying the Shaw Saville crest, a representative collection of which is displayed in the church. John Callan of Southwell designed the commemorative stained-glass window in 1981. The *Forest* was a large, fully-rigged Canadian sailing ship, displacing 1,422 tons, registered at Windsor, Nova Scotia. The *Forest* was given her name 'because it took one to build her'.

She also sank off Portland Bill. Having delivered timber to London, the *Forest* was returning empty with only minimal ballast and therefore rode 'high in the water'. Nine of her crew, including the 50-year-old master, Ephraim, and his 33-year-old mate, Robert McValine, were saved. The other 12 were drowned.

In 1877 a long-proposed extension of the branch railway from Portland to the dockyard, via the existing stone siding at Castletown, eventually started to take shape on the ground. Running for a mile, it was needed to bring coal for the new generation of steam-powered battleships, and came into use in 1878. The increasing institutionalisation of the island was now being reflected in its birth-rate and a Wesleyan School was built at Weston, in 1858, to accommodate 227 pupils.

The brigantine *British Seaman*, carrying coal from Hull to Gibraltar, 'went down like a stone' on colliding with the Greek barque *Anthippe* 15 miles south-east of Portland Bill on 3 October 1878. The brigantine seems to have been at fault, as she rammed into the stern of the barque, which put into Cowes for repairs.

The *Speedy*, carrying ingots of tin from Penzance to St Brieux, put into Portland Roads during a force 9 south-easterly gale on 7/8 January 1879. Her anchor failed to hold, however, and she was swept onto the shore near Ferry Bridge, in the company of the Weymouth fishing smack *Essay*, ending her days on the nearby Mere. On 1 November 1879 the Fowey smack *Exhibition*, carrying vegetables from Treguier to Weymouth, foundered off Portland Bill.

The 585-ton Newcastle steamship *Hesledon Hall*, carrying iron ore to Bilbao, ran into the London steamship *Terlings* in mid-Channel south of Portland Bill on 25 July 1880. With her bows stowed in, the vessel from the Tyne began to sink, and took five of her 13 seamen to their deaths.

One of the best descriptions of urban Portland was penned by Dorset architect, poet and novelist Thomas Hardy (1840–1928) in his Napoleonic epic *The Trumpet Major*, published in 1880. He was thinking of the steep 'Street of Wells', which rises from Maidenwell at the upper end of Chiswell Square, becoming the High Street as it climbs towards Fortuneswell in the general direction of Verne Citadel:

*The steep incline before her was dotted with houses, showing the pleasant peculiarity of one man's doorstep behind his neighbour's chimney, and slabs of stone as the common material for walls, roof, floor, pig-sty, stable-manger, door-scraper and garden stile.*

Portland's 'wild, herbless, weather-worn promontory' provided Hardy with the setting for his character Anne Garland to watch HMS *Victory* sailing down-Channel in 1805 for Plymouth and Cape Trafalgar, with Bob Loveday on board. By 1880, Fortuneswell was already expanding and changing, with densely packed terraces and lines of slate roofs in a triangle between two uphill thoroughfares. Hardy re-honed the vignette at the end of the decade for *The Well-Beloved*, which appeared in 1892:

## Harbour

*The Prince of Wales arriving in the royal yacht* (centre left) *to mark completion of the Inner Breakwater, with the Outer Breakwater beyond, from* The Graphic *of 17 August 1872.*

*Portland Harbour and the Channel Fleet from the torpedo range on the Bincleaves side of the water in 1900.*

*Training ship HMS* Boscawen (centre right) *adding a Nelsonian touch to Portland Harbour in the 1890s.*

*The towering rock, the houses above houses, one man's doorstep rising behind his neighbour's chimney, the gardens hung up by one edge in the sky, the vegetables growing on apparently almost vertical planes, the unity of the whole island as a solid and single block of limestone four miles long, were no longer familiar and commonplace ideas.*

Revd William Robert Waugh, the Congregational Minister at Chiswell from 1879 to 1892, rebuilt his Manse and proceeded to construct an astronomical observatory. It had its counterpart to the west at Rousdon Observatory, near Lyme Regis, from where baronet Sir Cuthbert Peek of the biscuit-making family published his *Meteorological and Astronomical Observations* from 1886 to 1895. Waugh submitted his jottings to the Dorset Natural History and Antiquarian Field Club in Dorchester. He observed the annual Leonid meteor showers each November, as well as markings on Jupiter and sunspot comings and goings. In 1901, when he was long retired and sporting a white beard of Biblical proportions, he described 'the somewhat sudden appearance' of a 'steely blue' new star 'in the constellation Perseus'.

The 'Forger's Slate', now displayed in Portland Museum, is an elaborate tribute to a popular prison warder, etched like a printing plate by an accomplished engraver who is said to have lost his freedom for copying a banknote. It is an intricate representation of the tomb with an even more elaborate border which carries the heading 'H.M. Convict Prison, Portland, Governor G. Clifton Esq' above the wheel of life, and a detailed epitaph:

*Memorial of the late Chief Warder Brooks. Who, while on duty on 19th January 1881 was seized with apoplexy and, mid universal regret, expired in 36 hours. Sacred to the Memory of William Thomas Brooks. Born 14th August 1822. Died 21st January 1881. Now is the axe laid at the root of the tree. Watch therefore for ye know not the day nor the hour.*

There was also official grief at his demise, the governor recording:

*It is with no ordinary feeling of regret that I have to record the sudden death of my faithful chief warder, Mr W.T. Brooks from an attack of paralysis, brought on from exposure while on duty during the immensely cold weather which prevailed at the beginning of that month.*

The medical officer, Dr George Herbert Lilley, added his respects in the prison's annual report:

*I regret also to record the death of chief warder W. Brooks from a very sudden attack of apoplexy; he was seized while standing by my side and talking to me; he was at once removed to the hospital, where he became*

*rapidly worse; and died in a few hours. The death caused the most profound regret, as* [he was] *held in the highest esteem alike by officers and prisoners.*

The *Rosebud*, a brigantine returning in ballast from Dieppe to Llanelli, was washed into the outer breakwater off Portland on 4 February 1881. The Dutch schooner *Fenna*, carrying a cargo of glass and iron from Amsterdam to Trieste, sank off Portland in a force 9 gale on 10 March 1881. The ketch *Corunesa*, in sail with potatoes from Hamburg to Penryn, sank 15 miles east of Portland Bill on 16 October 1882 after being in collision with the steamship *Darent* from Whitby.

A transitional type of iron-built sailing vessel, the *Waitara* embarked with her sister ship, the *Hurunui*, from Gravesend for Wellington, New Zealand, and they travelled together down-Channel through mist and rain on 22 June 1883. Then disaster struck, literally, as they bounced off each other in a disastrous double collision south of Portland. There were two impacts, just two minutes apart, as a result of which the *Waitara* was lost with 27 lives (though a contemporary report only accounts for her second officer, 12 passengers, and one 'stowaway'). The sinking happened so quickly that only 14 survived, being those able, lucky or young enough to climb up cables or into boats as they were lowered from the *Hurunui*.

On 8 August 1883 the coal-carrying schooner *Sapphire* was driven into Chesil Cove. Her crew were taken off by rocket-fired lifesaving apparatus. The next unscheduled arrival was the Norwegian barque *Christiana*, carrying floorboards from Drammen to Dartmouth, which was thrown spectacularly towards Cove House Inn by a hurricane on 1 September 1883. Two of her crew of ten were drowned, the other eight being saved by rocket-fired breeches buoy.

The *Folke*, a schooner, sailing from Newcastle to Lisbon with coal, coke and bricks, went down in what was described as 'the lightest of winds', 12 miles south of Portland Bill, on 14 November 1883. The brig *John Givan*, sailing with deal floorboards between Drammen and Swansea, sank following an 'unidentified' collision nine miles south-east of Portland Bill on 3 December 1883. The wind was rising towards a full gale, which aided the escape of what may be assumed to have been the culprit.

Prison life on Portland continued to take its toll on those who worked in the extreme cold and heat of some of the worst winters and best summers of the Victorian era. In sweltering conditions, frustration tended to turn to violence and one of the regular fights during the digging of the great ditch beside Verne Citadel ended in a death, though the post mortem blamed heart failure. Others took out their desperation on themselves, with suicide attempts running at the rate of 20 a year, ten per cent of which were successful. Methods ranged from hanging with a towel and self-mutilation with pieces of tin or zinc

# Harbour

*The Royal Breakwater Hotel on The Strip* (left) *facing stone wharves and the wooden pier* (centre) *at Castletown, with a steamer heading into the harbour, north-westwards in 1890 towards a wooden viaduct carrying the railway on to the island* (top right).

Above: *The Home Fleet, gathered off the coaling wharves at Castletown, in about 1930.*

Right: *Commemoration stone laid by Prince Edward in 1872, also inscribed for Prince Albert who sunk the first stone of the Inner Breakwater from the same spot in 1849.*

to the eating of 'poisonous roots'. One individual, serving a life sentence for murder, emasculated himself in 'a fit of depression'.

D.R. Bowler's study of *Portland Convict Prison* shows that although corporal punishment was normally reserved for violent offenders, five convicts were birched in April 1883 for idleness. Each received 24 strokes of the birch, a 4ft instrument of multiple rods, bound together to a regulation 7in. circumference. The prospect of the stick was also used to induce others to work harder, with ten lazy individuals being brought into the punishment room to witness the beatings. In May 1883, and in June 1884, severe floggings with the fearsome cat-o'-nine-tails were stopped by intervention of the medical officer and the prison governor, when the individuals were in danger of passing out.

The clay-boat *Coila*, with a cargo of Purbeck ball-clay en route from Poole to Runcorn, became a total loss 15 miles south-east of Portland Bill on 19 January 1884. That summer, on 2 June, the local cutter *Emma* was dredging for oysters in Lyme Bay, 15 miles west of Portland Bill. In calm water, out of a bright sky, she was 'run over' by a barque which was never identified.

The 3,082-ton Newcastle steamship *Britannia*, carrying cattle from New York to London, was in collision with the steamship *Bellcairn* from West Hartlepool on 31 July 1884. She went down 12 miles south of Portland Bill, with all of the stock, but apparently all 29 crew and the eight passengers were saved by the *Bellcairn*.

Chief among the Irish rebels imprisoned in The Grove on Portland, held on a life sentence from 1884, was Thomas J. Clarke. Convicted of conspiring with the Fenian or Irish Revolutionary Brotherhood to dynamite public buildings in England, he was released under an amnesty in 1898.

John 'Babbacombe' Lee (born 1862) became known as 'the man they couldn't hang' when the noose had been put around his neck three times in Exeter Gaol on 23 February 1885. On each occasion the trapdoor jammed as the lever was pulled. In tests it had worked perfectly and at the third attempt a warder jumped on and off the door as the hangman wrestled with the pulleys. The ordeal lasted a total of 45 minutes. Sentence was then postponed and afterwards commuted to life imprisonment.

Lee had been convicted of the murder of Mrs Keyse, a former lady-in-waiting to Queen Victoria, at Babbacombe, near Torquay. Her throat had been cut and her skull fractured in a frenzied attack, after which the killer torched her home on 16 November 1884.

Her footman, John Lee, who had a criminal record – for theft – became the obvious suspect, though he proclaimed his innocence throughout and no direct evidence was produced at his trial. An assortment of omens and dreams were said to have predicted the bizarre outcome at Exeter. A flock of white doves circling the prison yard was also taken to be a sign of his innocence.

On being reprieved, Lee was taken from Exeter to Portland Prison at The Grove, and was kept inside for 22 years. When he was eventually released it was as a living legend, with media attention and the release of songs, comic strips and even an early cinema film. The truth, which was that the evidence upon which he had been convicted was circumstantial, became twisted into ever more far-fetched fictions. These had either the dead woman's solicitor being blamed for the murder, or King Edward VII who, as the Prince of Wales, had been a frequent visitor to the house at Babbacombe. Lee made up for some of his lost years by marrying a nurse.

J.W. White noted in 1885 that Portland's wild asparagus crop was still alive and well, growing either side of Small Mouth, beside the estuary of The Fleet. On the other side of Chiswell, quarryman Hiram Otter (c.1855–1940) proceeded to create a coastal footpath south from Chesil Cove, beneath West Weares, to the headland at Tar Rocks and Clay Ope beyond it. He used his 'large and sinewy arms, with muscles of strong iron bands' to hand-jack immense boulders out of the way. Then he etched them with biblical inscriptions and the first lines of some of the Salvationists' most powerful hymns. He was the cheerleader of Portland's newly founded Salvation Army Corps. 'Alleluia!' he cried, when each of his texts was completed. Alleluia Bay became the local name for the indented coast between Chesil Cove and Tar Rocks. Silverwell, on the undercliff west of Priory Corner, was renamed Jacob's Well.

The Swedish steamship *Sudon* was lost just 400 yards south-east of Cave Hole at Portland Bill, while carrying non-ferrous metals in 1885, leaving remains across the seabed including her winches and boiler. The ship's bell has since been recovered.

The *Bournemouth*, the paddle-steamer that carried the new resort's name, was wrecked on the western side of Portland Bill, beneath the Higher Lighthouse, on 27 August 1886. Her bows stuck firm on the inshore rocks and all aboard were lowered to safety. Efforts failed to prise her clear and she was then battered to pieces by a series of westerly gales.

The Norwegian steamship *Nor* was washed up on the Chesil Beach on 18 January 1887. The crew were brought off safely by rocket-fired breeches buoy. The vessel remained intact for some time but later broke her back and was eventually smashed to pieces.

A soldier of the Dorsetshire Regiment slipped from the edge of the dry ditch beside Verne Citadel and fell to his death on 22 November 1887. Then, as now, the occasional escaped prisoner provided a little excitement in island life though it was the prison's boast that all were recaptured. On 5 December 1887 'a notorious burglar', 35-year-old William Keagh, slipped away from one of the gangs working in the

# Harbour

*North-east along the Inner Breakwater from the royal arms* (bottom right) *to the chalk cliffs at Chaldon Herring* (top left) *in 1972.*

*The Inner Breakwater* (left), *South Ship Channel* (centre right) *and Outer Breakwater* (beyond) *to the East Ship Channel* (centre left) *in 1972.*

*Fort Head* (centre) *and the Outer Breakwater, looking south to The Grove* (top left) *and Verne* (top right) *in 1972.*

*Fort Head, otherwise known as the Chequered Fort for its wartime dazzle-camouflage, seen from the western side of the East Ship Channel*

*'C' Head and the Northern Arm of the Breakwater which joins Bincleaves Groyne* (top left) *looking north-east from the North Ship Channel to Rodwell in 1972.*

*Ship from France Telecom taking on fibre-optic cable from the 'gleaming white' store of Global Marine Services at Castletown in 2001, in a view across Portland Harbour to the full length of the North Eastern Breakwater.*

quarries. He was duly recaptured the following day in the Harbour Master's store at Castletown.

The brig *Clara Nobella*, returning to her Llanelli home from London with a cargo of chemical fertiliser, was lost in a moderate offshore wind 25 miles west-south-west of Portland Bill on 3 April 1888. Later in the year, bound from Charlestown to Brussels with Cornish china clay, the ketch *Lady Sondes* went down off Portland Bill on 14 August. The Harwich ketch *Ada*, carrying paraffin from London to Exeter, sank in the Race off the Bill during a force 9 south-south-westerly gale on 12 December 1888.

Though originally authorised as the Easton & Church Hope Railway as long ago as 1867, and partly cut by the time the company's powers expired in 1872, the major work on the extension line from Castletown to Easton did not start until 1888. This would continue for the rest of the century, as the geography dictated a 3.5-mile loop below East Weare and Grove Cliff and then through the challenging geology of Portland itself in order to reach the village amid the quarrylands. Merrick Head of Pennsylvania Castle, looking forward to its completion, said that he was old enough to remember Governor Penn crossing to Portland in the Passage Boat, before the building of the Ferry Bridge in 1839, in a carriage and four.

The emerging Labour movement established an early presence in the heart of the Portland quarrylands with the opening of a Working Men's Club, in Reforne, in 1888. On the other side of the libertarian divide, in the convict quarries, prisoners from The Grove found they were to labour for their principal adversary, the Metropolitan Police. Plans were approved for a new headquarters to replace Scotland Yard, on a site beside the Thames Embankment, where work began, to designs by Norman Shaw, in 1890.

Work started at Southwell in 1890 on what was intended as the island's principal borehole for drinking water and went on until completion in May 1895. The project cost £6,000 and successfully broke through the strata of stone into underlying Kimmeridge clay, but this oily layer was impregnated with sulphurous chemicals which turned the water brackish.

The Whitehaven barque *Ehen*, sailing from Bremen to Bordeaux with a cargo of rice, ran into the rocks at Mutton Cove on the western side of Portland Bill in dense fog on 22 April 1890. One of the seamen climbed sheer cliffs – which virtually overhang the water – and happened to meet a Coastguard on patrol along the cliff path beside the Higher Lighthouse. A rescue operation swung into action, a rocket line enabling the remainder of the nine crew and Mrs Roberts, the master's wife, to be rescued by breeches buoy.

Two crewmen and a passenger were lost when the London barque *Ethel*, outward bound for Hobart, Tasmania, was in collision with the steamship *Umbilo* while becalmed 'in a mill pool' 25 miles south-west of Portland Bill. The *Ethel* proceeded to sink, though Captain Ross and the remaining 20 crewmen and passengers were picked up by the *Umbilo* on 24 June 1890.

On land, in poor weather early in August 1890, lepidopterists Mr and Mrs Nelson Richardson caught eight specimens of a small, hairy-headed moth which had never been recorded before in Britain. It was identified as *Tinea subtilella*, a species first taken and identified by Herr Fuchs on old vineyard walls in the Rhine in July 1878. Richardson gives a picture of Portland at the time of the introduction of William E. Metford's improved rifling for the breech-loading Martini-Henry rifle:

*I hope that the ensuing season may show that the resources of Portland are not yet exhausted, though so-called civilisation is doing its best to destroy the insects by making a new railway, and the collection of them, by the establishment of a new rifle range at which rifles are used, which, I am told, carry two miles. the shooting with which takes place straight along the undercliff.*

A fire aboard the Austrian schooner *Fannie C*, en route from Hamburg to Buenos Aires, caused her captain to run her into the Chesil Beach at Portland in order to save the lives of his ten crewmen. The vessel was carrying a cargo of unspecified 'combustibles' and became a complete loss on 3 October 1890.

Dense fog, swirling in a light offshore wind, caused the Stockton-on-Tees steamship *Thames* to run into Tar Rocks, south of Chesil Cove, on 2 January 1891. The 408-ton three-masted vessel was carrying a cargo of crushed granite roadstone and tin ingots from Newlyn to London. Captain Becherley and his 12 crewmen were able to scramble ashore. In March 1891 the Boston-built sailing ship *Senator Weber*, flying the Swedish flag, foundered off Portland Bill. Her crew were taken off by the Weymouth fishing boat *Lass*.

The brig *Annie Harris*, carrying ore from Swansea to West Hartlepool, sank after being in collision with the German steamship *Dresden* whilst becalmed 15 miles south of Portland Bill on 18 July 1891. Four of her seven crewmen were lost. The barque *Mysterious Star* went down closer to Portland on 13 October 1891. The same day, in a south-westerly gale, the Sunderland barque *Ora et Labora*, carrying deal floorboards from Nordmaling to Nantes, was driven ashore on the Chesil Beach at the back of Victoria Square. The ketch *Adolphus*, from Lyme Regis, foundered eight miles south of Portland in a force 8 north-easterly gale on 28 March 1892. She was in transit with limestone from Plymouth to Southampton.

Thomas Hardy's novel *The Well-Beloved*, first published as a magazine serial in 1892 and then as a

## Harbour

*Mere Tank Farm* (top left) *and the almost empty tarmac of former RNAS Portland helicopter base in 2001.*

*Two Royal Fleet Auxiliaries out in the harbour, in 2001, with two sections of wartime Mulberry Harbour inshore at Castletown* (bottom left).

book in 1897, is set on Portland. It features Avice's Cottage at Wakeham, one of the island's very few thatched buildings, as the home of would-be well-beloved Avice Caro, who dies and is followed by other unattainable Avices. Avice Caro's daughter is named Ann Avice Caro and her granddaughter Avice Caro. 'All men are pursuing a shadow,' Hardy responded, in defence of his improbable plot.

The novel's main male character, Portland sculptor Jocelyn Pierson, finds fame and fortune in London, returning to his native isle to fulfil his ideal of perfect womanhood. Despite his best intentions, each of his infatuations with successive generations of the Caro family predictably fail to reach the altar. The book was set in 1857 but extended forwards to 1897, which lay in the future when the magazine edition rolled off the press in 1892.

Built in 1892 between Verne Citadel and the Admiralty Quarries, the High Angle Battery provided Portland Harbour and the sea-lanes across Weymouth Bay with their main late-Victorian artillery defences. A total of 15 huge rifled muzzle-loaded cannon were mounted in barbettes set deep into the stone plateau above East Weares. The gun barrels were elevated steeply in order to achieve a trajectory over open ground to the east.

Two datestones carry the royal initials for Victoria Regina over tunnels that led to underground shell and cartridge stores, which were kept several hundred yards apart to minimise the danger of accidental explosion. Narrow-gauge railway lines go into the tunnels and around the rear of the barbettes. The guns comprised the following complement:

*Six 9-inch calibre (range 5 miles).*
*Two 12-inch (range 4 miles).*
*One 10-inch (range 5 miles).*
*One 9-inch (range 2.5 miles).*
*Five 7-inch (range 2 miles).*

All were designed to fire Palliser-type shells into the first generation of ironclad battleships. Each gun barrel had its own elaborate carriages and elevating gear which, as a combination, weighed in excess of 20 tons. They were never fired in anger. All were stood down and sold for scrap in 1910. Gun emplacements and some ancillary buildings, such as side-arms stores, have survived to become an ancient monument, and were restored as a community project in 1984.

A land-based Boys' Training Establishment for naval cadets was established on the north-eastern slopes of the island in 1892. Together with its vessels in the harbour, it housed a total of 1,600 'Navy boys'. Offshore, Training Ship *Boscawen* (the former HMS *Trafalgar*), was joined by a new-style ironclad battleship in 1893. HMS *Minotaur*, displacing 10,600 tons, had entered Portland Harbour earlier in her career, as flagship of the Channel Fleet in 1877. As a cadet training ship, however, she was re-named *Boscawen II*.

The *Bridport News* of May 1893 recorded a well-attended beating the bounds ceremony at the parish boundary between Portland and Chickerell, which may have challenged a few of the islanders' assumptions, the ritual of marking the boundary seemingly having been repeated a mile further north-west than was usual. Bounds were originally beaten so that children would learn at an impressionable age, via a stroke of the cane across the buttocks, the point beyond which it was unsafe to stray:

*The Portlanders seem determined to keep up their rights, which they annually maintain by an official visit to the well-known 'bound-stone' on the Chesil Beach. Holy Thursday, or Ascension Day, is, by custom, the day on which the ceremony takes place. This year the number attending seems to have been augmented for some reason or other, perhaps the fact of a new stone being used added importance to the affair. Be that as it may, there were many visitors, both by sea and land.*

*It is said the rights of Portlanders extend to the new bound stone opposite Fleet, but the public would like to be enlightened as to the nature of those rights. There is one right at all events which does not extend beyond the Portland side of the stone, that is, we are informed that the lord of the manor of Abbotsbury, or rather the Earl of Ilchester, does not interfere with or claim the foreshore. Not that such a right would be of any use whatever, seeing the difficulty of telling where it is. The shingle shifts with the weather, and with it the foreshore, if ever such existed except in fertile imagination.*

The Plymouth brigantine *Jane Francis*, carrying Cornish china clay to Hamburg, was the victim of a 'hit and run' collision in light winds on 22 July 1893, about 15 miles south-east of Portland Bill. The offending vessel, heading down-Channel, was alleged to have been an American sailing ship.

In 1894 the building of breakwaters resumed in Portland Harbour after a break of two decades. The Admiralty engaged in astute forward thinking, anticipating that the advent of the motor torpedo boat would change naval warfare by enabling sudden gunboat attacks on warships that were moored or berthed. The existing harbour works, conceived as a protection against the weather, were now seen as inadequate as a defence for the fleet at anchor. Only extended breakwaters could make the harbour safe. To that extent the naval thinkers were right, as the torpedo would become the principal weapon against shipping, though they would mainly come not from the surface but from a perfected form of 'submersible' and in some cases, unthinkably at this time, from the air.

The decision to enclose the whole of Portland Harbour was nothing if not ambitious. Two additional sections of breakwater, making landfall on the mainland shore halfway between Sandsfoot Castle and the Nothe Fort at Weymouth, were to enclose four square miles of deep water.

The steamship *Gertrude*, heading up-Channel, ran into Portland's eastern cliffs at Blacknor on 26 August 1894. She was under full power at the time, approaching in thick fog from Lyme Bay, as was demonstrated by the wreckage, which was literally lifted into the air with the bows projected above the rocks, though this see-saw effect had the stern sinking from sight. By good fortune, however, the *Gertrude* collided with Portland out of a calm sea on a windless day, enabling all 20 crew and passengers to be rescued. The vessel was carrying iron pyrites from Huelva to Rotterdam.

The author Beatrix Potter (1858–1943) brought her father to see Portland on 1 April 1895 but saw no point in coming again:

*Portland Island is a curiosity to see once. Very like Gibraltar only flat-topped. The top is one vast quarry and stony wilderness. The convicts did not particularly appeal to me.*

The sailing ship *Willowbank* sank near Portland on 12 December 1895. A year later, on the night of 4 December 1896, a gale toppled the chalk stack of Old Harry's Wife at Studland and washed away the old chain pier at Brighton.

The most notable Englishman to be held in Portland Prison at The Grove was Jabez Balfour, who arrived as convict V460 on 19 June 1896:

*There was no necessity to carve the words 'Abandon hope, all ye who enter here' over the entrance to Portland Prison. The massive cold great walls say that for themselves.*

As the Member of Parliament for Burnley, he built a business empire upon a web of deceit, which fell apart in 1892 when he fled to the Argentine. Balfour was eventually extradited to the United Kingdom and stood trial at the Old Bailey. A sentence of 14 years' penal servitude (of which 18 months were spent on Portland) was imposed for company fraud and corruption. His white-collar crime was ahead of its time, both in terms of what we now know as sleaze, and in the way he articulated the problems of being a fallen pillar of Victorian society:

*If the brutal warder of popular melodrama was ever a real person, he was to be found at Portland during my time there. That is many years ago now. Things have doubtless changed since then, but Portland as I knew it was a heart-breaking, soul-enslaving, brain-destroying hell upon earth. The tone of the officers' voices, their curt, dictatorial and offensive manner, their sneering laughs and gibes struck me as being in consonance with the place itself...*

*During our miserable hour of exercise the assistant warder who had charge of us on one occasion threw a stick down in our path and defied any man to pass it except on the left-hand side. I myself was twice reproved for looking up at the sky...*

*Once a prisoner in passing me smiled, the warder saw and was swift to shout, 'Now then, Balfour, smiling is not allowed here.'*

In 1896, the realities of a Portland convict's life were immortalised in verse by A.E. Housman (1859–1936) in an interruption to the otherwise rural progress of *A Shropshire Lad*:

*The star-filled seas are smooth to-night*
*From France to England strown;*
*Black towers above the Portland light*
*The felon-quarrier stone.*

*On yonder island, not to rise*
*Never to stir forth free;*
*Far from his folk a dead lad lies,*
*That once was friends with me.*

The 1839-built timber Ferry Bridge was replaced by an iron structure in 1896. Beside it, with George Eastwood as landlord, stood the Royal Victoria Hotel, typical of a series of modern-style roadhouses designed by Weymouth architects George Crickmay & Co.

Opposite, a series of waterside sheds were set to become a major naval munitions plant, with Whitehead Torpedo Works providing weapons for motorised gunboats and the first submersibles. The latter belonged to the next century, with Viscount Goschen as First Lord of the Admiralty refusing to sanction their deployment in April 1900, but his successor Viscount Selbourne reversed the decision a year later and authorised the building of five British vessels 'to assist the Admiralty in assessing their true value'.

Whitehead Torpedo Works was established by Robert Whitehead on the Wyke Regis side of Small Mouth in 1891. Whitehead had pioneered development of the weapon at Fiume, Italy, in 1867. A Torpedo Depot was established at Castletown in 1901 and HM Submarine Torpedo Boat No. 1 was launched at Barrow on 2 October that year. Generally known as *Holland 1*, she was built by Vickers at Barrow-in-Furness under licence from the Holland Torpedo Boat Co. To Alfred von Tirpitz, founder of the German Imperial Navy, these were unnecessary 'luxuries', and on this side of the North Sea Admiral Lord Charles Beresford dismissed them as 'toys'. Both were forced by events to change their minds.

Portland, being of national strategic importance, had to be supplied with a dependable supply of fresh water, but the search on the rock was proving fruitless. The solution, found in 1898, lay on the mainland, in the valley above Upwey Wishing Well, where a

500,000-gallon reservoir was built 545 feet above sea level. From here, via a ten mile main of 10in. pipe, a high pressure supply reached to Portland and extended across the whole island, including to Tophill and the 495ft highest point on Verne Citadel. The total cost of all these works was £45,896. A large booster reservoir was then constructed on the island at Verne Yeates in 1902 but remains only partly filled due to a crack. An additional borehole and secondary pumping station followed at Friar Waddon, north-west of Weymouth, below the Ridgeway Hill source.

The strand at Castletown, known as The Strip, developed as a long three-storey terrace with the Jolly Sailor and the 1898-dated tiled frontage of the Portland Roads Hotel. Next were the Royal Breakwater Hotel, The Albert (later called the Green Shutters) and the Sailors' Return. Beyond Castletown, in the dockyard, was the Depot including the Admiralty Slaughter House. Offshore, the Royal Navy bunkering boat *Patrick Henry* – one of the

harbour 'coal hulks' – sank at her mooring in Portland Roads during a gale on 9 March 1898. It was a blustery month and a similar 'cold wind' – blowing force 9 from the north-east – accounted for the collision of provisions cutter *Surprise* and the yawl *Lavona*, on adjacent moorings, on 25 March 1898.

Coincidentally, the 1,650-ton despatch vessel HMS *Surprise* was in collision with the 1,620-ton Cardiff steamship *Netley Abbey* – carrying coal to Kronshtadt – two miles south of the Shambles Lightship on 4 August 1899. There were no fatalities but the coaster sank later in the day.

Thomas Hardy always admitted he lived in his mind with the past and its conflicts, from Trafalgar to the Crimea, but the advent of modern warfare filled him with dread. News of rising numbers of casualties in the Boer War led him to produce a remarkable poem entitled 'The Souls of the Slain', in which the spirits of soldiers killed in South Africa fly homeward over Portland Bill like migratory birds.

## Fortuneswell

*Yew Tree Cottage, on the corner of New Road, as Alfred Burridge's Portland Academy in 1888.*

## Fortuneswell

*Fortuneswell* (right) *in 1891, linked by intermittent buildings in the High Street* (centre) *to the hamlets of Maidenwell and Chiswell* (left).

*Looking up the street in Fortuneswell to St John's Church and Trevaneon Eveleigh's Royal Hotel, in 1891.*

## Fortuneswell

*Fortuneswell* (right) *in 1839, with newly-built St John's Church though not showing the first Ferry Bridge* (centre background), *and the High Street running down to Maidenwell* (left).

*Army manoeuvres before the South African War, in 1898, marching up through Fortuneswell towards New Road* (left) *and Verne Hill Road.*

# Fortuneswell

*Naval cadets marching down into Fortuneswell from Verne Hill Road (right) in about 1895.*

*The Beehive Stores (left) opposite the shop-front of watchmaker and silversmith Arthur Ernest Comben (with blind).*

## Fortuneswell

*Portland Observatory with Revd William Robert Waugh, the Congregational minister at Chiswell, in 1899.*

*Chiswell (left) and Fortuneswell (right), from Priory Corner, to a naval background in 1912 with oil tanks and warships.*

## Fortuneswell

Left: *Looking down on Fortuneswell, in 1973, from terraces above the High Street to the roundabout in Victoria Square and cars queuing on Portland Beach Road* (towards top left).

Below: *Verne Citadel* (top left) *and Fortuneswell* (centre) *from the Chesil Beach in the 1890s.*

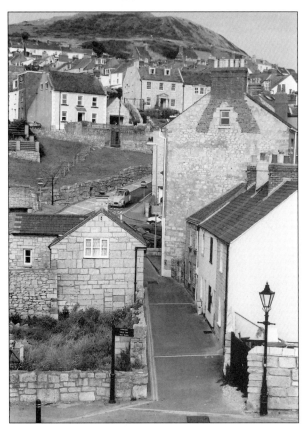

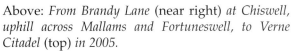

Above: *From Brandy Lane* (near right) *at Chiswell, uphill across Mallams and Fortuneswell, to Verne Citadel* (top) *in 2005.*

Above right: *Cove House Hotel and Chesil Cove, protected by waves of recently completed sea defences, in 1997.*

Right: *Cove House Hotel behind its walls, with the Chesil Beach beyond.*

# Fortuneswell

Above: *Upper parts of Fortuneswell from the High Street* (centre right) *to New Road* (top left) *in 1998.*

Left: *Three-storey flats at East Weare Road, Castletown, looking more like a doll's house in this telephoto shot from 2006.*

*John Maine's 'outdoor sculpture' of stone-built terraces* (centre)*, seen from above Chesil Cove in 1998, form a buffer-zone between Fortuneswell and West Weares.*

# ✦ CHAPTER 8 ✦

# *World Wars*

After Queen Victoria celebrated the diamond jubilee of what was now 'the longest reign on record', those 'imperial' works on the royal island and further developments across the harbour were having more than a visual impact on Portland's environment. A local botanist noted that a particularly vulnerable species was the wild asparagus. The Whitehead Torpedo Works was expanding across its prime habitat on the Wyke Regis side of the water and, on the other bank of Small Mouth, unlike the great drifts of maritime thrift, it was failing to colonise the railway bank. Few noticed and fewer cared at a time when war-works rather than ecology captured the spirit of the age.

From Portland it must have seemed that the British Empire was secure for ever, though in retrospect it could be argued that it had reached breaking point. There were already cracks that defied diplomacy, as the South African War had shown, plus the deeper danger of European powers clashing over their portfolios of overseas possessions and beginning to square up to each other on the home continent. Other empires, it was noted, were much less stable than ours, and any confrontation would be complicated by a web of treaty obligations. In this respect the British were particularly restrained, usually standing alone or in the company of a faithful old 'white ally' such as Portugal, or of the promising new 'yellow friend' in the shape of Japan.

Portland's branch railway reached its ultimate extent on 1 October 1900, when the line to Easton Station opened for freight traffic. The first passenger train arrived on 1 September 1902, but services were disrupted on 28 November 1903 when the station was destroyed by fire. It was rebuilt in 1903, as was the viaduct across Small Mouth, where the timber structure was replaced in steel.

The 2,385-ton Spanish steamship *Enecuri*, heading home to Bilbao in ballast from Hamburg, anchored in Balaclava Bay during a force 9 north-westerly gale but dragged her anchors and was washed onto rocks beside the Inner Breakwater, along which the captain and his 26 crewmen clambered to safety. The captain, however, disregarded warnings that the wreck was liable to capsize and returned to it the following day with his dog. Both were drowned as the vessel slid from its precarious perch.

The French smack *Auguste*, from Trouville, sank after being in collision with the Spanish steamship *Olazarri*, 25 miles west-south-west of Portland Bill, on 21 January 1901. There was only a light breeze at the time and the smack seems to have been fishing. Of the seven crew, five lost their lives.

The first two oil tanks between Portland Beach Road and The Mere were constructed in 1901 for innovative oil-burning escort vessels. Their number grew during the century to a total of 26, with 14 in a line that stretched for half a mile beside the A354, though they have since retreated back towards the harbour.

The Poole ketch *Star of Peace*, carrying oil cake from London to Bridport, was stranded while attempting to round Portland Bill on 5 February 1902. South Portland Working Men's Club in Reforne moved into the Coronation Hall in Moorfield Road, coinciding with a visit from the new King Edward VII on 3 April 1902. The actual coronation, planned for 26 June of that year, had to be postponed until 9 August in order for Dorset surgeon Sir Frederick Treves to perform a pioneering life-saving appendix operation on the monarch.

In Portland Harbour the Royal Navy cadet Training Ship *Boscawen II* was joined by a second ironclad battleship in 1902. The new arrival was the 6,621-ton HMS *Agincourt* which, on being berthed near her sister ship, also had her name changed, to *Boscawen III* (the *Agincourt* name was reissued in 1914 to the impounded Turkish warship *Sultan Osman I* on its being requisitioned by the Royal Navy). An earlier *Boscawen* (confusingly, the second of four ships to carry the name at Portland) remained in service, moored in the harbour as a sail-training vessel.

Offshore, the Norwegian barque *Patria*, sailing with timber from Frederikstad to Port Natal, lost a seaman who was washed overboard on 26 October 1903. Things then went from bad to worse as she was crippled by hurricane-force winds off Portland Bill. A yardarm was lost and all her canvas shredded. Defiantly, on realising he was being driven inshore by a rising tide, Captain Danielson told his 11 crewmen that their only chance was if he headed directly into the pebbles of the Chesil Beach at Chiswell.

Chesil Cove was 'crowded with spectators' as the *Patria* came towards them, 'eventually driving hard up the beach, engulfed in huge waves'. Coastguards fired a rocket line for a rescue by breeches buoy. As a result the crew all survived, though the injured second mate had a leg amputated the following morning and the cook 'went mad and had to be put in a straight jacket, his mind having gone.'

The artillery battery at Verne Citadel was stood down in 1903 and the barracks handed over to an infantry company. The decommissioned guns were removed for scrap in 1906. On top of the island, in 1903, a new Wesleyan School was built at Weston. In the far south, work started in October 1903 on the present-day 136ft high lighthouse at Portland Bill, and continued until 1905. This was to take the place of the old Upper and Lower lighthouses. Trinity House paid £300 for the site and the circular stone tower, with 153 steps, was built by contractors Wakeham Brothers from Plymouth. Three lights are set at 141 feet above sea level. Three tons of lenses float at the top of a liquid metal base of half a ton of mercury. Its night-time white flashes are, in fact, a group of four lights which reveal a beam every 20 seconds. An additional red light illuminates the water over the Shambles sandbank. Close to ground level, seaward of the tower, the fog horn is activated as visibility falls to less than two miles, and gives a blast of 3.5 seconds at half minute intervals.

Another new lighthouse was also being built at the eastern end of the North-Eastern Breakwater of Portland Harbour and came into use on 14 March 1905. Lloyd's Cottage, on the site of the former Lloyd's Signal Station, was rehoused in an Edwardian bungalow on Portland Bill, next to a compound which bristles with masts.

Completion of Portland Harbour, with four square miles of sea enclosed behind massive walls of stone, made it much more than the 'Harbour of Refuge' envisaged six decades earlier. Bigger than anything created in the colonies, it represented one of the peaks of British engineering achievement, and remains the largest man-made deep-water harbour in the world. The area sealed off by the four lengths of breakwater is large enough to contain the harbours of Malta and Gibraltar, together with Hyde Park and Kensington Gardens.

Portland Harbour became host to every type of craft in the evolution of the modern warship, 'from the old wooden walls with their spreading white sails, to the latest Dreadnought creation, a sort of monstrous floating fort', plus those primitive submarines. The earlier breed of iron-plated steam frigates were represented by the 6,170-ton HMS *Warrior*, which used steam auxiliary power as a last resort. Dating from 1860, the 380ft vessel had cost £400,000 and used transitional technology. When on the move, under sail, one funnel was lowered from sight and the screw propeller was lifted from the water. Maritime steam, at the time of its adoption in the middle of the nineteenth century, was regarded as little more than a means of emergency propulsion for times of calm.

The timber viaduct which carried the railway across the inner extremity of the harbour, at Small Mouth, was replaced by a steel structure in 1903. On 25 October 1903 a gale turned the Russian schooner *Anna Maria* as she attempted leaving Teignmouth for Lisbon with a cargo of china clay. Instead she was driven up-Channel by heavy seas and made landfall on the Chesil Beach. The vessel was doomed but the sea did her six-man crew a favour by felling the mainmast, which formed 'a bridge to the shore, along which the men clambered without delaying to collect any of their belongings.'

Even in this year of its so-called completion, this series of autumn and winter gales undid recent work on the breakwaters of Portland Harbour, which needed immediate repairs after being battered by the sea on 12 December 1903. Bincleaves Groyne, on the Weymouth side of the water, was to remain unfinished for several years while water lapped over it during the highest tides. Even these had been changed by the breakwaters, with high tide at Castletown in Portland Harbour now two hours later than that at Chiswell in Lyme Bay.

Edwardian municipal gardens at Easton Square were opened by Councillor H. Sansom in April 1904. They initially displayed the 'elegance of the era' but were subsequently reduced to what Stuart Morris described as 'bland suburban mediocrity' with the loss of bandstand, railings and trees.

Tout Quarries closed in about 1905, but there was still a look of heavy industrialisation across the island from Tophill onwards. The Admiralty Quarries had their own railway network, with rolling stock hauled by saddle-tank steam engines, which meant that Portland now, at the turn of the twentieth century, had six different railway systems – the original Merchants' Railway, the Admiralty Incline, the standard-gauge branch line, supply lines on the breakwaters and a closed-circuit network of little lines in the High Angle Battery.

The quarry system was long remembered for a dramatic accident in which the prison's own saddle-tank locomotive slid down a scree slope in what is now the Stadium area. The cable-operated Merchants' Railway, lowering stone to the quay at Castletown, had its own mini-disaster on 15 June 1904.

Four loaded stone wagons ran away and left the track at great speed, smashing through the Admiralty slaughterhouse, where the damage cost £300 to repair. The year of 1904 marked the virtual completion of modern Portland, and most of its labour force was withdrawn, causing closure of the Mission to Navvies.

Between 1905 and 1907 the ships of the Boys' Training Establishment – each sharing the *Boscawen* name – were withdrawn and replaced by the cruiser HMS *Sapphire* and a succession of smaller training brigs such as HMS *Martin* and HMS *Seaflower*. These distinctive vessels, with one gun-deck, two high masts, and a central funnel, had been regular visitors to Portland Harbour since the turn of the twentieth century.

# Lighthouses

*The Lower Lighthouse at Portland Bill, seen shortly before it became redundant in 1906, is now Portland Bird Observatory.*

*'A' Head Lighthouse on the North Eastern Breakwater of Portland Harbour, looking north-west to the Nothe at Weymouth (centre top) in 1972*

*Lighthouse (left) and the Trinity House seamark (right) with the Waverley paddle-steamer rounding Portland Bill in 1996.*

*The Upper Lighthouse at Portland Bill was also replaced in 1906, and famously became the home of birth-control pioneer Dr Marie Stopes.*

*Left: Three tons of lenses floating on half a ton of mercury, at 141 feet above the waves on Portland Bill.*

*Below: The last Shambles Lightship, beside the sandbank off Portland Bill, before replacement with an automatic buoy in 1971.*

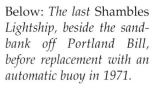

*Portland Bill Lighthouse from the south-west in 1973.*

The Padstow schooner *Deveron*, loaded with china clay and moored in Portland Harbour, sank after being in collision with the destroyer HMS *Conflict* on 19 June 1905. The Bridgwater schooner *Rollo*, carrying stone from Rouen to Plymouth, was lost on 6 January 1901 when she rammed one of the two original harbour breakwaters. The four crewmen scrambled ashore with their bags and were given refuge by Royal Artillerymen in Fort Head.

The 2,199-ton German steamship *Athen*, having picked up a cargo of coking coal in Cardiff for transit to Rio Grande do Sul, Brazil, was waiting in Lyme Bay for another vessel to join her when she was in collision with the steamship *Thor*, 11 miles south-west of Portland Bill. She sank after the incident, though the crew of 25 were taken off and returned to Hamburg.

Following the coming into operation of the new Portland Bill Lighthouse, Higher Lighthouse became a private house and the Lower Lighthouse was redundant. The destroyer HMS *Landrail*, also obsolete in 1906, was relegated to the receiving end of target practice by the Channel Fleet. The 950-ton vessel was towed from Sheerness to Portland Harbour for preparation for her new role, being stripped of combustible fittings and filled with ashes, dust, empty barrels and other semi-inert materials such as cork, in order to absorb impacts without being set ablaze. She was then towed out into Lyme Bay by the Admiralty tug *Camel*, and moored fore and aft.

Here she met her end from the combined firepower of the battleships HMS *Albemarle*, *Caesar*, *Exmouth*, *Prince George* and *Triumph*. They began the barrage at 7,000 yards and slowly closed to within 3,000 yards, each firing for about five minutes. The *Landrail* was afloat, however, and an initial inspection indicated that she was suitable for a repeat performance another day – after being returned to Portland for evaluation and patching – and was in the process of being moved on a long line from a destroyer when she began to heel over and sink in deep water, taking Signalman Leonard Wardley down with her. Others in the team were able to jump for their lives.

A major landslip in 1907 cut off rail services between Portland and Easton. Expansion of the community there continued, as a result of which a Methodist Church was built at Easton, in early-English style, over the winter of 1906/07.

Ordinary Seaman Frederick Charles Thompson, of HMS *Swiftsure*, was killed aged 18 in an accident on 13 February 1908. The tragedy was followed by the dignified theatrics of a full military funeral. The Hull ketch *Autumn*, in sail with railway parts from London to Newport, Monmouthshire, foundered while trying to enter Portland Harbour on 7 July 1908. The 785-ton steamship *Idlewild*, carrying coal from South Shields to Devonport, foundered nine miles south-south-east

of Portland Bill on 30 June 1908.

The timber viaduct across Weymouth Backwater was replaced in steel in 1908 and the following year the expanding suburbs of Westham and Wyke Regis were provided with the railway halts for which they had been petitioning. A passing loop, controlled by a signalbox, was constructed beside the existing station at Rodwell.

The Weymouth ketch *Fox* sank beside the northern entrance of Portland Harbour after being in collision with the Greek steamship *Zarifls* on 17 October 1909. The Weymouth pilot cutter *Spirit* was 'struck and sunk', killing James Zelley, off the outer breakwater of Portland Harbour on 15 January 1910. This accident was blamed on the Danish steamship *Jan* for approaching the pilot boat 'in a careless and unseamanlike manner'.

'The *Dreadnought* Hoax' is often mentioned in national newspapers as the greatest April Fool's joke of all time, but the inconvenient fact is that it happened a little earlier in the year, on 10 February 1910. The incident, involving the flagship of the Home Fleet in Portland Harbour, remains, in the national psyche, as enduring as the memory of Richard Dimbleby wandering through rows of 'spaghetti trees' on BBC television in 1957.

The brilliance of the *Dreadnought* deception lay in the crafting of its details. The key perpetrators were William Horace de Vere Cole (1881–1936), alias the man from the Foreign Office, and Miss Virginia Stephen (1882–1941), known to us as the writer Virginia Woolf. With three friends she posed as a male member of the Abyssinian royal family, having been fitted out by London tailor William Clarkson in oriental costume. The three spoke a mixture of Swahili and Latin (pronounced backwards) for the convenience of a 'German' interpreter.

The plot swung into action when de Vere Cole telegramed the Royal Navy at Portland with a message that purported to come from Sir Charles Hardinge, the Permanent Under Secretary for Foreign Affairs, who later in the year was created 1st Baron Hardinge of Penshurst:

*Commander-in-Chief Home Fleet, Portland. Prince Makalen of Abyssinia and suite arrive 4.20 today, Weymouth. He wishes to see* Dreadnought. *Kindly arrange meet them on arrival. Regret short notice. Forgot wire before. Interpreter accompanies. Hardinge, Foreign Office.*

The recipient aboard the battleship, at 3.45 in the afternoon, was Admiral Sir William May (1849–1930). He had just half an hour in which to put on full dress, arrange for a guard of honour to be mounted on board, and send a launch to Weymouth to collect the Africans. Meanwhile they were being escorted off the London train by civic dignitaries – namely the Mayor and Corporation of Weymouth

# Navy

*Railway* (foreground), *and sidings out on to the Inner Breakwater* (right), *together with the Naval Hospital and Coal Depot* (centre right) *at the eastern end of Portland Dockyard in 1892.*

*Naval boundary marker in Castle Road, beside the Victorian cemetery, carrying the symbols of Government (broad arrow) and Admiralty (anchor).*

*New Admiralty Camber, between The Strip at Castletown* (bottom left) *and Portland Dockyard, with training ship HMS* Boscawen *moored offshore.*

*Edwardian gathering of the Channel Fleet in Portland Harbour.*

# The Daily Mirror

THE MORNING JOURNAL WITH THE SECOND LARGEST NET SALE

No. 1968         WEDNESDAY, FEBRUARY 16, 1910         One Halfpenny

HOW THE OFFICERS OF H.M.S. DREADNOUGHT WERE HOAXED: PHOTOGRAPH OF THE "ABYSSINIAN PRINCES" WHO HAVE MADE ALL ENGLAND LAUGH.

*Colour party in Portland Naval Cemetery firing shots over the grave of 18-year-old Ordinary Seaman Frederick Charles Thompson of HMS* Swiftsure, *accidentally killed on 13 February 1908.*

*The* Daily Mirror *scooped the incredible story of 'How the officers of HMS* Dreadnought *were hoaxed' at Portland in February 1910.*

# Navy

Warship and the Floating Dock in Portland Harbour in the 1920s.

Submarine M2 *and her Peto float-plane which went down off Portland Bill on 26 January 1932, with the loss of 59 seamen and airmen.*

The Pens, *for escort vessels, between Castletown and New Admiralty Camber in the 1920s.*

The assault ship Intrepid, *which had been empty and redundant at Portsmouth, was hastily recommissioned in Portland Harbour in April 1982 and sailed to the South Atlantic for the Falklands War.*

*The Royal Navy back at Portland in 2006, in the shape of the tanker RFA* Brambleleaf *(A81, foreground) – a Falklands veteran – and a RFA landing ship.*

*The latest 'landing ship dock auxiliary vessel', RFA* Mounts Bay, *berthed at Portland (L3008, centre) in 2006.*

and Melcombe Regis – and ushered into a 'four-wheeler' and taxi-cab for the short drive to Weymouth Harbour. *The Daily Mirror* reported:

*All the princes wore vari-coloured silk sashes as turbans, set off with diamond aigrettes, white gibbah tunics, over which were cast rich flowing robes, and round their necks were suspended gold chains and jewelled necklaces. Their faces were coloured a deep brown with specially-prepared powder, and half-hidden under dark false beards and moustaches, while except in the case of the lady, their hair was dyed black and crisply curled.*

*The young lady's make up – she is described as very good looking, with classical features – was precisely the same as that of the other princes, save that her long hair was bound up tightly on top of her head, and she also wore a black curly wig. They also wore patent leather boots which, oriental fashion, tapered to a point, the ends projecting fully six inches beyond the toes. White gloves covered the princes' hands, and over the gloved fingers they worse gold wedding-rings – heavy plain circlets, which looked very impressive.*

*Prince Makalen, as chief of the royal party, had an additional ornament. This was the real Imperial Order of Ethiopia – a star-shaped jewel, in the centre of which was a sapphire-like piece of glass. It was suspended from a red, gold and blue ribbon, and was pinned on – with a safety-pin – to a gold chain round the neck. The metal was of Abyssinian silver plated with gold.*

Stepping out of the Admiral's launch and climbing the gangplank of the battleship, they were piped aboard to the strains of the Zanzibar national anthem, which was the closest tune the band could attempt, 'not knowing that of Abyssinia, if such a thing exists'. To the Navy's embarrassment it also lacked an Abyssinian flag.

Horace de Vere Cole (alias Herbert Cholmondely from Whitehall) led the party and shook hands with Admiral May and Captain Herbert Richmond, the chief officer of the *Dreadnought*. He introduced the visitors as Prince Makalen (Duncan Grant), Prince Sanganya (Virginia Stephen), Prince Mandok (Anthony Buxton) and Prince Mikael Golen (Guy Ridley). Herr George Kauffmann (Adrian Stephen) followed in beard and bowler as the German interpreter.

Prince Makalen talked gibberish as he inspected the Royal Marine guard of honour. Kauffmann, Virginia Woolf's brother, explained that the prince wished to know 'the difference between the red and blue marines'. The explanation was duly translated into gibberish as the party proceeded to tour the entire warship and alternately 'beamed with pleasure and glared ferociously'.

They declined offers of tea because 'the least moisture would remove the powder from their skin'. This was nearly unmasked on arrival back at Weymouth, as one of the princes slipped on a step and almost toppled into the harbour. Then a young Flag-Lieutenant escaped with his dignity intact by politely declining the award of the Imperial Order of Abyssinia. The masquerade was maintained all the way back to London.

The paddle-steamer *Brodick Castle*, the replacement for the *Bournemouth*, which was lost at Portland Bill in 1886, followed her predecessor's fate on 31 October 1910. Renamed *Peca Nova*, she had embarked upon what should have been her maiden voyage to Buenos Aires as an Argentinian cattle-barge. Under tow from Weymouth, her line broke in 'huge waves' as she rounded Portland Bill, and she was wrecked within sight of the *Bournemouth*'s grave.

The Llanelli steamship *Jason*, carrying ingots and pigs of iron, ran into the shore near Sheep Rock on 13 March 1911. Out in the Channel, 15 miles south-south-west of Portland Bill, the Glasgow coaster *Enriqueta* sank on 11 October 1911 after being in collision with the German steamship *Westphalia*. The *Enriqueta*, which was carrying coal from Hull to Kingsbridge, had a crew of ten, who were taken off.

'The Admiralty regrets...' a statement began on 6 February 1912 after the 1903-built submarine HMS *A-3* surfaced off the Isle of Wight under the approaching bows of 1,070-ton submarine and gunboat depot ship HMS *Hazard*. All 14 members of her crew went with the submarine to the bottom, but the wreck was raised in mid-March and the bodies were taken to the Royal Navy cemetery in their home port of Portsmouth. The end for the submarine came in 'Channel Firing', as commemorated in a Thomas Hardy poem, at the receiving end of the light 4-inch guns of the battleship HMS St *Vincent*, midway between Portland Bill and St Alban's Head.

The 2,571-ton Newcastle steamship *Myrtledene*, carrying iron-ore from Sagunnto, Spain, to Rotterdam, steamed at 8 knots into the rocks of Mutton Cove on 25 March 1912. Captain Mitchell thought he was 'at least 20 miles south of Portland' at the time. The vessel's hull was ripped apart and the engine room flooded, but no one was killed as she ended up wedged bow-first in offshore rocks below Blacknor. The steam tug *Verne*, from Portland Harbour, and the *Helper* from Weymouth stood by as the 25 crew and two passengers left in the ship's boats. The *Myrtledene*, which was launched on the Tyne in 1890, was originally named the *Harewood*.

The first great review of the Royal Navy at Portland, comprising the combined Home and Atlantic Fleets, was carried out by the new 'Sailor King' George V, from 8 to 11 May 1912. The event had been due to start on 7 May but the first day's activities were cancelled by fog. This also caused the royal yacht *Victoria and Albert* to arrive late from the Isle of Wight, and Winston Churchill stood in for the king as First Lord of the Admiralty. Political leaders were also present, headed by Liberal Prime Minister

Herbert Asquith, and the Conservative Leader of the Opposition, Arthur Balfour. They were treated to some superlative gunnery from the battleships HMS *Orion* and HMS *Neptune*.

The Fleet outgrew Portland as it assembled for a Royal Review. Usually the ships were gathered in a north-east to south-west grid that started at Bincleaves Groyne and extended into Weymouth Bay, with an inner line of small vessels such as minesweepers and motor torpedo boats, stretching for two miles into the open sea beyond the East Ship Channel and the harbour breakwaters.

When the fishing boat *Turenne* from Boulogne, steaming off Portland with a full catch on board for return to France, ran aground on Clay Ope, below Blacknor, on 12 February 1913, all 16 members of her crew scrambled ashore. The wreck was bought and patched by Portland quarry owner Fred Barnes, who took her around the Bill to Castletown Pier, where she was scrapped. The fish had already been salvaged, though they went to Billingsgate rather than Boulogne.

The big guns of 'Channel Firing' would certainly have been heard by Thomas Hardy at his Max Gate, Dorchester, home on 4 November 1913. The target for the day was the obsolete 14,100-ton battleship HMS *Renown*, renamed *Empress of India* on being decommissioned, which had been stripped and gutted. She was towed out of Portland Harbour to a mooring at the place of execution, in what is still the Lyme Bay sea danger area, where her peers discharged shells and torpedoes.

Engine breakdown caused the 2,035-ton Dutch steamship *Dorothea* to be driven ashore into Chesil Cove during a gale on 14 February 1914. She was carrying iron ore from Marbella to Rotterdam. A much smaller loss, also of metal, took place on 30 July 1914, when the Jersey schooner *Lucinda* went down 14 miles west-south-west of Portland Bill. She had set out into a gale from Cowes for Llanelli.

History is seldom what was considered to have been news at the time but it is often the myth that endures instead. Such is the case with Dorset's crucial role as the European powers went to war in the summer of 1914. The truth is far more interesting than the contemporary account.

The Royal Navy's 1st, 2nd and 3rd Fleets gathered at Spithead between Portsmouth and the Isle of Wight for a review by King George V and the First Lord of the Admiralty, 39-year-old Winston Churchill, on 17 July 1914. Exercises followed in the English Channel as the yachts at Cowes Regatta were joined by Prince Henry, brother of the Kaiser, who had called on his cousin at Buckingham Palace and been assured by King George that Britain would remain neutral in the event of a European conflict. Here at home the office furniture was being shuffled and Admiral Sir George Callaghan, Commander-in-Chief of the Home Fleet, was summoned by train to

Whitehall, to be told on arrival that he was being replaced by Admiral Sir John Jellicoe.

Whether misinformation or linguistic misunderstanding, this was far from political reality, as Churchill realised on 23 July when he dispersed the 3rd Fleet to its home ports. The 2nd and 3rd Fleets remained together and regrouped in Portland Harbour.

There they were said to have remained until the outbreak of war. Secret orders, however, had prepared them for action a whole week earlier on arrival at Portland. Personal effects were removed and put into store at the dockyard, though many of them would never be needed again. Red flags flew as ammunition was taken on board, including Dorset-made propellant charges from the Royal Naval Cordite Factory at Holton Heath, and projectiles from Whitehead Torpedo Co. Ltd at Wyke Regis. Frenetic activity succeeded in readying the warships in a matter of days.

Captain G.C.C. Crookshank had the eye, equipment and opportunity to picture the moment, though many of his glass negatives were lost to breakage or damaged by damp and dust. His ship was HMS *Agamemnon*, which went on, as we have now become accustomed to say, to enjoy a good war, ending with iconic status under Vice-Admiral Sir Rosslyn Erskine Wemyss by taking the Turkish surrender in negotiations which began on 28 October 1918. Launched in 1879 at Chatham, the ironclad turret ship displaced 8,492 tons and carried four 38-ton guns.

By noon on Monday, 27 July 1914, ships of the 2nd Fleet were leaving Portland and sailing towards training establishments around the country. The dreadnought *Bellerophon*, from the 4th Battle Squadron, was steamed towards the Bay of Biscay, heading for Gibraltar to be refitted in a dry dock there.

The remainder of the 1st Fleet – about to be re-designated as the Grand Fleet – waited off Portland until Wednesday, 29 July. That day the German Fleet began its mobilisation and the Admiralty and War Office responded by secretly moving the ships from Portland to a safer location. They were ordered to steam 'at high speed, and without lights' through the Straits of Dover, into the North Sea and onwards to Scapa Flow anchorage between the isles in Orkney.

The Admiralty feared that Portland was vulnerable to a surprise attack by German motor-torpedo boats. Operational ships were to be at their war stations before a declaration of war, 'therefore if possible before we had decided ourselves'. These were Churchill's own words. He later described these unfolding events, which he successfully concealed both from the German High Command in Berlin and the British Cabinet in Whitehall:

*We may now picture this great fleet with its flotillas of cruisers steaming slowly out of Portland Harbour, squadron by squadron, scores of gigantic castles of steel wending their way across the misty, shining sea, like*

# First World War

*Last picnic on the Chesil Beach, between Wyke Regis and Portland* (background), *in July 1914.*

*Ratings relaxing in a boat circling The Fleet, as the Fifth Battle Squadron prepare for war in Portland Harbour in July 1914.*

*Clearing personal gear and trunks from HMS Agamemnon when the Fifth Battle Squadron was put on a war footing in Portland Harbour, July 1914.*

*Taking off personal trunks from the battleship Agamemnon into a gear-boat at Portland.*

## First World War

*Inspection of midshipmen on HMS* Agamemnon, *in the process of loading cordite in Portland Harbour, July 1914.*

*'1A' labels on barrels of cordite, the propellant charge for naval shells, being loaded on to HMS* Agamemnon *in Portland Harbour, July 1914.*

*giants bowed in anxious thought. We may picture them again as darkness fell, 18 miles of warships running at high speed and in absolute darkness through the narrow Straits, bearing with them into the broad waters of the North Sea the safeguard of considerable affairs. The strategic concentration of the fleet had been achieved with its transfer to Scottish waters.*

Back at Portland, the old battleship *Prince of Wales* remained and was taking on coal in the harbour when the signal came through from the Admiralty that began the Great War. Everyone cheered, ratings recalled, before they resumed coaling with renewed vigour. Issued at 23.00 hours on Tuesday, 4 August 1914, and effective from midnight, the message read: 'Commence hostilities against Germany.'

The first loss, however, was to that old enemy the weather, rather than to the Germans. The 6,010-ton ironclad battleship HMS *Invincible*, demoted by the Admiralty and renamed *Fisgard II* upon reuse of her historic name, was under tow from Portsmouth with the tugs *Danube* and *Southampton* on 17 September 1914. As she took on increasing quantities of water, the 'scratch crew' had removed everything moveable from upper to lower levels in an attempt to restore stability. It was to no avail, however. Five miles off Portland Bill at 17.09 hours the former warship heeled over until she was lying on her beam-ends. Her four ship's boats and 24 lifeboats were available for an orderly evacuation, but although 43 of her complement survived the other 21 men were drowned.

Fears of German motor-torpedo boat or submarine incursions into Portland Harbour had already led to attempts at sealing its entrances with nets. The first version comprised thousands of small, round glass bulbs in floating cases. These were suspended on piano wire, with the idea that they would 'bob about' if activated by an intruder, but it was soon realised that by that time it would probably be too late to react.

The next development was torpedo nets, hanging like curtains across the channel, suspended from floats known as 'cats'. Tom Pike, who was at Portland at the time, understood that the arrangement worked well for the north and east entrances but failed at the South Ship Channel when the main tide flowed out from the harbour. There the nets ran sideways 'like drapes in the wind'. Five-ton anchors (called 'clumps') were attached to the bottom of the nets to overcome the problem.

However the experts had reckoned without the immense quantities of rubbish which float away from a huge battle fleet. This jetsam caused havoc:

*The nets were clogged, and at full tide they naturally flattened with the stream and lay useless on the surface, despite their heavy anchors. It used to be said that you could walk on the nets when they were filled with gash.*

The Admiralty decided there was no time for further experimentation. The southern entrance into Portland Harbour was to be abandoned and blocked. This would be achieved by sinking an obsolete battleship. Selected for scuttling was the redundant iron-clad HMS *Hood*, 14,000 tons, which went down on 4 November 1914.

The intention was that she would be raised after the war, but salvage was never attempted, and the hull and crushed superstructure are still there today. She had 'turned turtle', with her bilge keel showing above the surface at low water. Tom Pike told me:

*In about 1960 the situation changed and the masts, guns and funnels of the* Hood *were no longer capable of supporting her upside-down weight. They snapped and the big whale-back of her hull sank from sight. She must now be lying on her gunwales.*

In the event, Dorset's naval tragedy took place on the high seas, at 02.20 hours on New Year's Day 1915. The 15,000-ton battleship HMS *Formidable*, sailing last in line with the 5th Battle Squadron from Portland, was torpedoed in Lyme Bay, 20 miles east of Start Point. German submarine *UB-24* was responsible, with two torpedoes from close range, but itself only narrowly survived, having grazed the warship's heaving keel.

An orderly evacuation was carried out for two hours, as the battleship appeared to be stable, but at 04.39 she slipped under quite suddenly. Deteriorating weather had hampered the evacuation, and of the crew of 780, only 233 were saved, some in their own cutter, which took 20 hours to reach Lyme Regis. The Brixham trawler *Provident* carried out heroic rescues, as did the escort cruisers HMS *Topaze* and *Diamond*, which together brought a total of 80 survivors into Portland Harbour. For the remaining 547 officers and men the sea became their grave.

The ship's dog, an old terrier named Bruce, was also lost. He was last seen standing on duty beside his master, Captain Loxley, who remained with Commander Ballard on the bridge. Revd G. Brooke Robinson, former curate of Burton Bradstock and a prominent member of West Bay Swimming Club, who was chaplain on board, also went down with the ship.

There were 50 men aboard the boat washed up at Lyme but nine of them were dead or dying. Others had expired during the voyage from injuries and exposure, and their bodies had been pushed overboard. At Lyme the press found their second 'Man's best friend' story.

John Cowen had been left for dead on the floor of the Pilot Boat Inn in Broad Street. During the night, however, the landlord's cross-breed collie started licking his face and hands. Charles Atkins drew attention to his dog's agitation and a groan was heard to come from the body. From the jaws of

## First World War

*Shells in the foreground and barrels of cordite behind during the arming of the guns on HMS* Agamemnon.

*'Completing' with projectiles: 13.5-inch shells are prepared for action on HMS* Agamemnon *in July 1914.*

## First World War

*Continuing 'completing' by taking on board a torpedo, in the arming of HMS Agamemnon.*

*The obsolete battleship HMS Hood (centre) being prepared for scuttling to block the South Ship Channel into Portland Harbour against U-boat penetration in July 1914.*

*HMS Hood (background) in position to block the South Ship Channel into Portland Harbour in October 1914.*

*The White Ensign stiff in the air as the last church service of peacetime is held on the stern of HMS Agamemnon off Portland.*

*His Majesty's Ships Russell, Exmouth, Cornwallis and Duncan leaving Portland to join the Grand Fleet on 29 July 1914.*

*Right: HMS Hood, plus wires and nets, capsized across the former South Ship Channel to prevent entry by enemy submarines or motor-torpedo boats.*

disaster the press had their miracle to report:

*Immediately willing hands completed the work the dog had begun and in a short time Cowen sat up. Since then the dog and Cowen have been inseparable, and as Cowen is not yet allowed out, he and the dog spend most of the time before the kitchen fire cultivating the acquaintance so curiously begun.*

On the other end of the scale, for warships, the 162-ton HMT *Quail III* – the initials standing for His Majesty's Trawler – was run over and sunk by an unidentified vessel off Portland Bill on 23 June 1915. The Admiralty designated Portland Harbour as a War Anchorage and Trawler Station and placed it in control of English Channel sea-area XIII, which became known as Portland Command Area.

Across other waters, former Portland convict Thomas Clarke achieved international notoriety in the middle of the First World War when he issued what became his death warrant. This was in the form of the first and only edition of *The Irish Republic* newspaper, released in Dublin, to announce the Sinn Fein insurrection on 23 April 1916: 'The following have been named as the Provisional Government: Thomas J. Clarke...'

So began the announcement of what became known as the Easter Rising. Clarke's was the first of seven names. During the uprising, 2,000 rebels held the centre of the city for a week. Martyrdom came for Clarke – in front of a firing squad – on 3 August 1916.

Portland Royal Naval Air Station was established in The Mere marshes between the Chesil Beach and Portland Castle on 26 September 1916. It was initially designated as shore-base HMS *Sereptia*. The expansion that followed included a seaplane shed, while the lagoon beside the bunkering oil tanks became the home-base for the 12 Short & Wright float-planes of No. 416 and 417 Flights, which comprised 241 Naval Air Squadron in 1918.

Four 9.2-inch guns were installed in Blacknor Fort during the First World War, in Victorian emplacements midway along Portland's western cliffs, in a commanding position overlooking Lyme Bay. Amid all this military activity, civilian life was also undergoing change, with the building of All Saints' Church behind The Straits at Easton in 1916/17. This, the replacement Parish Church, was to succeed to the privileges, registers, rights and silver of the beautiful classical St George's in Reforne. It cost £13,000 and opened with a tide of bereavement and grief as memorial services were held to commemorate those who were falling in foreign fields. The sea in sight of the island was no safer.

On the evening of 3 August 1916 a German submarine surfaced beside the schooner *Fortuna*, 15 miles south-south-west of Portland Bill, and trained her deck-gun on the Falmouth vessel, which was carrying scrap iron from Le Havre to Swansea.

Explosive charges were placed on board and the sailing ship was scuttled half an hour later. Her crew were later picked up by the *Joanna*, also in sail, and landed at Plymouth. The same U-boat was also seen intercepting and sinking the sailing barge *Ivo*. At first light the following morning, 24 miles south-south-west of the Bill, it was the turn of the Bridgwater schooner *Ermenilda* and her four crewmen, who were picked up by a Russian steamship. They had been carrying 155 tons of granite from Guernsey to Poole.

The 1,342-ton West Hartlepool collier *Spiral* was also stopped on 4 August 1916 by a German submarine, identified as *UB-18*, 14 miles south-east of Portland Bill. The steamship was in transit from the Tyne to Bordeaux with a cargo of coal, which was the major strategic import to war-torn France, at the rate of 1,500,000 tons a month for the duration of the conflict.

The Norwegian 1,388-ton freighter *Daphne* was torpedoed and sunk by *UB-16* while steaming up-Channel off Portland, from Newport to Rouen, on 11 November 1916. She was also carrying coal, as was the 3,806-ton Bergen steamship *Finn*, torpedoed by *UC-26*, 40 miles south-west off Portland Bill on 19 November 1916. Her final voyage had been from the Tyne to Genoa.

Fishing boats, working 25 miles south-west of Portland Bill, were targeted by a German submarine on 28 November 1916. Crews were taken off the wooden smacks *Amphotrite* and *Provident*, which were then sunk by gunfire and scuttling charges.

Heavily armed but disguised naval vessels, designed to look just like the merchant ships from which they had been converted, were a bright idea adopted by Winston Churchill, First Lord of the Admiralty. Their deadly combination of theatrics and trickery paid dividends as these Q-ships accounted for a total of 12 U-boats. One of these successful actions took place 24 miles south-west of Portland Bill on 30 November 1916, when Q-ship *Penhurst* seduced the German minelaying submarine *UB-19* into surfacing in front of her. Screens were thrown aside and the White Ensign went up the halyard as the first of 83 shells pounded into the doomed U-boat. Of the Germans who jumped into the sea, 16 survived to be taken prisoner.

The day began inauspiciously for *UB-19*. Her earlier target near this spot turned out to be the German-owned schooner *Behrend*, flying the red ensign, which was en route from London to Brest with a cargo of guano fertiliser. Berthed at Arbroath on the day that the war began, the sailing ship had been confiscated by the Admiralty, and its sinking was the submariners' final contribution to the war.

Steaming up-Channel eight miles south-east of Portland Bill, the 5,620-ton tanker *Conch*, carrying 7,000 tons of benzene from Rangoon to the Thames refineries, was torpedoed and sunk at 22.30 hours on 8 December 1916. No warning had been given and

# First World War

Back at Portland from Scapa Flow, HMS Agamemnon's 'Torture Party' of 'Xmas 1914' sending 'Best Wishes For A Happy New Year From Us All'.

New Year reality aboard the Agamemnon on 1 January 1915 was the arrival of survivors from the battleship HMS Formidable, which had been torpedoed in Lyme Bay.

Loading a 21-inch torpedo into an H-class submarine at Portland.

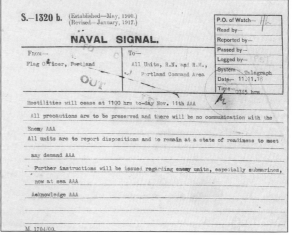

The end: 'Hostilities will cease at 11.00 hours today' was the signal the Flag Officer, Portland, received on 11 November 1918.

Above: Portland stone marks the graves of soldiers of the British Empire who fell on the Western Front, these being in Sarre Road Cemetery No. 2, where the Battle of the Somme began on 1 July 1916.

Left: Edwin Lutyens chose Portland stone for the national monument to 'The Glorious Dead' in Whitehall.

the first anyone knew of the presence of *UB-23* was a thud, followed by a great tower of flame as burning oil engulfed the bridge and destroyed all but one of the lifeboats. Of the crew, a total of 28 were killed – many of them Chinese – although a similar number were able to escape, mostly by jumping into the sea. The forward tanks continued to burn through the night and ship went down at 07.00 hours the following morning.

The 563-ton French barque *Union*, carrying rough timber from Aquin to Le Havre, foundered off Portland Bill on 28 December 1916, a casualty of the sea rather than the war, but the submarine menace remained. The next victim was the Danish schooner *Standard*, sailing with 347 tons of china clay from Fowey to Leith, 13 miles south of Portland Bill on 20 January 1917. She was followed by the 2,548-ton West Hartlepool collier *Romsdalen*, torpedoed by *U-84* ten miles south-west of the Bill while carrying coke from Newport to Calais on 17 February 1917. The same submarine used her other torpedoes on the 2,233-ton Liverpool steamship *Valdes*, passing seven miles south of the Bill on 18 February 1917. As she went down 11 seamen were lost on what was intended as a supply mission to support troops on the Western Front. They were carrying flour for bread and hay for the horses from Manchester to Cherbourg.

Geography played a part in the German submarine offensive during the second half of the war. Beachy Head, St Catherine's Point and Portland Bill joined Start Point and the Lizard as prime danger points where U-boats waited between shipping and the shore. The new generation of ocean-going enemy submarines were 240 feet in length and displaced 820 tons, carrying a 4.1-inch deck gun and 16 torpedoes. These were mainly deployed in the Western Approaches, but the Channel and North Sea were infested by smaller 100ft craft with double tubes and a total of four torpedoes, operating from Zeebrugge and Ostend. They could also lay mines.

'The position is exceedingly grave,' Admiral Sir John Jellicoe, as Chief of Naval Staff, warned the First Lord of the Admiralty and the War Cabinet in February 1917. He foresaw a situation in which it would be impossible to continue waging war if such losses continued. Admiral Sir David Beatty was persuaded to relinquish eight of his best destroyers from the elite Grand Fleet to sail south for the Channel on anti-submarine patrols, and Rear-Admiral Alexander Duff took command of a new Anti-Submarine Division. Other drastic measures included the secret arming of merchantmen – the disguised Q-ships – but the fear was that once their presence was known to U-boat captains, more shipping would be sunk on sight rather than being scuttled after the crews had been put in boats. The introduction of depth-charges and the convoy system did more than anything to reduce the losses.

The weather claimed the schooner *Macbain*, returning in ballast from Cherbourg to Fowey, 20 miles south-south-west of Portland Bill on 4 March 1917. She was followed, a short distance to the west, on 12 March 1917, by the 3,205-ton Liverpool steamship *Memnon* (formerly the *Plassey*), with a mixed cargo from Dakar to Hull. This time enemy action was responsible in the form of submarine *UC-66*. The same day, as she neared Portland with a delivery of coal from Barry, the 2,897-ton freighter *Tandil* was sunk by *U-85*.

The smack *Advance* was sunk by gunfire from a submarine 25 miles west-south-west of Portland Bill on 21 March 1917. Nearby, on 13 April 1917, the Fowey schooner *Maria* was stopped by a U-boat while returning to Cornwall with coal from Glasgow, and scuttled by explosive devices. Closer to the shore, seven miles off the Bill, the five crewmen of the schooner *Jessie*, carrying coal from Cardiff to Carentan, abandoned their ship after a German submarine fired warning shots across the bow on the afternoon of 27 April 1917. The 1,957-ton freighter *Gorizia* from Uruguay, nearing the end of a voyage from New York to Cherbourg. foundered and sank 20 miles south-west of Portland Bill in the early hours of 30 April 1917. An enemy submarine was active in the area that day, and proceeded to intercept the Fowey schooner *Little Mystery*, five miles to the south-east, as dawn broke. She was also bound for Cherbourg with coal from Cardiff, and the take-over by a scuttling party was hastened by the U-boat commander firing his pistol. One man was shot in the arm.

The 1,392-ton collier *Broomhill*, en route from Penarth to Sheerness, was captured at gun-point by German submarine *UC-61*, nine miles south-west of Portland Bill, on 10 May 1917. Two members of the crew lost their lives, but the rest were taken off as explosives were set to sink the vessel. The same day the 518-ton Norwegian steamer *Minerva* (formerly the *Marie*) was also sunk by a U-boat while in ballast between Caen and Swansea.

The Whitehaven schooner *Benita* was stopped and scuttled by a U-boat 15 miles south of Portland Bill, whilst carrying stone from Cherbourg to Poole on 20 June 1917. The same day, a mile to the west, the French sailing ship *Bidartaise* – in ballast from Cherbourg to Swansea for a cargo of coal – met the same end. On 30 June 1917, 22 miles west of Portland Bill, the 1,913-ton French steamship *Chateau Yquem*, in ballast from Dunkirk to Barry for Welsh coal, was torpedoed and sunk by *UB-40*. The Norwegian steamer *Uli*, in transit from Glasgow to Nantes with coal, was torpedoed and sunk further inshore in Lyme Bay, midway between Portland and Lyme Regis, on 4 July 1917.

The 5,842-ton freighter *Salsette*, owned by the Peninsular & Oriental Steam Navigation Co., was torpedoed by *UB-40* whilst outward bound from London to Bombay with general cargo. A total of 15 lives were lost when she sank, 15 miles south-west of Portland Bill, on 20 July 1917, though 259 passengers and crew were taken off. Approaching from the other direction, at the same spot that day, the 3,660-ton *Fluent* was torpedoed and sunk by *UC-65* as she neared completion of a voyage from New York to London with oats and steel for the war effort. Four miles off Portland Bill, the 654-ton Norwegian steamer *Veni* (formerly the *Dagmar*) was halted at gun-point and scuttled by a submarine. It was a busy day, the fourth local loss being the 1,916-ton West Hartlepool collier *L.H. Carl*, carrying 2,900 tons of coal from Barry to Rouen. She was torpedoed 14 miles south-west of Portland Bill at 21.30 hours, with the loss of two boiler men in the engine room.

Carrying coal for the Royal Navy, from Penarth to Portland on 26 July 1917, the 1,701-ton collier *Gregynog* was torpedoed and sunk in the Bristol Channel by *UB-86*, with the loss of three crewmen.

The 3,120-ton *Hazelwood* was struck and sunk by a German mine, laid by *UC-62*, while carrying a cargo of coal from the Tyne on 19 October 1917. She went down in Weymouth Bay, between St Alban's Head and Portland Bill, with the loss of all 32 persons aboard.

The 1,274-ton *Algarve* was torpedoed and sunk by *UB-38* 15 miles west-south-west of Portland Bill on 20 October 1917, whilst steaming from Rouen to Swansea in ballast. The master and his 20 seamen went down with the vessel.

The 5,704-ton steamship *Aparina* was torpedoed and sunk whilst heading from London to Barry Roads anchorage in the Bristol Channel, in ballast, on 19 November 1917. All 56 crew and passengers were killed as she went down midway between St Alban's Head and Portland Bill. The sinking was attributed to *UB-40*.

Portland's submarine depot ship HMS *Hazard* lived up to her name on 28 January 1918, when she was rammed by the hospital ship SS *Western Australia*. The *Hazard* sank but the *Western Australia* remained afloat and tended surviving casualties from both vessels.. There was enemy action that day, eight miles south-south-east of Portland Bill, where German submarine *UB-58* torpedoed the Guernsey ketch *W.H.L.*, which was in ballast between Cherbourg and Shoreham.

The last plotted position of the 2,128-ton steamship *Avanti* was rounding Portland Bill as she sailed close inshore to avoid German submarines while carrying iron ore from Bilbao to West Hartlepool. She was ambushed by *UB-59* on 2 February 1918 and sank off St Alban's Head with the loss of 22 men comprising Captain Davies and almost his entire crew. Only two were saved. The Royal Navy at Portland also lost three officers and 16 ratings that day, aboard the armed trawler HMT *Remindo*, on anti-submarine duties.

The 1,907-ton London steamship *Borga*, carrying coal from Swansea to Dieppe, was torpedoed by *U-55* in Lyme Bay at 11.40 hours on 1 March 1918. The vessel took water immediately and went down in a couple of minutes, with the loss of five of her crew, between Beer Head and Portland Bill.

The 943-ton French coaster *Polkerris*, carrying coal from Wales to Le Havre, was torpedoed and sunk ten miles south-east of Portland Bill on 4 March 1918. The 1,905-ton Belgian steamship *Martha* was torpedoed by *UB-80* and sank seven miles west-south-west of Portland Bill on 7 March 1918. The same submarine accounted for the 1,122-ton Norwegian steamer *Grane*, carrying coal from Swansea to Rouen, on 9 March 1918. The newly built 3,571-ton Liverpool steamship *Luxor* was heading the other way, in ballast from Cherbourg to Barry, when she was torpedoed by *UB-57* about 12 miles south of Portland Bill on 19 March 1918.

The destroyer HMS *Bittern* 'went down like a stone' off Portland, taking all 60 of her crew with her, at 03.15 hours on 4 April 1918. The 400-ton warship was in collision with the much larger steamship *Kenilworth* in Lyme Bay, south-west of Portland Bill. Visibility was almost non-existent due to thick fog, and neither vessel was showing any lights due to the danger of enemy submarines. Subsequent investigation blamed the steamer for sailing too far out into the English Channel on its course towards Start Point. The destroyer had been launched in 1897.

A huge explosion in the engine room rocked the 4,241-ton Glasgow steamship *Pomeranian* (formerly the *Grecian Monarch*) at 05.30 hours on 15 April 1918. Sailing inshore, nine miles north-west of Portland Bill, the ship was on the Lyme Bay leg of a voyage across the Atlantic, outward bound from London to St John, Newfoundland, where she was to have become a Canadian troopship. The vessel listed alarmingly and all but two of the crew, comprising Captain Maxwell and 56 men, went down with the vessel. The lucky couple were the purser and second engineer, who were found by a patrol vessel clinging to a plank caught in fore-rigging of a mast that had remained above the water. The sinking was credited to submarine *UC-77*. Then, at dawn, at 07.10 hours and also well inside Lyme Bay, 13 miles north-west of Portland Bill, the 601-ton Belfast steamship *Ailsa Craig* was torpedoed by *UB-80*. She was carrying coal from Cardiff to Granville. On this occasion, however, Captain Milliken and his crew of 15 were able to abandon ship in the only boat that remained usable.

The 1,001-ton London coaster *Bamse* (formerly the *Thomas Coates*) was torpedoed and sunk in Lyme Bay, 15 miles west-north-west of Portland Bill, by *UB-80* whilst in ballast from Rouen to Swansea for coal, at 23.50 hours on 17 April 1918. Four crewmen lost their lives but Captain Wilson and the other 13 men were picked up and taken to Torquay. The culprit this time was *UB-112*.

The 516-ton German submarine *UB-74* ended her brief career in Lyme Bay, four miles north-west of Portland Bill, on the night of 26 May 1918. The armed yacht HMY *Lorna* – the initials standing for His Majesty's Yacht – spotted her periscope and dragged her hull across the conning tower, after which she dropped three depth-charges. Four German sailors were later spotted in the water, shouting 'Kamerad!', but a further depth charge was released and the sole oil-soaked survivor died three hours later.

When the 1,303-ton Leith collier *Moidart* was torpedoed and sunk in Lyme Bay at 00.10 hours on 9 June 1918 by *UB-77* while carrying coal from Barry to Le Havre, 15 lives were lost. Her position was to the west of Portland Bill. On 11 July 1918 the 731-ton Norwegian collier *Kong Gottorm* was torpedoed and sunk by *UB-103* in mid-Channel, 30 miles south-east of Portland Bill.

The 1,895-ton Gibraltar steamship *Gibel Hanam* was torpedoed on 14 September 1918, about 15 miles south of a position variously given as Abbotsbury and Portland, whilst carrying coal from Swansea to France. Captain Sapp and all but one of his 22 crewmen were killed. Another collier, the 2.336-ton London steamship *Ethel*, was torpedoed by *UB-104* in Lyme Bay on 16 September 1918 but remained afloat and was taken in tow towards Portland Harbour. She rounded both the Bill and the Shambles sandbank but then sank on being pulled against the water into Weymouth Bay, four miles south-east of Portland Bill.

Despite the rate of attrition, after the United States had joined the conflict, the rate of transatlantic re-supply and replacement of lost shipping became unstoppable and the U-boats could no longer win the war at sea, despite having sunk Allied and neutral merchant vessels displacing a total of more than 11 million tons. By 1 October 1918, the Kaiser had asked his cousin, Prince Max, to negotiate an armistice as preparations were made to evacuate Ostend and Zeebrugge, causing the scuttling of four U-boats and five destroyers that were unable to sail. 'The navy does not need an armistice,' protested the new chief of German naval staff, Reinhard Scheer but, though undefeated at sea, they had lost the war at home. The actual Armistice was signed at 05.10 hours on 11 November 1918 and took effect on 'the eleventh hour of the eleventh day' of what was the 1,586th day of the First World War. Germany was blockaded and had collapsed. The Kaiser abdicated, influenza was sweeping the land, there was anarchy in the dockyards, sailors joined street protests, and returning heroes found themselves amongst mutineers who saw no point in further sacrifice.

The news was relayed by the Flag Officer, Portland, to all units of the Royal Navy and Royal Marines in Portland Command Area, by a Naval Signal:

*System: Telegraph.*
*Date: 11.11.18.*
*Time: 0745 hrs.*
*Hostilities with cease at 11.00 hours to-day, Nov. 11th*
*All precautions are to be preserved and there will be no communication with the Enemy.*
*All units are to report dispositions and to remain at a state of readiness to meet any demand. Further instructions will be issued regarding enemy units, especially submarines, now at sea.*
*Acknowledge.*

There were 28 armed trawlers based at Portland at the time of Armistice, with myriad other patrol and support vessels, including several requisition paddle-steamers which, because of their shallow draught, general stability, and precision reverse and turns, were excellent for inshore mine and wreck clearance. In December 1918 the full complement of more than 200 vessels attached to Portland Command Area gathered in the harbour for demobilisation and return to their civilian owners.

The Cenotaph – the empty tomb – that is the nation's premier war memorial in London's Whitehall, comprises great blocks from the Portland whitbed at Wakeham. These were cut, rubbed and gritted to shape. It stands 35 feet high and weighs 120 tons, with precise non-cemented joints that were claimed to be the finest worked on stone since the Parthenon was built above Athens in the fifth century BC. The other subtlety of design is that it does not contain a single vertical or horizontal line.

Every piece of stone was cut slightly out of true, so that if the apparent verticals are extended they meet at a point 1,000 feet into the sky. The horizontal-looking surfaces and joins are circumferentials of an imaginary circle that has its centre 600 feet beneath the ground. The design was the creation of Sir Edwin Lutyens (1869–1944), not originally as a column of stone but as a sketch for a temporary wooden saluting base that took him only a matter of hours to devise. The platform was needed for a march-past of troops through London in the peace celebrations of July 1919.

On 30 July 1919, Bonar Law's War Cabinet ordered the replacement of the timber structure with a permanent replica. The massive white blocks were cut from the northern side of Perryfield Quarries, on the western part of the land in the angle of old railway cuttings opposite the Mermaid Inn and Portland Museum at the Pennsylvania Castle end of Wakeham's wide street, under two little fields known as Pitt's Ground and Above Coombe. There were to be other Lutyens-inspired cenotaphs overseas for those without marked graves. Portland stone was also chosen, in uniform secular shapes carrying restrained formulaic wording, as standard memorials for those million men of the British Empire who lay in formal cemeteries. Tens of thousands of such blocks were shipped to the Western Front. Those bodies that remained unidentified were to be described as an 'Airman, Seaman or Soldier of the Great War' who was 'Known unto God' in eloquent and evocative words devised by the poet Rudyard Kipling.

The Greek steamship *Preveza* was driven ashore in Chesil Cove on 15 January 1920 and her boilers remained lying in the shingle for more than a decade. The following day, in a combination of swirling fog and heavy seas, the 202-ton armed trawler HMT *James Fennell* ran aground on Tar Rocks, between Priory Corner and Blacknor. The naval vessel was near the end of a homeward voyage from Gibraltar to Portsmouth. Portland fisherman 'Sunny' Sanders heard the shouts of the crew and ran to their aid, but had to clamber over outcrops while telling them to stay put. On reaching the shore he caught hold of a hawser and line, which he secured in the stones. Holding on to the cable, 16 ratings splashed their way to the rock pools, a distance of 30 feet, but on following them the captain slipped into the sea. Sanders jumped in to rescue him.

Construction of the Cenotaph was carried out by Holland, Hannen & Cubitts Ltd at a cost of £7,325. Lutyens waived any fee for his most famous work. It was unveiled by King George V on Armistice Day at the eleventh hour of the eleventh day of the eleventh month, on 11 November 1920.

The retired battleships HMS *Colossus* and HMS *Collingwood* were seconded to the Boys' Training Establishment at Portland on 22 September 1921. Both were veterans of the Battle of Jutland, during which Colossus was hit by two German 12-inch shells, and the future King George VI served in A-turret on the *Collingwood*. Out in Lyme Bay, in November 1921, the Caernarvon schooner *Mary* was lost 12 miles west-north-west of Portland Bill.

A recurrence of landslip problems between Portland and Easton, in 1921, was compounded when a train set fire to the ballast. This largely comprised ash and coal slag from the dockyard, and was set to smoulder for weeks. As a result, stone ballast had to be substituted.

The Floating Dock moored between Castleton dock jetty and the Coaling Pier was in use from 1922 for the repair and refitting of submarines and escort vessels. This facility remained a familiar feature of Portland Harbour until after the Second World War – when it was known to the Royal Navy as Auxiliary Floating Dock 19 – but was then towed away, such work becoming 'concentrated' at Devonport in 1959.

In the 1920s it was reported that one of Portland's veteran warships, the unique HMS *Warrior*, was to be preserved in Portsmouth Harbour. In Portland, the Royal Navy's first iron-plated steam frigate had been 'for many years the guardship in the harbour, and is considered the most pleasing model of the armour-plated, sail rigged class'. The aspiration for preservation came to pass, but not until 1986, before

which the *Warrior* languished as a bathing jetty in Milford Haven. Built in 1859/60, HMS *Warrior* was designed to be powered by sail as well as by steam, with the former remaining. The 48,400 square feet of canvas required a crew of 600, along an upper deck that was 400 feet long. Below there were 80 muzzle-loaded guns, once more preserved in situ, though now as fibre-glass replicas on replacement carriages.

The 456-ton London tanker *Scandinavia*, carrying liquid petroleum gas from Thames Estuary refineries to Manchester, attempted putting into Portland Harbour during a gale but was driven onto the rocks of the central breakwater, 400 yards south of Fort Head. Captain Campbell and his crew were taken off by the tugs *Petrel* and *Pilot* from the inside of the breakwater. The 13 men reached its outer edge by swimming through troubled waters that had been smoothed, literally, by leaking oil.

There is an old adage that 'one wreck attracts another' – as it does through the rubbernecking of crashes on motorways – which came true twice over on 22 February 1923. Both the 513-ton steamship *Cragside* and the ketch *Phoenix* ran into the outer breakwater during the night, close to the remains of the *Scandinavia*. This steamship was directly responsible for a further victim on 3 April 1923, when the crew of the Weymouth drifter *Freewill* lost control of the hawser from her bow while trying to lift an iron plate from the shipwreck in a heavy swell. As a result the fishing boat was drawn down and battered against the breakwater. She became 'its fourth wreck in four weeks'.

The contraception pioneer Dr Marie Stopes (1880–1958) chose Portland for her holiday home. This was in thatched Avice's Cottage, adjoining No. 217 Wakeham on the corner of Church Ope Road, both of which she later gave to the island for use as a museum. In 1923, pregnant with her only son, she moved into the former Higher Lighthouse. Marie refused to wear a bra or corset and threw her physical energy into swimming the treacherous tide-race off Portland Bill which one day almost claimed her life. Portlanders remembered her 'wild red hair' and recalled with distaste her open philandering with young men. She exalted them in *Love Songs for Young Lovers* in 1939, though by this time the morality of the public Stokes, in a string of books, was receding into memory.

'Poor Harry,' was her exercise in eccentricity by proxy, as young Harry Verdon Stopes-Roe was dressed in bizarre clothes, denied any education and received cruel indifference when it came to his choice of a mate on the grounds that the girl in question was short-sighted and therefore genetically unfit for breeding according to Marie's eugenic philosophy.

Humphrey Verdon Roe (1878–1949), the second husband she married in 1918, provided the cash that launched Britain's family planning clinics. The first, in 1921, was the Mothers' Clinic for Constructive

Birth Control. Humphrey served with the Royal Flying Corps in France and was wounded on active service. His autobiographical *Who's Who* entry explains his wider contribution to aviation, in founding plane-makers A.V. Roe & Co. Ltd which, during the Second World War, provided Britain with the Avro Lancaster bomber:

*From 1909 onwards, when flying seemed to be a dream, his foresight and faith in its future led him to devote the whole of his capital and talents to helping his brother, Sir Alliott Verdon-Roe, to establish the Avro biplane.*

'The Admiralty regrets,' an official statement began as the events of 10 January 1924 were confirmed. HM Submarine *L-24*, built at the end of the First World War, had been rammed by the 29,100-ton battleship HMS *Resolution* in Lyme Bay, 11 miles south-west of Portland Bill. Fully loaded, the battleship would have displaced about 33,500 tons, compared with about 1,000 tons for the submarine. The *L-24* sank instantly, with the loss of all 43 officers and men. Among them was Chief Petty Officer E.F. Buck, whose son, far from being put off joining the Royal Navy, himself became a submariner in the Second World War.

'A slight bump' – all that was felt on board the *Resolution* – was logged on the bridge at 11.13 hours. The worse was feared, however, as a periscope had been sighted shortly before the impact, followed by a patch of oily water, spreading across the sea in the battleship's wake. There was a major exercise in progress, involving not only the Atlantic Fleet but also auxiliaries, submarines and aeroplanes, from No. 10 Group of the Royal Air Force based at Lee-on-Solent. Attacking 'Red' forces were testing the readiness of 'Blue' defenders. The unfortunate submarine was presumed to have passed below the bows of the battleship and was identified as the *L-24* when this vessel failed to return to Portland after the exercise had been cancelled. There was no prospect of even attempting a rescue, as search vessels and divers failed to establish the position of the wreck until the end of the month.

The first HMS *Osprey* at Portland was a ship rather than a shore base. The command ship of the 1st Anti-Submarine Flotilla, the *Osprey* was commissioned on 1 April 1924 as the headquarters craft of the Royal Navy's Anti-Submarine School. In 1927 its headquarters staff moved from ship to shore, and the name followed. HMS *Tiger*, a veteran of the Battle of Jutland, was stationed at Portland from 1924 to 1929 as the Royal Navy's principal Gunnery Practice Ship, for offshore firings in Lyme Bay and the English Channel ranges.

In the fading light of a January afternoon in 1925 the Royal Navy's Atlantic Fleet sailed out of Portland Harbour on a mission to destroy one of its own capital ships. This was the 25,000-ton battleship HMS *Monarch*. Unlike most of the vessels that have gone down in the cause of target practice, before and since, however, there was nothing defective or obsolete about the *Monarch*. She was only 15 years old and had an eventful war record, with the elite 2nd Battle Squadron, from the Battle of Jutland to the Scarborough Raid.

The destruction of HMS *Monarch* was highly political. She had been formally sacrificed under the provisions of the Washington Treaty, an international accord limiting naval armaments. Signed in 1922, the treaty was the strategic arms limitation enactment of its day. There was a three-year lapse before implementation of the provisions. The Admiralty decided that the *Monarch* should be destroyed by her peers.

The empty ship of the line was first hit with a series of seaplane attacks, which did little damage, and she then survived a pounding from the 6-inch guns of a line of light cruisers. These hardly dented her armour, the steel of which was a foot thick. Next came the battleships, firing from 12 miles, each salvo weighing six tons. Eight shells were fired and some hit the *Monarch* but ricocheted to land in the sea miles away. This process lasted all day and the battlecruisers carried on into the night, illuminating their target with great sheets of light stretching across the horizon.

HMS *Monarch* took it all. The Royal Navy's photographic ship – the aptly named HMS *Snapdragon* – sailed round to record the details of the damage. The final moments were approaching. The battlecruiser HMS *Repulse* sailed in from her firing position to within a mile of the Monarch. She fired into the crippled hulk, aiming at the water-line, tearing a hole to let the sea into the hull. The *Monarch* listed and gradually sank from the glare of the searchlights.

The Belgian trawler *Noree*, on a fishing trip down the Channel from Ostend, was lost 11 miles south-east of Portland Bill on 25 February 1926. Perhaps because of seasonal inattention due to the demands of the date, the steamship *Burutu* collided with French sailing ship *Eugene Schneider* off Portland Bill on Christmas Day in 1926. The latter came off worse and proceeded to sink.

The former Higher Lighthouse – renamed Branscombe Lodge – became the home of Dr Marie Stopes, after she had handed over her Wakeham property for an island museum, in 1929.

The small Victorian steamship *Forester*, from Cardiff, having set off back to Swansea from Poole in ballast after delivering coal, was forced to put into Portland Harbour to escape mounting seas on 12 January 1930. The vessel was not only in distress but was out of control as she drove through the anchor lines of the Atlantic Fleet, bounced between their mooring cables and then hit a breakwater. The crew of six, plus a stowaway, jumped and scrambled to safety as the *Forester* 'turned turtle'. The men

# Capital Portland

*Broadcasting House, in Portland stone in Portland Place, continues to be acclaimed as the iconic building of the twentieth century.*

*St Paul's Cathedral, by surviving the Blitz, became the symbol of national survival.*

*Newly cleaned columns of St Paul's Cathedral, once more the most striking example of Portland stone in the capital.*

*Sir Christopher Wren's grand design for St Paul's from the famous west font.*

Left: 'St Paul's' inscribed on blocks of Portland stone arrived in London in 1972 for repairs to the national monument.

were safe but terrified, cowering under spumes of spray for several hours as they waited until the Weymouth Lifeboat was able to come close enough to take them off.

The 127-ton motor vessel *Innisinver*, heading from Par in St Austell Bay to Boulogne with china clay, collided with 'floating wreckage' five miles south-west of Portland Bill on 9 September 1930. She proceeded to sink as the crew abandoned ship.

The *Madeleine Tristan*, a three-masted French schooner carrying 50 tons of grain from Treguier to Le Havre, was battered onto the shingle of Chesil Cove on 20 September 1930. They were so far off course that even the 'regular grandfather of the sea', as her captain was described, remained confident that he was on the northern coast of France until being disabused of this by English voices. He had done his best for the survival of his men, realising that the general situation was already lost, by driving the vessel into the top of the beach. Here the sea washed her sideways and she took years to break up. So strong was the south-westerly wind at the time that the first rocket-fired safety line to the stricken vessel was blown inshore and landed on the roof of nearby Underhill School.

Cleall's Dairy, run by Frederick Cleall, was next door to Flew's Stores in Chiswell. Both delivered across the island, the milk being poured from a pint measure into jugs on the doorstep. Avice's Cottage, the picturesque thatched corner house at the south end of Wakeham immortalised by Thomas Hardy, opened its doors to the public as Portland Museum in 1930. Donated to the island by birth control advocate Dr Marie Stopes, it had been derelict for some years.

By the beginning of the 1930s, submarine disasters were becoming almost commonplace, and only a month after the loss of the *Poseidon* the Admiralty had to issue another ominous statement:

*News has been received this evening that submarine M-2 dived about 10.30 this morning off Portland and since then no further communications have been heard from her.*

The Royal Navy's big submarine *M-2*, launched in 1919 with a 305ft hull and a battleship-size 12-inch gun, was refitted and recommissioned as an aircraft carrier in 1927. She had a hangar attached to her conning tower. This was for a catapult-launched Peto reconnaissance seaplane, produced by George Parnall & Co.y at Bristol, with a 28ft wingspan that folded to only eight feet.

Experimental flights achieved a maximum speed of 113 miles per hour and endurance times of two hours in the air. A crane on the submarine retrieved the Peto at the end of its flights. What seemed like hopeful progress – establishing the combination of submarine and aircraft as long distance 'eyes of the fleet' – abruptly ended on 26 January 1932, three

miles west of Portland Bill. On board were 49 submariners, plus nine RAF aircraftmen who attended to the hangar, the seaplane and the flight-deck, and Peto's pilot.

The *M-2* had dived with its hangar doors either faulty or open (or both). From the hangar, the sea entered the hull of the vessel through a hatch which had also been left open, and it sank like a stone to 17 fathoms. Rescue vessels were soon on the scene but could do nothing. All 60 personnel had drowned.

The position of the submarine was fixed on 3 February 1932 and the tiny seaplane was raised by divers five days later, but out of respect for the dead it was decided that it should be scrapped. The project had died with the *M-2*. Attempts continued to salvage the huge submarine, but were eventually abandoned on 8 September 1932. She was left as a tomb and divers report that the hull is still intact and that the hangar doors remain open. The *M-2*'s gun-carrying sister ship, the *M-1*, already lay to the west, off Start Point, where she sank with her crew after colliding with a freighter on 12 November 1925.

The flagships of the three leading European nations made news simultaneously on Thursday, 3 January 1933. 'I thought we touched the bottom of the ocean,' said singer John McCormack, as he stepped ashore in New York from the 51,656-ton German liner *Bremen*. Commodore Ziegenbein, the commander, added:

*Some waves were 82 feet high, two feet higher than the bridge. The winds were higher than the greatest velocity the instruments could measure, which is 100 miles an hour. They must have reached 125 miles an hour.*

For the British there could be pride:

*The Bremen's difficulties emphasised the magnificent achievement of the Cunard liner* Mauretania, *the only big passenger ship to arrive on time this week. Yet for four days the British liner forced her way through huge seas and was buffeted by a hurricane. The veteran greyhound of the Atlantic averaged 22.69 knots, making the voyage from Cherbourg in 5 days 16 hours 18 miles.*

Meanwhile, instead of being safely home in Cherbourg, France's £3,000,000 luxury liner *L'Atlantique* had become a blazing inferno three miles east-south-east of Portland Bill. The fire started when the liner was off the Casquets, in the Channel Islands, and from there she had drifted to the eastern edge of Lyme Bay. Evacuated and empty, it seemed for a while that she might become Dorset's most spectacular shipwreck of all time, which was the opinion of the *Daily Mail*'s Weymouth correspondent when he arrived on the Bill at sunrise:

*As the news spread excited watchers on shore came and saw billows of smoke pouring from the vessel high into*

# Capital Portland

*The Ionic frontage of the British Museum, described as the 'most imposing in the metropolis', was completed in 1847.*

*County Hall – seen from the London Eye in January 2000 – was built for London County Council between 1912 and 1933.*

*Portland stone, appropriately carved with the square and compass symbol of the trade, on the frontage of Freemasons' Hall in 1933.*

*the skies, and shimmering waves of heat arose around her from the glowing hull. British, French and Dutch tugs circled about her, their crews trying to get a line aboard and bring her under control.*

*For six hours the heat and smoke held them at bay, and the* Atlantique, *uncontrolled and helpless, was until late in the afternoon a plaything of the tide, the north-west wind, and dangerous Channel currents. Fears ran high near midday that the* Atlantique *would drift inside the Shambles bank, and on the turning of the tide be borne aground on the Dorset shore.*

*Almost imperceptibly, however, she drifted away from Portland and out into the Channel. She presented a pitiful spectacle at close quarters. She listed heavily to port and her bows dipped; her hull was red hot above the water line; parts of her interior were bared to the air and her foremast lay across her ruined deck. All that remained of her palatial 'street' of shops and other lavish equipment were unrecognisable remnants.*

*It was late in the afternoon that the men from the tugs, braving the heat and choking smoke, got aboard her. A Frenchman was the first to do so, and the first thing he did was to hoist a French ensign on the ruined monster's remaining mast.*

Several hours passed before hawsers were successfully secured. For a time the boarding party were forced back as the fire erupted again, and narrowly escaped with their lives. The financial imperative behind these desperate efforts – and the inherent risks of towing her back across the Channel – was to avoid the heavy salvage charges that would be incurred were the liner to be beached on the Dorset shore. Because of the heavy list she had to be towed broadside, as the reporter continued:

*At 4.45 I saw her slowly disappear on the horizon near St Alban's Head – the rearguard of a slow, sad procession. Forty hours after she had caught fire she was still burning furiously deep down in her tortured hull.*

From here, off Purbeck, L'Atlantique was slowly towed through the night, southwards, on the 80-mile journey to Cherbourg. She was to make it back, against all the odds, shadowed by the French minelayer *Pollux*. The warship had been ready, with guns and torpedo tubes, to sink the liner if she became a danger to shipping.

The sailing vessel *May* was 'struck and sunk' by what was thought to be a New Zealand steamship after leaving Portland Harbour on 21 May 1933.

Portland stone was being used for three prestigious projects in the capital. Broadcasting House, the headquarters of John Reith's British Broadcasting Corporation in Portland Place, carried its motto in letters devised and carved by the sculptor Eric Gill: 'Nation shall speak unto nation.'

The County Hall offices of London County Council, begun in 1912 and suspended as a result of

the First World War, were completed beside the Thames in 1933. More symbolic, as it carried the square and compass symbol of the trade, was the Freemasons' Hall in Great Queen Street. At the dedication of this 'New Masonic Temple' in July 1933 the Duke of Connaught, as Grand Master, noted that it had cost nearly £1,000,000 to build, 'which was the price of St Paul's Cathedral'.

Relegated to use as a coal-hulk, the 830-ton former paddle-steamer *Countess of Erne* broke her mooring in Portland Harbour in strong winds on 16 September 1935. The vessel drifted across the harbour and was washed into the rocks of the outer breakwater, where she sank, facing the East Ship Channel.

It was as King Edward VIII that the Duke of Windsor (1894–1972) visited Portland on 12 November 1936 to review 40 ships of the Home Fleet. It was his first and last visit, as sovereign, to the Royal Navy. His train arrived on the island, pulling into the station yard to an inauspiciously wild reception. It was 4.25a.m. and there was a full gale in progress. Waves were breaking over the Chesil Beach and there was two feet of water across the rails in the siding beneath the royal train. Victoria Square and the harbourside roads at Castletown were also flooded.

The king remained sleeping, however, until eight o'clock. The royal car then had to force its way into the dockyard along a narrow corridor between floodwater on one side and cheering children on the other. He embarked from Castletown on the royal yacht *Victoria & Albert* to cross the turbulent waters amid warships heaving and straining on their moorings. The echo of a 21-gun salute reverberated from the Verne as the sun broke through and smiled down on the Commander-in-Chief's barge as the royal party proceeded between lines of battleships and cruisers. They lunched in the flagship, the battleship HMS *Nelson*.

That evening, King Edward attended a concert party aboard the aircraft carrier HMS *Courageous* and then hosted a dinner for senior officers aboard the *Victoria & Albert*. The following afternoon thousands of people lined the streets of Weymouth as the king drove to the main station to board a train for Paddington. The sun shone once more during an enthusiastic send-off and for his return to London and his troubles. A month later, under pressure from Prime Minister Stanley Baldwin, he abdicated in favour of his younger brother, the Duke of York, who became King George VI, with Princess Elizabeth as heir to the throne.

Overseas the wider world was falling apart. Britain was impotent to intervene after the Japanese machine-gunned the British Ambassador to China, Spain began imploding and the Czechoslovakian problem was set to run. As Neville Chamberlain's government edged towards rearmament, Portland inevitably figured in the process, and in 1937 Verne

Citadel became an infantry training centre. Anti-aircraft rockets, using 3-inch tubular charges produced in Dorset by the Royal Naval Cordite Factory at Holton Heath, were brought to Portland for testing from Blacknor Fort between 1937 and 1939. The experiments were conducted by the Explosives Research Department of the Royal Arsenal, Woolwich. They were fired from two saucer-shaped pads of concrete which survive between the coast path and the cliff edge of either side of the fort, with clear views across Lyme Bay.

Gun-laying predictors monitored the fall of shot in an extended series of successful proving trials. These were discontinued and moved to Aberporth, Wales, when it became clear that Blacknor would be needed by the Royal Artillery as a coastal defence battery for the duration of the emergency that was developing into the Second World War.

The rockets went into production with a 25-pound shell, both for anti-aircraft salvoes of 19 rockets in a cluster and for air-to-sea anti-ship purposes. An improvised version had a 60-pound warhead for use against tanks, railway locomotives and other land targets. The rockets were also used in assisting aircraft to take off from merchant ships.

The Royal Navy's 6th Destroyer Flotilla of Tribal-class vessels, led by HMS *Mohawk*, sailed for Liverpool Bay on 2 June 1939. There, the previous day, the new submarine HMS *Thetis* had failed to surface from her first dive, with 90 men trapped aboard. Although the stern of the submarine was raised and four of her crew had got out through an escape chamber, its upper hatch had then jammed through an operational error. As a result the remainder of the 53 crewmen and their 50 passengers – including caterers for what should have been cele-bratory trials – were doomed. It was also distressing for those on the water, who could hear that their comrades were alive inside but could do nothing to save them.

King George VI visited Weymouth and Portland on 9 August 1939 for a review of the Reserve Fleet. Few sailors saw their king, however, as he stood on Bincleaves Groyne. He, at least, could see some ships but most were a blur and smudge on the horizon, obscured by drizzle and mist. The Mayor of Weymouth apologised for the weather. 'Don't worry, Mr Mayor,' the king replied, with a laconic allusion to world politics, 'it's raining everywhere.'

Portland's black-out and sirens were tested in a 'mock battle' on 13 August 1939 which involved forces on air, land and sea, as well as civilian units such as the Observer Corps, Air Raid Precautions, and Local Defence Volunteers.

Only 40 hours after the declaration of hostilities came the first U-boat kill to be claimed off Dorset during the Second World War. Commanded by Lord Louis Mountbatten, the new K-class destroyer HMS *Kelly*, leading the 5th Destroyer Flotilla from Portland, depth-charged a suspected enemy subma-rine in Lyme Bay on 5 September 1939. Substantial wreckage came to the surface. The *Kelly* had earlier missed the tracks of two torpedoes fired at her in Weymouth Bay by only 30 or 40 yards.

The first major explosion to be heard in south Dorset during the Second World War took place just 13 days into the conflict, on 16 September 1939, as the 6,000-ton Belgian passenger liner *Alex van Opstal*, homeward bound to Antwerp from New York, hit a German mine off the Shambles. Though the vessel listed badly she remained afloat long enough for all 49 crew and eight passengers to be rescued by a passing Greek steamer. They were brought into Weymouth.

On 7 October 1939 the Dutch freighter *Bynnendyk*, returning to Rotterdam from New York, was blown up by a German mine off the Shambles sandbank. The 52 crewmen abandoned the blazing wreck and watched her sink from their rescue vessel, which took them to Weymouth.

The Greek steamship *Elena R* was sunk by a German mine off the Shambles sandbank on 22 November 1939. More fortunate, though mined and listing, the Kingfisher-class destroyer HMS *Kittiwake* was able to limp back into Portland Harbour on 22 November 1939. On the last day of the first year of the war, Winston Churchill visited Portland as First Lord of the Admiralty, and went on to see in the new year with old and new relatives at Minterne House, from where the Honourable Pamela Digby had been recently married to Winston's son, Randolph.

The 750-ton Royal Navy trawler HMT *Hartlepool*, with a Durham crew from there and South Shields, was fitted out in Portland Harbour on 5 January 1940 for experimental wireless tests. The equipment, comprising a Mark III high-frequency transmitter and HRO receiver with aerials, was installed in the chartroom and operated by 45-year-old John Darwin – a cousin of the Victorian naturalist – from Section VIII of MI6, the Secret Intelligence Service, at Whaddon Hall, Buckinghamshire. He came with instructions from Richard Gambier-Parry and left Captain William Powlett to assess its anti-submarine potential.

For the rest of the month, apart from at sea, the weather brought about the suspension of warfare, as frost and blizzards were capped by a record snowfall on 27 January 1940, not that the details appeared in public weather reports. Meteorology was a depart-ment of the War Office and such forecasts remained a state secret for the duration of the war.

Batteries of 9.2-inch anti-ship guns were emplaced on and below the cliffs of East Weares in the spring of 1940, but after the Germans poured into the Low Countries and France, the main threat was from the air, as the Luftwaffe moved forward to airfields across the Channel and Portland became a front-line parish. Adolf Hitler's other achievement,

## Second World War

A 9.2-inch anti-ship gun in a Royal Artillery coast defence battery, below East Weares, in 1940.

Luftwaffe bombs falling towards Fort Head and the Outer Breakwater of Portland Harbour.

Night watch, with searchlight and binoculars, from East Weares as England feared invasion in the summer of 1940.

Leading Seaman Jack Mantle VC, buried in Portland Naval Cemetery, was posthumously awarded the Royal Navy's first Victoria Cross to be won inside United Kingdom territorial waters.

Left: HMS Foylebank, sunk by 'Stuka' dive-bombers, in Portland Harbour on 4 July 1940.

the overthrow of Neville Chamberlain's government, was more than offset by the appointment of Winston Churchill as Prime Minister. His Dorset visits were set to continue.

The former Peninsular & Oriental steamship *Himalaya*, which at 3,438 tons was the largest vessel in the world when she was launched in 1853, was requisitioned as a troopship during the Crimean War and spent her retirement in Portland Harbour. Here she was the Navy's principal coal-hulk. This task ended when a Junkers Ju.88 bomber dropped four sticks of bombs on her, of which three exploded, on 12 June 1940. They left a wreck which lies scattered across the seabed.

HMS *Foylebank*, an anti-aircraft auxiliary converted in 1939 from a civilian freighter, was moored in Portland Harbour when the dockyard was targeted by the Luftwaffe for Dorset's first major attack during the Second World War. Daylight dive-bombers left 60 dead in her burning wreckage on 4 July 1940, including Leading Seaman Jack Mantle, who stuck to his pom-pom, firing at the Junkers Ju.87 'Stukas' as he and the ship were torn apart. He was posthumously awarded the Victoria Cross, which had the distinction of being the first won by the Royal Navy from an action inside United Kingdom territorial waters. Jack Mantle, who was living in Southampton but had gone to school at Affpuddle, in Dorset, is buried in the Naval Cemetery on the Verne Common hillside, overlooking the dockyard and harbour.

Offshore, on 4 July 1940, the 1,796-ton Dutch steamship *Deucalion*, in ballast between London and St John's, Newfoundland, was sunk by a wave of 'Stukas' about 20 miles south-south-west of Portland Bill.

The sea off Portland saw numerous casualties throughout the Battle of Britain. Most of the aircraft belonged to the Luftwaffe but they were joined by many defending Spitfires and Hurricanes from Fighter Command. My catalogue of such crashes from Dorset's *War Diary* makes no claim to be exhaustive but shows the extent to which Portland was a front-line landmark and target:

*9 July 1940 – Spitfire of 609 Squadron.*
*11 July 1940 – Spitfires L1069 and L1095 of 609 Squadron and Hurricane N2485 of 501 Squadron.*
*12 July 1940 – Hurricane P3084 of 501 Squadron.*
*25 July 1940 – Spitfire K9901 of 152 Squadron.*
*11 August 1940 – Hurricanes L2057, P3783, P3885 and R4092 of 601 Squadron.*
*13 August 1940 – Hurricanes P3348 of 213 Squadron and P3177 of 238 Squadron.*
*15 August 1940 – Hurricanes P2872 and P3215 of 87 Squadron.*
*25 August 1940 – Hurricanes N2646, P2766 and P3200 of 213 Squadron and Spitfire R6810 of 152 Squadron.*
*27 August 1940 – Spitfire R6831 of 152 Squadron.*
*30 September 1940 – Hurricanes P3655 and P3088 of 56 Squadron and Spitfire L1072 of 152 Squadron.*
*10 October 1940 – Hurricane P3421 of 58 Squadron.*

'Stuka' leader Hauptmann Friedrich Karl Freiherr von Dalwigk zu Lichtenfels, the 33-year-old Staffelkapitan of 1 Gruppe, Stukageschwader 77, was shot down in his Junkers Ju.87 and killed over the sea off Portland on 9 July 1940. The credit was claimed by Pilot Officer David Moore Crook in a Spitfire of 609 Squadron from RAF Warmwell. Von Dalwigk, who joined the Luftwaffe in 1933, was posthumously awarded the Knight's Cross on 21 July 1940.

The war on the waves was also taking its toll. The Vichy French liner *Meknes* was sunk off Portland by German submarine *U-572* on 24 July 1940. She was carrying 1,100 neutral French sailors, of whom some 400 were killed.

E-boats, Schnellboote from the Kriegsmarine, began their contribution to the German war effort on 26 July 1940. The motor-torpedo boats sank three merchant vessels between Portland and the Isle of Wight. 'E' stood for 'eil' – fast rather than enemy – but came to mean both. Aircraft, submarines, mines and E-boats remained a threat for the next five years.

The most significant single event was the dive-bombing of the 1,375-ton destroyer HMS *Delight* on 29 July 1940, 20 miles south of Portland Bill, and her subsequent sinking on being towed into Portland Harbour. Later decryption of intercepted Enigma-coded radio traffic revealed that she had been sunk as a result of 'Freya reports', which confirmed to Air Ministry scientific intelligence that the Germans had operational coastal radar stations. The immediate response was that the Admiralty suspended coastal convoys in the English Channel, which was placed off-limits to destroyers during daylight hours.

An approaching attack was plotted by Ventnor radar station at 09.45 hours and rightly estimated at '100 plus' as more than 150 Luftwaffe bombers and fighters headed for Portland Harbour. Many of the bombs fell on that target, but harmlessly, from 10,000 feet. In all, 32 devices hit Admiralty property on Portland and 58 exploded inside Weymouth borough. Their effect was minimal, being a contained fire which failed to ignite No. 3 oil-tank at The Mere, the loss of 200 tons of fuel elsewhere along the pipeline and the destruction of a shipwright's shop at Bincleaves.

During this raid a Junkers Ju.88 bomber crash-landed almost undamaged on 'The Castles' clifftop beside Blacknor Fort after being crippled in a dog-fight. The crew were taken prisoner and the 'kill' was claimed by Pilot Officer John Murray Strickland, in a Hurricane of 213 Squadron from RAF Exeter. The aeroplane (markings B3+DC) belonged to Kampfgeschwader 54, and carried their death's head Totenkoph emblem on the fuselage just aft of the transparent nose.

## Second World War

Cove House Hotel landlady Elizabeth Comben (centre) making her farewell to United States Navy personnel on the eve of D-Day.

Engineer company at Castletown approaching American landing ships 374 (left) and 376 on 4 June 1944.

Tracked vehicles and trailers entering the gaping jaws of American landing ships, bound for Omaha Beach, at Castletown on 4 June 1944.

Crew of U-249, the first German submarine to surrender at the end of the Second World War, line up on deck off Weymouth on 10 May 1945 before entering Portland Harbour.

Signal Corps men of assault unit 'Queue Uf' waiting for orders to file on board United States landing ship 374, at Castletown, on 30 May 1944.

Squadron Leader Terence Lovell-Gregg (1913–40) heroically led the Hurricanes of 87 Squadron from Exeter into impossible odds over the sea off Portland at the height of the Battle of Britain. There was no hesitation or deviation. 'Come on chaps, let's surround them,' were his last words. 'Shovel', as he was nicknamed, and his handful of flyers were outnumbered 15 to one by the Luftwaffe, as they hurled into action from 18,000 feet at 18.00 hours on 15 August 1940. The New Zealander's fighter was shot to pieces but he might have survived if the burning aircraft had not clipped an oak tree in the wood beside Abbotsbury Swannery. He was attempting to make a forced landing. Instead he fell to his death and is buried in the military plot at Warmwell churchyard.

Having been intercepted by Spitfires from RAF Warmwell, a wave of 30 Heinkel He.111 bombers dropped their loads from 16,000 feet above Portland Bill and headed home for France on 15 September 1940. Effectively, the Battle of Britain was over, and Operation Sealion for the invasion of England was postponed indefinitely, as was confirmed by Hitler in a deciphered message dated 17 September 1940. Operation Sealion was dubbed Operation Smith by Churchill in order to conceal the Enigma-coded source of such intercepted information.

HMT *Recoil*, an armed trawler, was sunk off Portland by a German mine on 28 September 1940. A large explosion was heard on the island. The destruction was so complete that no bodies or wreckage were found from what had been the captured enemy vessel *Blankenburg*. The key task for the trawlers was minesweeping, which had turned into the most dangerous activity on the ocean wave, short of going under it as a submariner.

HMT *Kingston Cairngorm*, the next loss to the German minefield, on 17 October 1940, was followed on 22 October by MV *Hickory*, a diesel-powered civilian vessel. The Dutch freighter *Maastricht*, sailing in convoy FN 366, was sunk by German E-boats to the east of Portland Bill on 23 December 1940. One of the escorts, the Royal Navy armed trawler HMT *Pelton*, was also lost.

Relatively speaking, apart from the occasional raider and other bombs jettisoned by Luftwaffe crews as they attempted to escape back to France, 1941 saw a lull in the conflict for Portland, apart from some direct hits on the railway. Somewhat optimistically, thoughts in Dorset military and scientific establishments were turning from a defensive to an offensive war, and the pressure was off on the English coast once Hitler had turned on Russia and America was provoked into joining the action by the Japanese 'day that will live in infamy' at Pearl Harbor.

In February 1942, arising from the sinking off Portland of HMS *Delight* in 1940, an audacious raid was practised off Portland and Redcliff Point, Osmington, to bring back a German Wurzburg radar apparatus of the kind that had caused her demise. C

Company of the 2nd Battalion, the Parachute Regiment, dropped onto the French coast between Le Havre and Fecamp, and were taken off by sea with their prize. This went for Air Ministry evaluation to the Telecommunications Research Establishment at Worth Matravers, which then had to be hurriedly evacuated inland to Malvern through fears of a German retaliatory raid on Dorset's key scientific base above Chapman's Pool.

A natural event which began at 11 o'clock on the morning of 13 December 1942 would have caused much more distress but for the fact that it was wartime, with emergency services fully mobilised. Water was beginning to seep through the Chesil Beach as the sea continued to rise. At noon the first waves poured over the top, into Chiswell, and within a short time the 'slight layer of water' across Victoria Square had risen to over five feet. There 'only an inch or two of the letter box... was showing above the flood and letters floated out on the tide'.

The stout stone wall beside the beach road was breached, being reduced to rubble at numerous points, and several yards of the adjacent railway line were also swept away. Sleepers had floated off into the harbour and rails were buckled. The gasworks was put out of action for 36 hours and boulders were strewn across the low-lying part of Chiswell.

The first buildings to be flooded had been the remains of houses on the west side of Chiswell and Big Ope. These had been reduced to ruins by the flood of 1824 and many were never repaired. Because it was a Sunday, most workers were at home, and started to take practical steps. R. Flann of No. 109 Big Ope told reporters that many people had lifted floorboards and nailed them across the doors when the sea started seeping through the Chesil Beach. Then they started to relax as the tide 'pitched off' but to everyone's surprise the first waves came over the top of the pebbles:

*I had just got into the Cove House Inn, which is on the highest part of the beach. There wasn't much of a wind blowing although the south-south-easterly storms had been piling up the water in the bay. The sea was making a terrific roar as huge ground swells swept up the beach. Then I heard an even louder roar and the sea hit the side of the house.*

*It must have been 60 feet high. The front door of the inn was shut but the wave rushed through the window and caught me square in the chest. I was thrown up against the bar, but I got away with only a cut on the back of my hand. I was lucky; I have never seen such waves in my life.*

The Comben family, the landlords of Cove House Inn, took refuge upstairs. They came down three hours later to find the till filled with water, windows smashed and glasses and cigarettes swept from the shelves. The frontage to the inn was washed away.

The Combens spent the rest of the afternoon clearing up the mess. At seven o'clock punctually they opened again.

Mr J. Galpin, a fisherman of Three Yard Close, watched the waves hit Cove House Inn and saw water pouring down the roof and walls:

*The people who built that place must have known what they were about. I was on the cliffs watching. Chiswell was covered in a cloud of spray. I saw the first great wave come rushing across the bay. A two-ton logwood which came out of the old Rand, a sailing ship wrecked many years ago, was picked up like a straw. The logwood smashed into my hut, which contained five tons of old iron saws, and took it through a stone wall as if it had never been there. The remains of the hut were thrown down several yards away.*

*An old boat was swept over three 6-foot walls right out into the road a hundred yards away. The hut, as you can see, is just matchwood. All my gear was inside and everything I get my living with is gone, except my boat, which I had taken to a safe place.*

Among the homeless was 73-year-old Mr L. White, who had gone to sea in sailing ships. He remembered the wrecking of the Norwegian barque *Christiana* at the end of the previous century:

*I was then washed out of another house on the beach. But it wasn't as bad as this. There hasn't been such a bad day since 120 years ago, when a lot of people were drowned.*

Mr White was told that his cottage, in a narrow alley close to the beach, would have to be demolished. Silt and yellow clay were a foot deep on the floor and the water had covered his coal fire which went out in a cloud of steam. All his clothes were ruined. Like many others, he was helped by members of Portland Women's Voluntary Service, who were soon on hand with hot dinners, tea, bedding and clothes.

National newspapers sensationalised the floods with stories to the effect that the Chesil Beach had been 'breached' or 'washed away'. Nothing of the kind had happened; the sea started by filtering through the 42ft high bank and later came over the top as well. Some pebbles washed down into Chiswell but there is no evidence that the sea has ever torn through the Chesil Beach, though the waters have revealed its core of blue clay.

In the winter and spring of 1943/44, BUKO (West) was the Build Up Control Organisation for the 1st United States Army and 2nd British Army, with headquarters at Portsmouth, under the control of Brigadier (later Major-General Sir) Gerald Duke (1910–92). There was also a BUKO (East) but that was a bogus logistical operation set up in Dover to deceive the Germans into believing that the main attack on D-Day would come in the Pas de Calais.

Efforts on the ground in Portland and Weymouth were co-ordinated by the 14th Major Port of the Transportation Corps of the United States Army.

Disaster struck United States forces, seven miles west-south-west of Portland Bill, on the night of 27-28 April 1944. A convoy of tank landing ships taking part in the big Exercise Tiger practice landings at Slapton Sands, Devon, were intercepted by German E-boats in sight of the coastal gun battery at Blacknor Fort, Portland, which was ordered not to engage the enemy vessels because of the number of American servicemen who were in the water. LST507 and LST531 had been sunk and LST289 was damaged by a torpedo. Five other tank landing ships escaped as the German vessels withdrew with the arrival on the scene of HMS *Azalia* and HMS *Saladin*.

Divers and British motor-torpedo boats, based at Portland, recovered bodies in the morning and established that no officer privy to the 'Bigot' secret – plans for the invasion of Europe – had been rescued by the Germans and taken to France for interrogation. Bodies were piled up on the dockside at Castletown. A total of 441 United States soldiers, mainly engineers, were killed or drowned and 197 seamen also lost their lives. A few bodies in Royal Artillery uniforms were also recovered. Detailed eye-witness accounts and the positions of the two sunken tank landing ships are given in my book *Dorset–America*, which went to print as this title was being completed.

Lance-Corporal Tecwyn Morgan, who was 31-years-old at the time, told me that everyone was sworn not to mention the disaster to anyone:

*It has played on my mind for decades. What they are saying just isn't true. We could virtually see it all from our coast battery on Portland, and then the bodies being unloaded at Castletown, before being packed in tunnels. There were no funerals. I've talked before to reporters, including Captain Murphy of Associated Newspapers and Scott Wilkinson, but nothing ever appeared in print.*

No German pilot was allowed to see and live to report the existence of the great invasion fleet that was being amassed in western creeks and harbours from the Fal to Southampton Water. One such fatal interception, above Portland, took place at midnight on 14 May 1944. The Allied pilot concerned, Flying Officer Gilbert Wild, told me he was in a Beaufighter Mark VI night-fighter of 68 Squadron from RAF Fairwood Common on the Gower peninsula at Swansea. His radar controller at Hope Cove, Devon, talked him towards 'a high-flying bandit' at 25,000 feet above the English Channel on an approach that was to cross the coast over Portland.

Reading from his wartime combat report, Gilbert Wild said that, with co-pilot Frederick Baker, he came to within 25 yards' range and gave a 2.5-second burst of cannon fire, which ripped through its fuselage and port engine. On circling and returning for a second approach, the Beaufighter closed to 150 yards and gave a 4-second burst from directly behind. Smoke and flame followed as the intruder fell to 10,000 feet and proceeded to drop into the sea. The pilot called 'Murder' over his radio and the radar operative confirmed that the enemy aircraft had disappeared from his screen at 'fix' Z 0560. Take-off from Fairwood Common had been at 22.22 hours on 14 May and the Beaufighter's return was logged at 01.30 hours on 15 May. Four cannon, mounted on the fuselage, had fired a total of 787 rounds of 20-millimetre ammunition, and wreckage off Portland confirmed the 'kill'.

Dorset was the 'concentration area' for the marshalling of men and material for V Corps (Force O) of the 1st United States Army which sailed from Portland and Weymouth for Omaha Beach – between Pointe du Hoc and Colleville – on the Normandy coast in Operation Overlord on the night of 5 June 1944. This Corps comprised the 1st United States Infantry Division, the 2nd United States Armored Division and two elite Ranger Battalions. Commander-in-Chief of Allied Land Forces on D-Day was General Sir Bernard Law Montgomery (later Field Marshal and Viscount (1887–1975).

For a brief moment in what did not become history, Prime Minister Churchill was authorised by the Allied Naval Commander, Sir Bertrand Ramsey, to sail on HMS *Belfast* from Weymouth Bay to Normandy on 'D-Minus 1'. On the morning of D-Day he was to return across the Channel in a destroyer, in plans which horrified the Chiefs of Staff, who proceeded to block the arrangements. King George VI wrote to Churchill that much as he also wanted to be there himself, he realised that it was the duty of the pair of them to stay at home and steer the ship of state from the safety of the shore.

It was a wise decision, for although both the *Belfast* and the destroyer survived, the battle for Omaha beach turned into a close-run thing. V Corps lost 2,000 men on what became the bloodiest of the invasion beaches. Weymouth and Portland's joint part in the story are commemorated by stones and plaques in each town. They were unveiled on 3 December 1947 by Colonel Sherman L. Kiser, wartime Port Commander, and his Sub Port Commander, Major Harold G. Miller of the 14th Major Port of the United States Army:

*The major part of the American assault force which landed on the shores of France 6 June 1944, was launched from the Weymouth and Portland Harbors. From 6 June 1944 to 7 May 1945, 517,816 troops and 144,093 vehicles embarked from these harbors. Many of these troops left Weymouth Pier. The remainder of the troops and all vehicles passed through Weymouth en route to Portland points of embarkation.*

Among them, as a war correspondent, was the author Ernest Hemingway who sailed in the USS *Dorothea L. Dix* from Portland Harbour amid a sea of Aldis lamps flashing the same message in Morse code: 'Three dots, one dash. Those are the lights tonight. Constantly. The letter is "V" for Victory.' One cross-Channel item was left behind, namely a pair of concrete caissons (codename Phoenix) for one of the two temporary harbours (codename Mulberry) which were towed across to Normandy to provide instant port facilities on the sandy shores. It still stands offshore at Castletown.

A week after D-Day, at 04.45 hours on 13 June 1944, the destroyer HMS *Boadicea* was sunk off Portland. The 1,360-ton warship was attacked by a Junkers Ju.188 bomber, which released two aerial torpedoes into her port side. The second hit the forward magazine and the resultant explosion removed the front half of the ship. The stern was inundated and sank within minutes. Only 12 of the crew survived. They were picked up by HMS *Vanquisher* and taken to Portland. The *Boadicea* had been escorting convoy EBC8 and was zig-zagging at 9 knots at the time the bomber approached. It was initially mistaken for a friendly RAF Beaufighter.

Then, at 19.11 hours on 15 June 1944, the frigate HMS *Blackwood* was lost off Portland. Belonging to the Royal Navy's 3rd Escort Group, she was hit by a torpedo from German submarine *U-764*, again causing heavy casualties. Of the survivors, 35 were wounded. The bows and stern of the warship were left jutting out of the water, and remained afloat through the night until, dawn when radar contact was lost at 04.10 hours.

*U-984* torpedoed another escort frigate, HMS *Goodson*, on 24 June 1944. She was towed into Portland Harbour but the damage was deemed to be irreparable. On the night of 24/25 June 1944, the German submarine *U-1191* was spotted and sunk by the frigates HMS *Affleck* and HMS *Balfour* as it attempted to shadow the Normandy supply routes across Lyme Bay. Another enemy submarine, *U-269*, was sunk by HMS *Bickerton*, also between Start Point and Portland Bill, on 25 June 1944.

An additional reason for this naval activity was that several big warships had gathered in Portland Harbour for Rear Admiral Deyo's Portland Task Force. They sailed on 25 June 1944 to bombard the German defenders in the French port of Cherbourg. Split into two formidable bombardment groups, the fleet comprised three battleships (United States Ships *Texas*, *Arkansas* and *Nevada*) and four Royal Navy cruisers, protected by nine escort destroyers.

The 33,900-ton battleship HMS *Rodney*, carrying 16-inch guns, left Portland Harbour on 12 August 1944 to bombard the solidly built German batteries on the occupied Channel Island of Alderney. She was escorted by the destroyers HMS *Jervis* and *Faulkner*.

*LCT A2454*, a tank landing craft, was washed-up

## Second World War

*The 16-inch guns of the battleship HMS Rodney, seen in Portland Harbour, which sailed to bombard German positions in Alderney and France in the summer of 1944.*

*Two Phoenix caissons from a wartime Mulberry Harbour, at Castletown in Portland Harbour, in 2006.*

Left: *Colours of the United States Navy being presented to St John's Church, Fortuneswell, at a post-war service in August 1945.*

on the Chesil Beach at Wyke Regis in mountainous seas of 15 October 1944. The state of the sea prevented both the Weymouth Lifeboat and a Portland dockyard tug from coming round Portland Bill to its aid. Ten of the craft's British crew were drowned, despite heroic efforts by six members of Fortuneswell Lifesaving Co., who ran along the pebble bank from Portland to fire a rocket-line into the stricken vessel.

Two of the rescuers, Coastguard Treadwell and Captain Pennington Legh, were also swept to their deaths. Only four sailors were saved – two of them by the lifesavers who lost theirs in the process. The four surviving members of the rescue team were awarded Lloyd's silver medal for lifesaving but one – V.F. Stephens of Wyke Regis – died in a car crash before he could receive it. Cyril Brown of Portland, who struggled through the waves to free a fouled line to the landing craft and then had to be hauled ashore himself and taken to hospital, was awarded the Stanhope Medal for the bravest deed of 1944.

The German submarine *U-772* was attacked and sunk by Allied aircraft off Portland Bill on 30 December 1944.

The submarine threat remained long after the main war had moved eastwards into the Reich. The 5,222-ton London freighter *Everleigh*, outward bound in ballast for New York, was torpedoed and sunk between Portland Bill and St Alban's Head by *U-1017* on 6 February 1945.

*U-249*, the first German U-boat to surrender at the end of the Second World War, initially signalled her intention to the Royal Navy after coming to the surface off the Lizard and hoisting a black flag. A rendezvous was arranged in Weymouth Bay, where the submarine resurfaced and then followed the frigates HMS *Amethyst* and HMS *Magpie* into inshore waters on 10 May 1945. The five officers and 43 crew of *U-249* lined up on deck as Commander Patrick Wylie Rose Weir of the Royal Navy took command in the conning tower and replaced her main flag with the white ensign. She then entered Portland Harbour. The vessel was carrying ten unfired torpedoes.

The second surrender that day was *U-825*, as Grand-Admiral Karl Doenitz's undefeated commanders began to form an orderly queue. The third, via Weymouth on 10 May 1945, was *U-1023*, which then joined the others at Castletown. Submarine *U-776* attempted to surrender at Freshwater, Isle of Wight, but local officials refused the offer and she was redirected to Portland Harbour on 16 May 1945.

The largest arrival in Weymouth Bay was the 45,000-ton American battleship USS *Missouri*, which visited both Southampton and Portland before sailing home. It was a depressing day in the rain on Portland for the United States Ambassador, Gil Winant, on 22 August 1945. He had come to unveil the official memorial to the Americans in Dorset, in

Victoria Gardens, but was preoccupied by personal matters. Winant shot himself after returning to America as a result of an unrequited infatuation with Sarah Churchill, the daughter of the wartime Prime Minister.

The *Minerve*, formerly the Free French submarine *P-26*, was being towed to the breakers from Portsmouth to Cherbourg when the line parted off Portland. She drifted ashore onto the rocks, below what is now the Admiralty Underwater Weapons Establishment, on 19 September 1945.

The old Greek steamship *Thira*, in ballast from Solvesborg to Alexandria, lost power and began to sink after her engine room flooded at 03.00 hours on 6 January 1946 when she made a second attempt at rounding Portland Bill. The earlier attempt had to be aborted due to mechanical difficulties and the vessel put into Weymouth for repairs over Christmas. What was described as a 'scratch crew' of 13 Egyptian, Greek and Sudanese sailors, were taken off by the Portland dockyard tug *Pilot*.

The 5,008-ton London freighter *Merchant Royal*, carrying steel from Saint John, New Brunswick, to Hull, collided with the homeward-bound USS *William B. Travis* midway between Start Point and Portland Bill at 02.30 hours on 3 July 1946. By mid-morning the freighter was under tow towards Portland Harbour but she continued to fill with water. The lines had to be released at 16.45 hours seven miles south of Portland Bill, as it became obvious that the vessel would sink.

Evaluation of helicopters in an anti-submarine role was carried out on Portland in 1946, when shore base HMS *Osprey* was revived at The Mere. Having been built in 1937, and surviving Fleet service throughout the Second World War, the 840-ton Admiralty tug *Buccaneer* became a victim of friendly fire on 26 August 1946. The tug was towing a target across Lyme Bay during battle training practice when it was accidentally hit by what was described as 'a wide' shot from the new 2,315-ton destroyer HMS *St James*. The 4.5-inch shell did what its makers expected, and the *Buccaneer* proceeded to sink, nine miles west of Portland Bill.

Test pilot Alan Bristow (born 1923), serving with 771 Naval Air Squadron, made aviation history off Portland on 6 September 1946. In a record-breaking flight he brought a Fleet Air Arm Sikorski R4B Hoverfly down onto the makeshift floorboards of the flight deck of trials ship *K253*. This was the frigate HMS *Helmsdale*. It was the first helicopter landing in the world on a naval escort-vessel at sea.

Departing in rough weather, against adverse forecasts, the 1,919-ton Danish trawler *Marguerita* set off home from Milford Haven for Christmas in Copenhagen. They paid the price on Portland Bill, where the crew of seven lost their lives as the vessel was driven into the rocks in 'impossible conditions' on 11 December 1946.

The 1,062-ton Royal Navy submarine *P-555* (ex-American lease-lend vessel *S-24*) was scuttled for an asdic training target, four miles north-west of Portland Bill, on 25 August 1947.

Captain Ned Hale (1907–88) was the post-war deputy director general of the Underwater Weapons Establishment on Portland from 1947 to 1950. During the D-Day landings he had served on Admiral Ramsay's staff for Naval Operation Neptune, and was then posted to the British Pacific Fleet as chief of intelligence in 1946. Captain Hale left Portland to command HMS *Daring*, as Captain (D) of the Second Destroyer Flotilla, in 1951.

Tragedy struck the crew of the aircraft carrier HMS *Illustrious* on 17 October 1948 when 29 ratings were drowned in Portland Harbour. They were attempting to return to their ship after a day in Weymouth when their pinnace was swamped in heavy seas. A total of 22 survivors were rescued, which took some explaining, as the boat was only permitted to carry a total of 40 people (not 51). Midshipman R.A. Clough, who was among those drowned, was blamed by the subsequent enquiry both for the overloading and having failed to turn back on hitting rough water.

The last military unit to hold Verne Citadel, appropriately – because they had built it – were the Royal Engineers. As they left it, in 1948, the fortress was handed over to the Home Office Prison Service for the accommodation of medium-security male inmates.

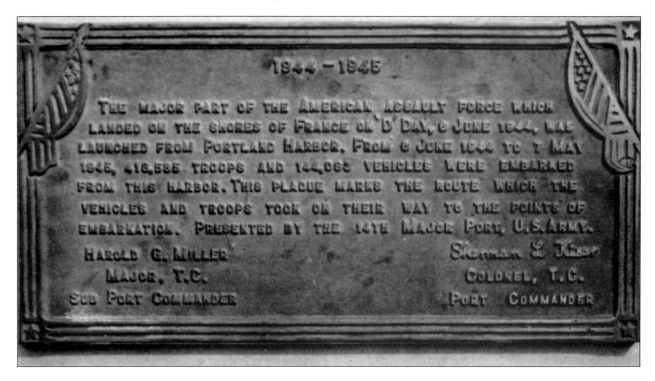

Above: *Portland plaque – with the original wording of August 1945 – which was revised to acknowledge Weymouth's contribution to the end of the war.*

Left: *Luftwaffe bomb from The Grove defused in 1995, now displayed at Portland Museum.*

# CHAPTER 9

# *Recent Times*

Ann and Francis Davison set off from Fleetwood in the ketch *Reliance* on 17 May 1949 'to sail the world and find our paradise'. This, as it cruelly turned out, was a dream that ended in Cave Hole, near Portland Bill, which provided momentary refuge on 3 June 1949. Francis then lost his grip of the rocks and was drowned. Ann, however, managed to climb the cliff to reach the Lighthouse and Coastguard Cottages, and lived to tell the tale in *Last Voyage*. The ketch was left wedged half inside Cave Hole for several months before she broke up completely.

The Admiralty Underwater Weapons Establishment was built across Barrow Hill, Southwell, between 1949 and 1952. It became one of Britain's most important top-secret installations – at the cutting edge of submarine warfare as ballistic missiles were redeployed from the air to the ocean depths – for the duration of the Cold War.

Clumps of wild asparagus were still growing around Portland Harbour in 1951, though it was apparently in decline and a decade later botanists failed to find the plant. The sandy turf of Hamm Beach, beside Portland Beach Road, was designated a site of special scientific interest by the Nature Conservancy Council for its attractive sea-holly, rare vetches, cranesbill and purple broomrape. Common maritime plants, there and through Chiswell, included sea-pink and tree mallow. Both botany and ornithology were back in vogue, and seaside access was practical again as, de-mined and stripped of coils of barbed wire, the Dorset coast was fully accessible for the first time since the Defence Regulations of 1940. In 1951, as London celebrated the Festival of Britain, bird-watchers gathered on Portland Bill, near the Coastguard Cottages, to celebrate the conversion of the old Lower Lighthouse into Portland Bird Observatory.

Easton's railway to Portland closed on the evening of 1 March 1952. The last scheduled passenger train between Portland and Weymouth steamed off the island at midnight on Sunday, 2 March 1952, hauled by locomotive No. 30177. The rails were left in place, however, as the line from Portland dockyard to Weymouth was retained both for freight and naval use, which included the occasional royal visit.

HMS *Sidon* was one of five Fleet submarines berthed alongside their depot ship HMS *Maidstone* in Portland Harbour as they prepared for torpedo-firing exercises on 16 June 1955. HMS *Springer*, moored outward from Sidon, cast off at 08.20 hours. Seconds later there was a thud and ringing alarm bells, as a grey plume of smoke rose from Sidon's conning-tower. Inside her hull, 13 of the crew of 56 lost their lives – but all would have done so had they not been on the surface – as the severity of the explosion was such that it ripped clothes from the crew, living and dead, and sent a cloud of debris and dust skywards through the hatch.

The location of the blast was in or beside a torpedo tube, causing the vessel to drop at the bow, and its seriousness was confirmed as the submarine proceeded to sink, in shallow water, at 08.45. The 'chemical blow', due to premature detonation of volatile high-grade hydrogen peroxide propellant, was repeated towards the end of the century by the Russian submarine *Kursk* in the Barents Sea. In neither case was a warhead attached or involved.

Though recovered and refloated, and not beyond repair, *Sidon* now carried a reputation and was therefore relegated to the role of underwater target. She was scuttled in Lyme Bay in 1957, seven miles west-north-west of Portland Bill, for use in asdic and other anti-submarine exercises.

The sixteenth and final Shambles Light Vessel, which was replaced by an automatic buoy over the winter of 1971, went into service in 1955 and was described by G.S. Thomson of Trinity House:

*This vessel was built in 1954 by Philip & Son of Dartmouth and has a red hull, light tower amidships and the name of the station – Shambles – painted in white capital letters 6 feet high on the sides. The vessel is 137 feet 3 inches in length, with a 25 feet beam and a builder's tonnage of 345 tons. This navigation light is electric of the multi-catoptric type, using a system of mirrors in conjunction with a number of 100 volt 350 watt lamps.*

*The fog signal which gives two blasts every 60 seconds is a diaphone operated by compressed air provided by compressors driven by 38 horsepower diesel engines. The light has a range of 25 miles and is shown at a height of 40 feet above sea level. The light character is two white flashes every 30 seconds. The light vessel has a crew comprising the Master and six Lightsmen and total complement of eleven. The Master spends one month on board and one month ashore while the Lightsmen spend one month on board and two weeks ashore.*

There was also a natural history discovery of note

beside Small Mouth, which could now claim to have Britain's only known colony of the Mediterranean scaly cricket *Mogoplistes squamiger*. It was confirmed as a British species in 1955 after Bernard C. Pickard found five adults at the high-tide mark. They live under pebbles between the tide lines in a most unusual habitat for a cricket.

In *Operation Portland*, published in 1972, convicted spy Harry Houghton described how, in the spring of 1956, he was drinking with a Russian agent he knew as Roman in the Crown Inn, Puncknowle, when a female colleague from the Underwater Weapons Establishment on Portland arrived in the company 'of a naval bod from the local shallow-water diving team'. Something that was said caused Roman to leave immediately for London. The significance was that Soviet Prime Minister Bulganin and Communist Party Secretary Krushchev were sailing to Britain on board the cruiser *Ordzhonikidze*, which was escorted by the destroyers *Smotryashchi* and *Sovershenny* and berthed at Kings Stairs, Portsmouth, on 18 April 1956.

As Roman assumed from careless talk in a remote Dorset public house, a British operation was being planned to inspect the hull of the Russian cruiser, as a result of which two wire jackstays were fitted to run the full length of the vessel below the waterline. These were for the use of underwater sentries to hold onto in the strong tides of Portsmouth Harbour, a team of six having being assigned to guard the *Ordzhonikidze*. They did not have to wait long, as a frogman in a black diving suit was seen at 07.30 hours on 19 April 1956 between the *Smotryashchi* and the *Ordzhonikidze*.

As a result, there was a struggle in which Commander Lionel 'Buster' Crabb was captured alive, although he later succumbed to his injuries or asphyxiation. 'Commander Crabb is presumed to be dead as the result of trials with certain underwater apparatus,' the Admiralty announced. According to Houghton, he had been tasked to fit a limpet-like device, which would have indicated the type of sonar which the Russians were using and then dropped harmlessly to the seabed. The attempted intelligence operation caused major diplomatic embarrassment, for which Prime Minister Anthony Eden was forced to apologise. The remains of Lionel Crabb's body, still in its rubber diving suit but lacking head and hands, were eventually found in Chichester Creek on 9 June 1957.

Work started in 1958 and continued until 1965 to build substantial stone sea defences, faced in concrete with an anti-wave profile, to protect Chesil Cove and the community of Chiswell at the southern end of the Chesil Beach.

The new nuclear age of underwater warfare touched Portland Harbour in October 1957, when Defence Minister Duncan Sandys and the First Sea Lord, Louis Mountbatten, welcomed USS *Nautilus* on her first visit to Britain. On her next visit to Portland dockyard, on 10 August 1958, she made history by surfacing in Weymouth Bay after the first voyage under the North Pole. She had sailed from Pearl Harbor, Honolulu, and submerged off the Hawaiian Islands before heading for the Bering Strait and the polar ice-sheet. The potentially perilous voyage into the unknown, during which there could be no prospect of rescue, ended in the English Channel after completion of the first water-borne transit of the northern hemisphere.

Dr Marie Carmichael Stopes died on 2 October 1958 at the age of 78. Her home at that time was Norbury Park, near Dorking, but she wanted her ashes brought back to her spiritual home on Portland. Her son, Harry Verdon Stopes-Roe, cast them from Portland Bill into the waters from which she had once been so lucky to escape.

Portland's connection with the Royal Navy moved with the times in 1959. Following further draining of The Mere, in the angle between the ferry road and Portland Castle, a naval helicopter station was formally opened by Admiral Sir Manley Power, Commander-in-Chief Portsmouth, on 24 April 1959. Forming part of shore-base HMS *Osprey*, it was designated as a Royal Naval Air Station for the Operational Flying School, No. 815 Naval Air Squadron being stationed there. The climax of the week was a royal visit by the Queen and Prince Charles, after which the final royal train departed from Portland dockyard, heading for Windsor, on 29 April 1959.

The 730-ton Hull coaster MV *Lesrix*, carrying coal from Goole to Hayle, had as its master Captain Semison, who was a veteran of dozens of wartime convoys and had survived three sinkings. His luck ran out on 1 November 1960, when *Lesrix* was last seen heading down-Channel into the eye of a storm, 15 miles west of St Catherine's Point, and can be presumed to have passed the Isle of Purbeck but failed to reach Portland. The quantity of debris washed up on the Bill, including hatch-covers and lifebelts, indicated that all eight crewmen had been lost with their ship.

Soviet penetration of the top secret Admiralty Underwater Weapons Establishment was confirmed with a series of convictions at the Old Bailey on 22 March 1961 during which Lord Parker, the Lord Chief Justice, sentenced 39-year-old Gordon Lonsdale 'whose identify may never be known' to 25 years in jail. Lonsdale was the 'directing mind' of the Portland spies of whom his counsel observed, in mitigation: 'At least it can be said of this man that he was not a traitor to his own country.'

The Russian agent, who pretended to be a Canadian businessman, had been gathering information on the new hunter-killer nuclear submarine HMS *Dreadnought*. That he was caught owed more to the complacency of his associates than the vigilance of the Security Service, MI5. Their first insight came via the CIA, from the debriefing of defector Colonel Michal Goleniewski of the Polish Intelligence Service, who claimed that details of British anti-submarine defences were being revealed to the Soviets.

Meanwhile, in the autumn of 1959, Detective Constable Leonard Burt of the Weymouth police had received a tip-off that Admiralty clerk Harry Houghton, who worked at Portland naval base, 'was regularly visiting the Polish Embassy in London'. Burt found that Houghton's £14 a week salary stretched to sustained profligacy, including regular bouts of binge drinking with naval records clerk Ethel 'Bunty' Gee. Both were under police surveillance, with sightings of Houghton and his new off-white Renault Dauphine being communicated under the code 'Off-White' in case radio frequencies were being monitored. 'Ours is a dangerous business,' wrote Harry Houghton on an incriminating Christmas card to Bunty Gee.

Hosking and Hoskins were also on their case. Bridport-born *Daily Express* crime reporter Percy Hoskins heard that 'fatherly dockyard policeman' Fred Hosking 'was Britain's lone spy-chaser'. The 60-year-old Admiralty constable was keeping an eye on Houghton after having been handed a sheet of notepaper which a civil servant had found on his desk. Scrawled by brush in tracing ink were the words 'You dirty Jew', with a black swastika daubed in one corner.

The recipient, who was not Jewish, suspected the culprit was Houghton, because of 'a personal grudge'. Harry Houghton's movements revealed a predictable pattern of London trips, taking Gee there on the first Saturday of each month, and an MI5 watcher saw him hand a bag to a stocky middle-aged man near Waterloo Station. That person was Gordon Lonsdale. The British spook, William 'Jim' Skardon, followed Lonsdale to a bungalow at Ruislip that was the home of Helen and Peter Kroger. A full MI5 team implemented their usual travelling circus of callers, including phoney salesmen and gardeners, plus a contrived problem with the telephone to gain entry for 'tap and bug'.

Antiquarian bookseller Peter Kroger traded from No. 190 The Strand, and specialised in 'Americana from the North Pole to the South Pole', which took him to book fairs across Europe. He had respectable international credentials, though these were compromised by a side-line in pornography. 'Books with microdots,' Skardon quipped after a visit to Kroger's stand. The spooks also found that Harry Houghton had been fired from a previous job with the British Embassy in Warsaw and assumed that he was initially blackmailed into spying for the Russians.

The trap was set and sprung on the first trip to London by Houghton and Gee in 1961, outside the Old Vic Theatre on Saturday 7 January, as they approached Lonsdale. His pockets were stuffed with banknotes. Cheap groceries in Gee's bag camouflaged the real shopping, which comprised microfilm of 310 classified Admiralty documents, including

construction details of HMS *Dreadnought*. The Krogers were next to be arrested.

Appropriately, a tin of Yardley Invisible Talc which MI5 operators found at Ruislip contained hidden compartments, and a hip flask had a concealed insert for sprinkling iron oxide onto magnetic tape in order to read Morse code. A microdot reader was incorporated into a tin of face powder. There was a Minox camera, £6,000 in cash and a cache of classified documents which spilled from books and had been stuffed under floorboards.

The Krogers' fridge contained a short-wave radio and there was another buried in the garden, though the latter was missed by MI5 and not discovered until 1977 by new owners of the bungalow.

Something similar applied to the identities of the leading spies. Only when an American journalist spotted a press picture of Peter Kroger did MI5 realise that they had been watching the most successful partnership in espionage history. Helen and Peter Kroger were, in fact, FBI-listed 'missing persons' Lona and Morris Cohen, who had disappeared in 1950, immediately before Ethel and Julius Rosenberg were arrested. They were together in a ring, co-ordinated by Russian master-spy Colonel Rudolf Abel, which included agent 'Perseus'. Their information enabled the Soviet Union to develop and explode an atomic bomb in 1948.

As a direct result of the Portland spy scandal, a three-man Committee of Inquiry into Breaches of Security was established by Prime Minister Harold Macmillan. It was chaired by Sir Charles Romer (1897–1969), a former Lord Justice of Appeal, who sat with retired civil servant Sir Harold Emmerson and Vice-Admiral Sir Geoffrey Thistleton-Smith.

Lonsdale, whose real name was Colonel Conon Trifomovich Molody (born 1921), was exchanged in 1964 for the British spy Greville Wynne. Helen Kroger (1913–92) and Peter Kroger (1910–95) were swapped, very unequally, for Gerald Brooke, whose only offence had been to distribute anti-Communist leaflets in Moscow. The Krogers settled in the Soviet Union and moved to Helen's family home near Lublin on the Polish border. Houghton and Gee were released from prison shortly afterwards.

There remains some speculation about another Portland spy. Sir Roger Hollis, as director-general of MI5, discontinued investigations into a further aspect. Someone else had to be involved because information from Portland covering operational details of the new submarine could not have originated with Houghton or Gee, as neither had nuclear clearance. Such matters came into the public domain with publication of Peter Wright's *Spycatcher* – alleging long-term penetration of MI5 by an 'undiscovered mole' – in 1987. Leonard Burt, the Dorset policeman on the case, became the county's Assistant Chief Constable and retired to Ferndown.

The 499-ton Dutch coaster MV *Evertsen*, carrying

# Cold War

*Commander Lionel 'Buster' Crabb, who dived to his death beneath a Russian cruiser on 19 April 1956, after the operation had been compromised by a chance remark to a Portland spy and his Soviet handler.*

*HMS Sidon with her commander, Lieutenant Verry, on the deck in white jumper (right) as rescuers arrived after a disastrous explosion in Portland Harbour on 16 June 1955.*

Below: *Verne view in 1965, over the Naval Cemetery, to frigates F49 and F51 and the cruiser HMS Tiger, docked at Portland with a Royal Fleet Auxiliary in the harbour.*

## Cold War

*Portland sheep* (foreground) *and secrets* (background) *at the Admiralty Underwater Weapons Establishment, Southwell, in 1981.*

*Castletown view to the section of Mulberry Harbour* (left), *a Rothesay-class frigate, and a minesweeper, beside the stone pier* (right) *in 1975.*

*On-duty officer passing an off-duty Portland Roads Hotel on The Strip at Castletown in 1975.*

*Minesweeper P297 leaving Portland Harbour beside 'C' Head, through the North Ship Channel, in 1984.*

china clay from Fowey to Rotterdam, was in collision with another Dutch motor vessel, *Favoriet*, off Portland on 24 June 1961. The nine members of the *Evertsen*'s crew and their three passengers were rescued by the *Favoriet* as the former went down 17 miles south-east of Portland Bill.

Portland and ornithology became synonymous in 1961 with the conversion of the Lower Lighthouse into Portland Bird Observatory. It is the one place in southern England where melodious and icterine warblers make dependable annual appearances. Some 2,000 migrant birds make their landfall into waiting mist nets, from which they are extracted, weighed, recorded and ringed. Regular specialities include the aquatic warbler, the sub-Alpine warbler, and the yellow-browed warbler. Occasionally there is excitement, at least among visiting 'twitchers', as they rush for news of an American arrival that has been a freak windfall from the jet stream.

Hawker's chief test pilot, Alfred William 'Bill' Bedford (born 1920), achieved a world aviation record for Portland on 8 February 1963 with the first vertical landing by a fixed-wing aircraft onto an aircraft-carrier. The plane was the Hawker Siddeley P1127 Kestrel, prototype of the Harrier, and the vessel HMS *Ark Royal*. She was sailing at 5-knots to the east of the Shambles.

Anti-submarine warfare was also taking on a new look in 1963 with the bringing into naval service of the Wasp helicopter. Its low-level dragonfly-like buzzing became a ubiquitous sound over and around Portland Harbour for the next quarter of a century.

Three special passenger trains for railway enthusiasts ran over the Portland branch line on 27 March 1965. The last train to use the line was a goods train, from Portland to Weymouth, on 9 April 1965. Rails from Easton were lifted in 1966 and its station demolished in 1972. Destruction of the remainder of the line began with demolition of Portland goods depot in 1969 and the removal of the track to Weymouth in 1970, with the viaduct across Small Mouth being demolished in November 1971.

Work began in 1967 and carried on until 1970 to drain and surface the remainder of The Mere for an extension of the Royal Naval Air Station. New accommodation blocks were built on the slope to the south-east. The steam-yacht *Patricia II*, carrying ballast, sank 17 miles south-west of Portland Bill on 13 May 1967.

The steamship *Nasad* was lost nine miles south-south-west of Portland Bill on 16 August 1968. A Royal Navy Whirlwind helicopter crashed at Portland on 9 October 1968.

Another Whirlwind helicopter, also flying with the Navy, ditched in the sea off Portland on 20 June 1969. On 3 August 1969 the fishing boat *Marie-Antoinette* struck a floating object – log or timber – and was holed, sinking four miles east-south-east of Portland Bill.

In 1969 I published an appeal for someone to provide me with the secret recipe for Portland dough-cake. From Portland I received cries of incredulity, such as a letter from Mrs Lillie Moore of Wakeham, who demanded: 'Do you seriously think any self-respecting Portlander would give you the recipe?'

The Tomkins family did, however, through Mrs Mary E. Bradley in Durweston, who wrote:

*I returned yesterday from Odstock Hospital. Near me was a lady from Portland and friends brought her sister. As I had no visitors that afternoon they were pleased to leave the sisters together and talk to me. We talked Portland and then I suddenly remembered your request for Portland dough-cake. The lady had made 30 pounds at Christmas and distributed it amongst friends and neighbours. This is the recipe the Tomkins ladies checked and double checked between them and gave me:*

*2 pounds of dough (as for bread)*
*1.5 pounds of currants*
*1 pound of lard*
*quarter pound of butter (only if a very rich mixture is desired)*
*quarter pound of brown sugar*
*quarter pound of mixed peel*
*1 teaspoon of nutmeg*

*Apply the least possible plain flour to your hands to knead the mixture. Press out naturally and cook. We didn't go into oven temperatures as it was taken for granted that cooks would know it had to be slow cooking at moderate heat.*

After the Tomkins sisters returned to the island they wrote to Mrs Bradley and divulged another of the secret tastes of Portland, its rice-cake:

*We thought you might like a recipe for a rice-cake. It is a lovely cake. I do cook mine for 45 minutes in a gas oven at a high regulo of number four then down to number two, just like a fruit cake, for a couple of hours. My friend suggests that we use this mix of lard, butter and margarine, to avoid it becoming too rich:*

*10 ounces of self-raising flour*
*4 ounces of lard*
*2 ounces of butter*
*4 ounces of margarine*
*4 ounces of brown sugar*
*1 pound of currants*
*4 ounce of ground rice*
*2 eggs*
*1 teaspoon of vinegar*
*1.5 teaspoons of nutmeg and spice*
*1.5 teaspoons of bicarbonate*
*2 ounces of peel*
*1.5 cups of milk.*

Three were killed and four saved when a Royal Navy Wessex helicopter crashed in the sea off Portland during the photographic reconnaissance exercise on 20 May 1971.

One of the island's three links with the mainland, the railway viaduct over The Fleet estuary at Small Mouth, was demolished in 1971.

The sixteenth and final *Shambles* light vessel was withdrawn from service on 30 September 1971, having been replaced by *Lanby I*, the acronym of the first Large Automatic Navigation Buoy, ordered by Trinity House. The system had been devised for the United States Coast Guard in 1965, and developed in Britain by Hawker Siddeley Dynamics. The first, chosen for operational testing off Portland Bill, cost £160,000. New technology inevitably came with its teething troubles and the light vessel had to return to the sandbank, in November 1971, whilst faults were rectified before the buoy could become a permanent substitute later that winter. Meanwhile, on 20 December 1971, Dick Crumbleholme and the Weymouth Lifeboat resumed their traditional role for one last time as the lightship's Father Christmas.

A Royal Navy Sea King helicopter ditched in the sea off Portland on 13 January 1972. Another naval helicopter, a Wessex, was lost off Portland on 16 February 1972.

HMS *Matapan*, a 2,750-ton destroyer launched in 1947, which had gone to sea for only six days before been 'mothballed' at Devonport until 1969, spent her later life at Portland. Totally refitted at a cost of £2,500,000, she replaced the 2,340-ton frigate HMS *Verulam* in Portland Harbour during the winter of 1972. The vessels were fitted out as floating electrical laboratories for sonar and other experimental tests carried out by the island's Underwater Weapons Establishment. Submarine detection equipment was fitted in the *Matapan*'s redesigned bulbous bow which, together with anti-rolling stabilisers along the hull, required plate riveting – as distinct from welding – to be employed in Portsmouth dockyard for the first time in years. A large helicopter deck was also fitted to one of the oldest warships in service use. Her name commemorates Admiral of the Fleet Sir John Cunningham's great victory over the Italian navy at Cape Matapan in 1941.

A total of 825 tons of Portland stone (10,000 cubic feet, valued at £7,500) was donated by the Bath & Portland Group Ltd to the 'Save St Paul's' restoration appeal. The first consignment, of 50 tons, was shipped in a traditional Thames sailing barge, the *May*, owned by Silvertown Services Lighterage and skippered by Reg Martin and his mate, Keith Stocks, on 7 August 1972. History was being repeated. Her first recorded visit to Castletown Pier had been on 31 October 1903, when she took on board 137 tons of block stone; her last on 6 March 1933, with a cargo of 125 tons. Capital loads of this size were out of the question in the 1970s due to licensing restrictions.

The first block to be loaded on the *May* in 1972 was one bearing the wine-glass quarry mark of Sir Christopher Wren, which was recovered by the Royal Navy, using a helicopter, from the ruins of King's Pier. It was four cubic feet in size (about six hundredweight). Delivery in central London was to Sunlight Wharf, near the Mermaid Theatre, which was the closest such facility still in use. After the historic voyage the remainder of the stone destined for St Paul's left the island by road, in 60 loads, between 1973 and 1980.

Since time immemorial – for most of the second Christian millennia – Portlanders have used their energy and expertise to place and replace marker stones on the parish boundary with Chickerell in the inhospitable nothingness of the Chesil Beach. The practical purpose of establishing this line, two miles beyond Small Mouth, was to reassert the claim to fishing rights and free use of the beach for hauling ashore valuable shoals of mackerel. In 1974, however, the team of fishermen and quarrymen had a much easier task, as the Royal Navy loaned a Wessex helicopter of 516 Naval Air Squadron to drop new stones into position.

A 'Flock Book' for Portland sheep was opened in 1974, to ensure that the strain remains a pure breed, after which each animal has carried an ear-tag with its number.

Veteran Navy flyer Captain David 'Paddy' McKeown, who retired in 1977, was the commander of Portland Royal Naval Air Station. His 35 years' flying service had taken him up in 52 different types of aircraft for a total of 4,500 hours airborne, and involved 800 deck landings on 16 different aircraft carriers. He had survived a mid-air collision in a Corsair over southern India in 1945. He was mentioned in despatches when flying a Sea Fury from HMS *Ocean* in the Korean War, and again in 1956 whilst flying Sea Hawks from HMS *Albion* at Suez.

The Sea Harrier, developed from the P1127 Kestrel, became a frequent sight hovering and flying above and around Portland. It was found to take off with increased efficiency, at less speed, from ski-ramps rather than traditional flat decks. These added fixtures appeared on the bows of the aircraft carriers HMS *Invincible* in 1978 and HMS *Hermes* in 1979. They were then incorporated as standard in the next generation ships, HMS *Illustrious* and the next *Ark Royal*, which were being built.

The futuristic aircraft made its operational debut with the Fleet Air Arm at Yeovilton, Somerset, on 19 September 1979, when 700A Naval Air Squadron was commissioned as the Sea Harrier Intensive Flying Trials Unit. Later, 800, 801 and 899 Naval Air Squadrons were issued with Sea Harriers, as were a couple of RAF squadrons with their version of the aircraft. Most would be combat-ready and heading for the South Atlantic, along with the Sea King helicopters, within a week of the Argentinian invasion of the Falkland Islands on 2 April 1982.

Portland's extreme natural events of recent times began in December 1978, when the sea seeped through the pebbles of the Chesil Beach on a scale not experienced since the Second World War. Lower parts of Chiswell were inundated and the road link with the mainland was completely awash. Damage would have been much greater but for the benefit of Portland's geology – providing one of the best building stones of these islands – which meant that none of the tightly packed homes collapsed. The Royal Navy came to the rescue with Lynx anti-submarine helicopters, which had just come into service, and Zodiac inflatables.

Then, to everyone's surprise, on 13 February 1979, the sea began to rise again in Lyme Bay and continued to do so – in a much more dramatic fashion – until waves surged over the top of the Chesil Beach. Several hundreds of tons of shingle were swept into Chiswell. Several parked cars floated along the street in a swirling surf that left Victoria Square flooded to a depth of four feet. Most of the water came over the pebble bank above Masonic Hall but there was also general seepage along a much wider front.

Portland's mystery flood of 1979, which came out of a relatively flat sea and was regarded at the time as a 'freak weather event', found an explanation in the winter of 2004. Having investigated the great Bristol Channel inundation of 20 January 1607, Professor Michael Disney came up with a scenario which may also apply to the sea having surged over Chesil Beach and engulfed the Chiswell district of Portland in 1979.

Photographs support anecdotal evidence that waves crashed over the 25ft high pebble ridge, carrying seven feet of water across at a time, with a force that maintained the wave form and carried shingle into streets and homes. I was there shortly afterwards and saw upturned cars and other debris. What continued to mystify emergency services was that no one had predicted such a spectacular event. Although atmospheric pressure was low, which allows sea levels to rise, the wind was a light easterly. This was the opposite direction from the south-westerly waves. There was no extreme local storm nor the forecast of an exceptionally high tide.

The puzzle was partially explained at the time by measurements from an automatic buoy beyond the Scilly Isles. This showed wave patterns of a size to be expected by a deep depression in mid-Atlantic, on 11 February 1979, but with crests that were abnormally far apart. The crucial difference appears to be the signature of a tsunami caused by 'monstrous submarine landslides' of the kind that Professor Disney describes from 1607, when thousands were drowned. Publication of his research overlapped the appearance of an equally unexpected Boxing Day wave across the Indian Ocean on Boxing Day in 2004.

The *Crystal* was built as an acoustic calibration vessel. Moored in Portland Harbour towards the Outer Breakwater, she has operated as the offshore arm of the Admiralty Research Establishment. Her lines are unlike those of any other vessel, resembling a row of terraced houses, though with very few windows and a flat roof. This rises into a tower block at one end. Both the outer and inner sides are sloping and the underside has a flat bottom.

HMS *Alacrity*, a 3,250-ton Type 21 frigate on war games off Portland, lived up to her name on 31 March 1982. Captain Christopher Craig's warship was one of the first to be ordered to sail after the Argentinian invasion of the Falkland Islands. Her immediate destination was Plymouth, where she hoisted the red flag to signify the loading of ammunition. The *Alacrity* then joined the frigate HMS *Antelope* off Gibraltar and was there at 03.00 hours on Friday 2 April 1982 when Sir John Fieldhouse, the Commander-in-Chief, Fleet, sent the signal from the Royal Navy's command bunker at Northwood ordering Operation Corporate.

The 12,120-ton assault ship *Intrepid*, lying empty in Portsmouth Harbour, was quickly brought back into service and went to Portland to be recommissioned and sent off to war under the command of Captain Peter Dingemans. Carrying a 75-ton landing craft, she arrived in the operational area on 13 May 1982 and slipped into San Carlos Water with the men of 3 Para.

Operation Corporate was 'the code name for everything that followed'. Those were the words of its recipient, Admiral Sir John 'Sandy' Woodward aboard HMS *Antrim*, who found himself in control of what had become the Falklands Battle Group. 'We did not even have charts of the Falklands aboard the Flagship,' he recalled in his memoirs, *One Hundred Days*. The aircraft carrier HMS *Hermes*, which became the flagship, entered the operational area with *Alacrity* as one of her escorts, on 25 April 1982.

Royal Navy pilot Prince Andrew, Duke of York, who trained at Yeovilton and Portland, was airborne in a helicopter attempting to decoy and deviate Exocet missiles off the Falkland Islands when the 18,000-ton Cunard roll-on roll-off container ship *Atlantic Conveyor* was hit on 25 May 1982. A total of 12 men died, including Captain Ian North, and a fire-fighting crew were rescued by helicopter, but the remaining 134 survivors owed their lives to HMS *Alacrity*. Captain Craig 'brought her right up to the floating time-bomb which was the *Conveyor*' in order to fire life-lines over the rafts in which the crew had abandoned ship, to tow them clear.

Commodore Christopher Palmer – as he became on appointment as commanding officer at RNAS Yeovilton – was a Falklands veteran mentioned in despatches. He then joined 702 Naval Air Squadron at Portland as a Lynx instructor in 1983, and was

## Events

*Victoria Square and the Royal Victoria Hotel* (left) *under water in the winter of 1906.*

*Tragedy ended the round-the-world voyage of the ketch* Reliance, *inside Cave Hole in June 1949.*

operational flying instructor to Prince Andrew.

Portland Sculpture Trust was formed in 1983, establishing stone carving and sculpture workshops that have literally left their mark in and around the otherwise disused Tout Quarries, where rock art has added a new dimension to the landscape. Representations of animals and symbols can be discovered across huge abandoned boulders and rock-faces. It is as if a tribe of cave artists and aborigines have survived on Portland since primeval times and crawl out from under their stones in some crepuscular reincarnation to make magic marks before going to ground at dawn. Such images make one look at a quarry in a different way. Others echo architectural landmarks carved out of the quarry itself.

Through Portland Town Council, the trust negotiated a 30-year lease of Tout Quarries, which has been run by Hannah Sofaer with Paul Crabtree, Robin Downton, Charles Frampton, Jonathan Phipps and Neville Walbridge. The ground is owned by Hanson plc, as the holding company of operators Bath & Portland Stone.

Navy flyer Captain Anthony Wigley was killed when his Wessex Mark V helicopter crashed on one of the breakwaters of Portland Harbour on 3 December 1984.

Christopher Craig, the bold captain of HMS *Alacrity* in the Falklands War, returned to Portland in 1986 as the commander of the island's Royal Naval Air Station, HMS *Osprey*. It was a noisy summer that year as construction work began at Chiswell and Castletown on a £5 million flood alleviation scheme to put an emergency drain under the Chesil Beach. It has been designed to come into use when the sea next breaks over it, through a mile of under-pebble culverts, the outfall being an open ditch across to the harbour at Castletown. Pile-driving on the Chesil Beach was likened to plunging one's hand into a bucket of marbles.

In 1987 the aggregates and construction company ARC Southern presented an acre and a half of dramatic slanting clifftop, known as Cheyne Weare, to Portland Town Council for a picnic area, at a peppercorn rent of £1 a year. A spoil heap on this section of the historic Southwell landslip had been cleaned up and provided with seaward-facing stone benches, looking over Weymouth Bay to St Alban's Head and the Isle of Wight. 'Cheyne Weare has been the best place for generations for the island's fishermen to spot shoals of mackerel,' quarry manager John Reay said at the hand-over ceremony.

Beside Chesil Cove, in 1986, the Chesil Gallery and Portland Town Council commissioned John Maine to create a 'living landscape sculpture' as one of Shaftesbury-based environment charity Common Ground's 'New Milestones' projects. John Maine had just finished his circular 'Arena' in Portland stone as a centrepiece for London's revitalised South Bank.

On Portland, between 1987 and 1993, he built five terraces across the scree slope below West Weares. Each retaining wall was inspired by the stone occurring at that point, with the stone used in the construction following the same sequence as the beds in the quarries above, namely basebed, whitbed, roach, slat and topstone. The terraces rise and fall to reflect wave patterns down on the beach.

Wasp helicopters of 829 Naval Air Squadron made a farewell flypast over Portland Harbour on 11 January 1988 on being decommissioned after a quarter of a century's service as the 'war horses' of the Royal Navy. Ten helicopters took part in the formation flying. They were replaced over the following two months by the Yeovil-made Lynx, which came into military use in 1978. The Cold War was coming to a close and Christopher Craig left Portland in 1989 in time to command Royal Navy 'Forces Afloat' in the Gulf War of 1991.

Ten coleopterists were delighted to find more than a hundred specimens of *Omolphus rufitarus* in 1989. This half-inch long beetle is one of Britain's rarest insects. It is only known from the Portland and Weymouth end of the Chesil Beach shingle but none had been recorded since 1926. Howard Mendel spotted the first, crawling on a thrift flower in a purple clump of *Ameria maritima*:

*I was overjoyed to see it there. We found it in far greater numbers than we ever dreamed. No one knows its history. The larvae seem to live in the soil beneath the plant.*

Another survey revealed the continuing presence of the moth *Sterrha degeneraria*, known as the Portland ribbon wave. It has its only British colonies here and at Torbay and is only otherwise known from central Europe, which says something for coastal micro-climates, though its food plant has not been identified.

Portland helicopters departed for the Persian Gulf in the autumn of 1990 after Saddam Hussein invaded Kuwait. Lynx helicopters of 815 Naval Air Squadron were deployed on the type-42 destroyers HMS *York*, *Gloucester*, *Cardiff*, *Exeter* and *Manchester* – listed in order of arrival – and the Leander-class frigate HMS *Jupiter*. No. 829 Naval Air Squadron provided Lynx for the type-22 frigates HMS *Battleaxe*, *Brazen*, *London*, *Brave* and *Brilliant*. A total of 14 such Lynx Mark-3 helicopters were 'modified and enhanced' for use in the Gulf and operated in three groups (W, X and Y) which 'were praised for their deadly accuracy in attacking Iraqi gunboats' during what became the first Gulf War.

The fishing boat MV *Antigua Star* foundered and sank three miles west of Portland Bill on 28 August 1992.

Defence cuts in March 1993 claimed Portland-based 829 Naval Air Squadron (motto 'They shall

# Events

*Sea Fury fly-past for Sea Hawk WV991 and Captain Paddy McKeown on his retirement at RNAS Portland in May 1977.*

*The sea breaking over the Chesil Beach in Portland's tsunami of 13 February 1979.*

not escape'). The squadron was amalgamated with its sister squadron, 815 Naval Air Squadron, which was also based at Portland. It took control of all 37 Lynx helicopters in service with the Royal Navy. By this time their practice vessel, *RNAL 50* – the Royal Navy Air Landing ship moored in Portland Harbour – had logged more than 100,000 deck landings which was far more landings (and therefore take-offs) than any other vessel in the Royal Navy.

Redundancies in one Portland family were alleviated in December 1993 when 50-year-old school cleaner Judith Smith won more than £2 million on the football pools. She had forgotten to fill in her coupon in the previous two weeks. A spokesman for Littlewoods declared her win to be 'the fourth biggest ever recorded'. Resigning from her £38-a-week job, Mrs Smith said it would 'give someone else the chance to earn a few bob'.

Completion during the year of John Maine's artistic earthworks beneath West Weares had been marked in May 1993 by Chesil Gallery hosting a celebratory exhibition entitled 'Henry Moore and The Sea'. The Henry Moore Foundation provided funding for finishing the innovative 'outdoor sculpture' project and followed this by loaning examples of Henry Moore's work for a special display at Margaret Somerville's gallery, between the sea defences and Pebble Lane.

Poole-based Sergeant Richard Stephen Howard (1963–94), of the elite Special Boat Squadron, was killed when diving in the sea off the breakwaters of Portland Harbour on 21 April 1994, whilst participating in overnight live-firing exercises with the Royal Marines. He was the navigator of a top secret SDV mini-submarine which was implicated in dragging him under water.

The modern German submarine *U-14* was nearly claimed by the Royal Navy off Portland Bill in a collision that was a timely reminder in events to mark the fiftieth anniversary of the end of the Second World War. The 500-ton diesel-electric vessel was at periscope depth when it was hit by the starboard propeller of the 4,000-ton frigate HMS *Battleaxe*. Two torpedo tubes and a ballast tank were damaged, but the pressurised hull was not ruptured. Both craft returned to Portland, under their own power, from war games in which Nato powers were participating.

There was another reminder of the conflict as bomb disposal expert Captain Michael Lobb (born 1968) spent 31 hours without sleep on Portland to defuse an unexploded wartime bomb in a controlled explosion that immobilised its detonator at 08.15 hours on 3 April 1995. He was fêted as a local hero by 4,000 Tophill residents as they returned to their homes. Throughout his ordeal, Captain Lobb of the Royal Engineers had a letter in his breast pocket from local schoolgirl Laura Gates: 'I think you and your Army are very brave and I would like to thank you for your help.'

Captain Lobb, by now enjoying champagne and congratulations after showing off his trophy in the middle of the Portland United football pitch at The Grove, told reporters:

*The low point of the operation was when I spent six and a half hours drilling a hole into the outer casing of the bomb. It took much longer than I expected but once it was finished I knew I was on the home run.*

Nine so-called 'Refuseniks' risked arrest and then injury by insisting on remaining in their homes. They were eventually allowed to stay, after signing disclaimers, while police cordoned off the island to prevent looting. 'That bit was quite easy,' an officer said. 'The barriers are already there, but we normally use them to try and prevent prisoners leaving rather than mainlanders arriving.'

Portland was in the process of parting company with the Royal Navy, which prepared to move its Flag Officer Sea Training westwards to Devonport. For 40 years, every operational surface ship in the Royal Navy had passed through Portland, and its weekly Thursday 'war games' in the English Channel, in which ships and their crews were subjected to simulated 'red on blue' attack. 'Wreckers' disabled vessels to ensure the realism and rigour of on-board scenarios. Their last 'victim' was the new type-23 frigate HMS *Argyll*, which sailed out of Portland for Plymouth on 21 July 1995 as Rear-Admiral John Tolhurst and his 250-strong staff were joined by 11 returning admirals for a farewell ceremony which climaxed in a 13-gun salute. There were protests in the press. Rear-Admiral Patrick Middleton and Captain John Trinder, a former Commander Sea Training, defended Portland as having provided 'the finest basic sea training for warships and their crews in the world.'

Onshore, in its final matelot days, this was The Strip at Castletown in my vignette from that summer:

*There's the office of the Naval Welfare Organisation, opposite St Paul's Church, and one of the earliest slot-machine laundries. Whereon come the boozers, many with pennants and other nautical memorabilia, including the Albert Inn, the Breakwater Hotel, the Sailors' Return (now an annexe to the Breakwater), the Portland Roads Hotel, and the Jolly Sailor. That little list tends to outgun the opposition, the Sally Ann, as the Salvation Army Red Shield Hostel is known. Sandwiched between the three-storey late Victorian and Edwardian façades are the reminders that these are the Navy's watering holes - buildings such as HM Customs House, and the shop-fronts of shipping agents, plus Grieves & Hawkes of Savile Row for the stylish officer.*

The Ministry of Defence sold the 350 acres of Castletown dockyard, Mere Tank Farm, adjacent land, and four breakwaters of Portland Harbour to

## Events

*Liz Box's dramatic shot of the moment the sea surged over the Chesil Beach into Chiswell on 13 February 1979.*

Left: *Water streamed through houses and shops into Chiswell on 13 February 1979.*

Right: *An island once more, as the sea washed Portland Beach Road into the harbour, beside Mere Tank Farm (left).*

Langham Industries plc and Portland Development Partners for £2 million in 1995, against a counter-bid from Roil (UK), which proposed establishing what was described as 'a marine disposal centre'. The winning bid was not the highest, which led to an investigation by the Serious Fraud Office into what was called a 'cut-price sale' in *The Times* of 11 September 1995, but no charges resulted. Portland Port Ltd, which took possession, was established as the local operating company, which originally planned to create a roll-on, roll-off ferry terminal.

The Old House at Maidenwell, between Chiswell and Fortuneswell, ceased to be a romantic ruin after plans were passed for its restoration in 1996. The eighteenth-century Palladian mansion had the look of incompleteness rather than collapse, with some saying the builders had run out of money, though others insisted it had been the home of Dr Motger. John Murphy gave me the version he tended to believe, which he had heard from an old Portlander in 1977:

*He tells of the rich old lady who decided to have a house built. Her plans extended further than the years left to her and she died before the final building stage. Relatives showed no inclination to continue with her project, and the building was abandoned. Only the garden was used and the giant cellars turned into store rooms. The last owner died just four years ago, leaving no heirs. On day the property will go to the Crown.*

My indelible memory of the Old House was as an informal adventure playground. When I made my inspection I was received at the front door by a young girl – astride a white pony. That was at a time when scotch whisky advertisements told us 'You can take a White Horse anywhere'.

Burgeoning prison numbers, set to break through the 60,000 level, put Portland back into the frame for a solution plucked from history. To a background of controversy about Dickensian hulks, Britain's first prison ship since Victorian times was towed across the Atlantic and berthed in Portland Harbour in March 1997. The slab-sided, five-storey vessel named *Resolution*, was once owned by the Bibby Line, and accommodated 1,100 soldiers in the South Atlantic after the Falklands conflict. In 1989 she was converted into a drug rehabilitation centre for 500 inmates by New York City Department of Corrections.

Abandoned on the Hudson River since 1994, *Resolution* was bought by the Home Office Prison Service in December 1966 for what was designated as a 'floating detention facility'. An unnamed civil servant told Richard Ford of *The Times*: 'This is a last resort for the service.' On being acquired and renovated by the prison service, at a cost of £4 million, *Resolution* was given the less loaded name of Her Majesty's Prison *Weare* (the Portland word for

cliff). The vessel was carried across the Atlantic on the heavy cargo barge *Giant 4* in an operation similar to that which brought Brunel's *Great Britain* back to Bristol.

Though *Weare* was the first and only floating accommodation for convicted British prisoners in the twentieth century, Irish republican detainees and internees were held on HMS *Maidstone*, moored in Belfast Lough in the 1970s, and the Sealink ferry *Earl William* housed immigrant detainees at Harwich in 1987. Conditions on *Weare* were several steps forward from those described by Charles Dickens. The Victorians would have expected a chapel and even a mosque, as well as a library for self-improvement, but might be surprised to find a gymnasium, two swimming pools and four squash courts.

By 1998, some 1,500 individuals in the Portland population of about 5,000 souls were prisoners. 'Local people are saying that the Isle of Portland is becoming the Devil's Island of Britain,' planning committee chairman Jim Churchouse told Sean O'Neill of the *Daily Telegraph*. The Borstal, reformed into a Young Offenders' Institution, also exceeded a 1,000 roll-call and reflected changing times with an ethnic mix that was rooted in the drug, knife and gun culture of inner-city life.

A clump of female wild asparagus was rediscovered growing beside Portland Harbour in 1997. The 70-year-old plant *Asparagus prostratus*, described as 'edible but unpalatably bitter' by Simon de Bruxelles in *The Times*, was in little danger of being eaten alive by humans or anything else, but the lack of such grazing had caused its laid-back fellows to be overwhelmed by the competition, in the form of vigorous vegetation. It became apparent, after much searching, that this was 'Britain's loneliest vegetable', the nearest male specimen being in a colony 175 miles to the west, in Cornwall. Artificial insemination, using introduced pollen, has since been carried out by Tim Rich of the National Museum of Wales, who outlined the dilemma for botanists:

*We used to have six sites in Dorset but over the years they have reduced up to the point where there is just one girl left. Their habitats have been removed by a variety of things. Here in Dorset quarrying has had a damaging effect and a torpedo factory [Whitehead Torpedo Works at Small Mouth] was built on one site. One site in South Wales has been washed into the sea and the plants no longer exist in Anglesey. They are getting rarer.*

Commercial refitting and repair began at Castletown in March 1997 with the arrival of the Airtours cruise ship *Sundream* at the Outer Coaling Pier for an intensive £6 million refit which took six weeks.

Portland Port Ltd became a statutory harbour authority on 1 January 1998. Ship visits during its ownership had increased from 12 vessels in 1996 to

## Events

*Graffiti in the underground railway from cartridge and shell stores at High Angle Battery included this tribute to 'Daisy' from Valentine's Day in 1994.*

*Captain Michael Lobb spent 31 hours defusing this German bomb on Portland in April 1995.*

*A Coastguard helicopter alone on the tarmac after the closure of RNAS Portland, looking across to Mere Tank Farm (far right) in 2001.*

193 in 1998, supporting a total of 500 jobs, as managing director Commander R. Best reported. Some 20 maritime businesses continued to expand in 1999. Portland Bunkers International Ltd includes a major strategic oil store comprising four underground tanks below the lower slopes of the Verne, and utilises 16 above-ground tanks in double rows beside the main road onto the island at Mere Tank Farm.

The other conspicuous presence from 1998 is the 'gleaming white' store of Global Marine Services, forming its United Kingdom base and housing 20 tanks which contain 2,000 miles of submarine fibre-optic cable. This business formerly traded as Cable & Wireless Marine, with depots at Southampton and Middlesbrough, both of which were closed and their activities transferred to Portland. Central to these were the cable ships CS *Sovereign* (covering the North Atlantic) and CS *Monarch* (the North Sea), which were now 'home-ported' at Portland. Other cable-laying vessels also began arriving at Portland for equipping or refitting before setting off all over the globe.

The Defence Evaluation and Research Agency retained its Noise, Electronic Warfare and Degaussing Ranges and the Royal Navy returned in style to Portland in July 1999 in the shape of HMS *Sutherland*. She was the Guard Ship for a royal visit by the Duke of Edinburgh to commemorate the 150th anniversary of the laying of the first stones of the Inner Breakwater by his precursor, Prince Albert. Prince Philip also relaunched and renamed the former Fleet Club at Castletown as Britannia Passenger Terminal. The terminal boasts a propeller from the redundant royal yacht *Britannia*, to reinforce the island's connection with an earlier *Britannia*, a Navy training ship based at Portland in the 1860s. Cruise ships pull into Portland for excursions across Dorset and Wiltshire, from Corfe Castle to Stonehenge and the Cerne Giant to Stourhead. *Funchal* was the first arrival to land passengers, in 1998, and *Explorer* followed in 1999, with 30 'ship calls' then being planned for the millennium.

Supply and support vessels of the Royal Fleet Auxiliary, including RFA *Olwen*, RFA *Argus* and RFA *Sea Crusader* returned to the Outer Coaling Pier at Castletown in 1999. Cosens Engineering manufactured two pollution control vessels, which were dispatched on a heavy lift ship from Q Pier for delivery to a Middle East customer. Manor Marine also expanded its business from traditional dockyard tugs and Royal Marine landing craft to a speciality in servicing and repairing the new breed of fast aluminium Incat-type cross-Channel ferries.

The seabed pens in the shallow sheltered waters around the mouth of The Fleet lagoon at Ferrybridge were established by Abbotsbury Oysters on offshore land of the Ilchester Estates.

Portland stone featured in a national scandal in 2000, when the new inner-court of the British Museum was prepared for its opening by Her Majesty the Queen. Portland stone had been specified – to match the elegant façade and general Georgian surroundings – but when the work was nearly completed someone realised that cheaper Caen stone from Normandy had been substituted for that which supposedly came from Portland. No one had noticed, apparently, so there was embarrassment all round.

It was unfortunate timing, as a renaissance and revival in the working of Portland stone had been achieved by Portland Sculpture Trust. Between its formation in 1983 and soon after the turn of the millennium, some 2,000 children and adults passed through the dusty doors of the former Drill Hall, between Portland Heights Hotel and Easton village, to take up traditional tools. Five, to be precise, Jonathan Phipps said, as he displayed the basic kit issued to wannabe sculptors. To quote him from my notebook, of April 2001, for a feature which appeared in *Purbeck the Country Magazine*:

*The pitcher is for starting to 'rough out'. The punch is for drawing form and shaping. The claw tool makes waves and enhances texture. The chisel is there for fine detail. The boaster comes last and is used for levelling and smoothing surfaces. These five tools are applied with a lump hammer, to begin with, or a dummy hammer for detail.*

The Drill Hall buildings have been leased to the trust by Albion Stone, operators of Independent Quarry at Tophill, where 40 acres of deep workings reach the fine-quality basebed or bedway of Purbeck-Portland strata. This layer, being fine-grained with few shells, is of superlative quality and eminently suitable for carving, both for restoration work on London buildings and in teaching the next generation of sculptors.

In the process, quarry manager Mark Godden coupled practical skills with geological expertise, as he explained the mechanics of production to a fresh intake of schoolchildren. The quarrymen follow deep gullies in a grid of joints, which run approximately from west to east and north to south, allowing the stone to be extracted as naturally large blocks. These, ideally, have minimal fossil content but occasionally there are spectacular discoveries.

One of the largest finds of recent years at Independent Quarry has been a 10-feet diameter tree-trunk of a cycad fern similar to those of the famous Fossil Forest on the cliffs beside Lulworth Cove. It was a remarkable discovery, still with the petrified remains of the actual trunk inside the root-bole, non-eroded and destined to be the pride of a Jurassic collection. Mark Godden pointed out that it dated from the time before the general drift of plate tectonics had brought Britain into cooler climes, when our dinosaurs were living in a position on the planet that had a climate such as is now found in the Middle East.

Another incredibly rare find featured a fusion of broken stalactites and calcite from the base of a former cave. This provided another exhibit for Mark Godden's geology lesson:

*It suffered catastrophic damage which must have happened during the last Ice Age, when freezing and melting caused the stalactites to shear and fall into a heap, where the calcite has cemented them together. I've never seen anything quite like it before.*

Another surface, with ripples and the shape of salt-crystals from a seaside lagoon, captured an extreme weather event in stone. The surface was formed in just one afternoon 150 million years ago, when extreme heat and hyper-saline conditions caused rapid evaporation of moisture from exposed mud. Fossil traces of minute life forms that existed on this salty shore indicate that there was a very high summer rainfall which caused a sudden flash-flood. 'It's a snapshot in time,' the quarry manager told students, as he ran his fingers across a block of stone a couple of feet across and an inch thick. The visible surface was the moment, he explained, but the under-lying stone was its history and pedigree, because it represented gradual accumulated sedimentation from at least three centuries of geological time.

After its time as Pennsylvania Castle Hotel, the clifftop mansion became a private home once more, latterly for multi-millionaire Stephen Curtis (1958–2004), director of the Russian oil firm Menatep. He took over from ousted oligarch Platon Lebedev, who was arrested in 2003 on charges of tax evasion and fraud. Having told an uncle he would be dead 'within two weeks' and that 'it would be no accident', Stephen Curtis was killed a fortnight later with his pilot, Max Radford (34), on 3 March 2004.

Their helicopter, which was based at Bourne-mouth Airport, Hurn, crashed when they were en route back to Portland from the lawyer's Mayfair offices. Pravda quoted witness reports that 'the heli-copter exploded in the air and crashed to the ground'. An accident investigation blamed a naviga-tion error caused by poor weather, but this was disputed by the pilot's father, Dennis Radford (72). He insisted at the inquest before Bournemouth coroner Mr Sheriff Payne, in 2005, that the possibility of sabotage had not been properly probed and that airport security at Hurn was lax. The verdict, however, was one of accidental death.

Pennsylvania Castle also has connections, if only by lending its name, with a mining and oil exploration company on the other side of the Atlantic. Pennsylvania Castle Energy Corporation came into the news over the Christmas holiday in

2005, when 12 men were found dead in a West Virginia coal mine.

By 12 August 2005 only a skeleton staff was left on prison ship *Weare* after the last inmates departed. The chief inspector of prisons, Anne Owers, described it as 'merely an expensive container' which lacked training facilities, and the landlord of the nearby Royal Breakwater Hotel, Robert Smail, expressed relief that loss of revenue would be balanced by not having 'prisoners coming in here after they've been released and getting wasted'. What to do with the empty ship was another matter, as it remains moored towards the eastern corner of the dockyard, though Mark Leech of the *Prisons Handbook* suggested it should be towed out to sea and sunk.

John Newth, visiting Portland Port for a feature in his *Dorset Life* magazine, found the British Antarctic Survey's supply ship *Ernest Shackleton*, en route during our autumn for the brief South Atlantic summer. Following her to beyond the Equator was the RMS *St Helena*, which is the island colony's lifeline. On the other end of the spectrum, in Dorset and Devon waters to explore the Jurassic coast World Heritage Site, was the cruise ship *Hebridean Spirit*.

The huge container ship *Fort St Louis*, carrying the letters 'CMA CGM' in outsized capitals, was being fuelled just inside the East Ship Channel from the tanker *Brabourne*. Another tanker, *Crescent Beaune*, was moored at the new Bunker Berth beside the Inner Breakwater. The cable ship CS *Sovereign* was taking on coils from the Global Marine store beside the Inner Coaling Pier.

Occasional visitors to Queen's Pier at Castletown now include Royal Navy warships and accompa-nying vessels of the Royal Fleet Auxiliary. One such combination in 2005, appropriately, was Type-23 frigate HMS *Portland*, with RFA *Orangeleaf*, plus the sail training ship *Pelican*, of London. Having retrieved the naval link, many locally held their breath as just one vote in July 2005 secured interna-tional laurels for London over Paris. The spin-off is that Portland Port is now preparing to be London-by-the-Sea, having been chosen to host the yachting events of the 2012 Olympic Games.

Oddly, for a place that no longer has a railway and has to be reached through the streets of a conurba-tion, mainline steam locomotives have returned to Portland. They are brought by road, to be stripped and rebuilt in a yard at Tradecroft, off Wide Street behind the Sculpture Park at Tout Quarry. Getting them there and back again involves a tricky negotia-tion of the steep inclines at New Road and Priory Corner. Seeing them on the summit of the island, surrounded by Dorset's biggest expanse of industrial dereliction, shows yet again how the unexpected is normal for Portland.

## Portland Bill

*Pulpit Rock, on the south-west side of Portland Bill, in 1898.*

*Portland Bill, south-west from the boat-haul at Red Crane, to the Trinity House seamark (centre left) and Lighthouse (centre right) in 1974.*

# Portland Bill

*Fishermen's huts and the coast path on the eastern edge of the Bill.*

## Portland Bill

*Sunset from Portland Bill, across Lyme Bay, photographed by Frederick G. Masters.*

# Subscribers

Mr and Mrs M.D. Adams, Weston, Portland, Dorset
Mr Bob Alexander, Weymouth
Brian and Marlene Allebone, Weare Close, Portland
Tracy Allen, Portland
Mr Hugh Arnold, Portland
Stan and Brenda Bates, Sheffield
Mr Jack Batty, Portland
Patricia L. Benson, Portland
Mr Christian Bird, Dicky, The Duke
Charlie T. Bower, Portland
Alan Brewer, Portland
Mr Geoffrey Charles Browne, Dorchester
Steven (Squeaker) Browne, Portland
Wendy M. Buckingham (née Saunders), Portland
Mervyn E. Burden, Portland
Mrs C. Burge (née Ansell), 100 years old November 2006, families originated Portland 1900
Chris Burke
Margaret C. Burt, Portland
Poppy Butcher, Weymouth, Dorset
Mr Allan T. Carey, Portland
Barry Carr
R. and S.M. Chapman, Portland
Andrew Chick, Portland
William F. Chick, North Finchley, London
Tim, Denise, Kim and Ryan Clark, Portland
Mr Frank Clarkson
Jenny Cockerill/Day, Portland
Pauline Colebrooke, Portland
Brian M.J. Cook, Portland
Darren L. Cook, Bristol
Matthew C. Cook, London
Dave and Jen Cooper, Portland
Gerry Copeland, Portland
Ron Craddock, Portland
Mr Andrew Peter Craft, Portland
Mr Peter Craft, Easton
Paul Dagg, Portland
Joanne Day, Portland
Wayne Day, Portland
Jim Dolbear, Portland
Dorset Library Service
Julie Dyson (née Thorne), Portland
Justin Elliott, Portland
Simon A. Elliott, Royal Air Force
Graham Flann, Weymouth
Mr Carl Flew, Southwell, Portland
Mr Stephen and Mrs Michelle Teague Forder, Portland
Ian Fuller, Grove Point, Portland
Tony and Jayne Gamble, Hucknall

Megan Geater (née Stone), Portland
Melvin Gillham, Portland
Yolande E. Gillham, Portland
Gleave, Portland
Simon and Sue Gledhill, Portland
Lindsay Graham Glenn, Portland
Mark Godden, Portland
M. Gooch, History Department. Royal Manor Arts College, Portland
Marilyn Goodall, New Zealand
Adam Gould, Portland
Alexander Gould, Portland
Curtis Gould, Portland
June Green, Portland
Benjamin John Griffiths, Portland
Bernard L. Grout
Monica Harle (née Warland)
Edward G. Harrington, formerly from Portland
Gordon B. Harrington, formerly from Portland
David Harris, Sweethill Lane, Portland
Janet Harris, formerly from Portland
June Hayhurst, formerly from Portland
Fritz and Joyce Heritier, Portland
Kenneth John Hinde, Portland
The Hollinshead Family, Wakeham, Portland
Major Leslie C. Hooper, Portland
Mr Robert Horgan, Portland
S. John Hoskins
Sheila Jean Hudgell
Jean M. Hull (née Cutting)
Rosmarie J. Husain, Portland
Linda Hutton (née Felmingham), Portland
Ronald Jarvis, Portland
Brian Kendall, Wotton-Under-Edge
M.A. Kilfoyle, Portland
Michael R. Lane, Portland
Brian and Moira Lee
Trevor and Jean Lee, Freshwater, Isle of Wight
Margaret Legg, Portland
Brian and Elizabeth Leonard, Portland
David J. Lewis, Portland
Henry Ley, Portland
Derek Llewellyn, New Zealand
Carole and Arthur MacKenzie
Barsby Mark
Michael J. May, Portland
Doreen McGann, Portland
Irene and Ray Meddick, Portland
Sally L., Mark, Connor J., and Lillie A. Merson, Portland
Bob Milverton, Portland

Michael G. Mincham, Portland
Maureen Mintern
Michael J. Monks
Mr Charles William Moore, Portland
Hazel Morris, London, Ontario
Mr Barry Mullins, Portland
Thomas Mustard
Peter and Frances Osborne, Sweethill Road, Southwell
Stewart Osborne and Carol Taylor, Cheyne Court,
  Weston Street
Brian H. Otter, Portland
John Otter, Poole
Michael Otter, Shepton Mallet
David J. Owen, Portland
Mr Brian Palmer, Portland
Caroline M. Partridge, Portland
John Patrick, Portland
Ken Pearce
Martin and Lorraine Pering, Portland
Ian J. Phelps
Gail, Lewis, and Bridie Pickering, Portland
John W.G. Powell, Portland
Warwick Powell, Poole
Charles E. Richards, Portland
Colin Richards, Portland
Mrs Hazel R. Roberts, Ashley Heath
Philippa Roberts, New Zealand
Mr R.J. and Mrs G. Roy, Portland
Lorraine D. Sainsbury, Portland
A. Samways, Portland
B. Samways, Newark, Nottingham
T. Sharpe and Family, Portland
Nigel A. Shaw, Portland
S. and D. Shearn
A.B. Shergold
Dan and Maureen Sherren, Portland
Brian C. Shorey, Portland
Marie Sinclair
Mr Graham Michael Smith
Graham John Smith, Teddington
Lyndsay Anne Squires
Adrian and Dawn Stanford, Portland
Mr Brian J. Stewkesbury, Portland
Anthony Lee Stickland, Portland
Martin Stone, Portland

Michael J. Stone, Portland
Rab Stone, Portland
Roger George Stone
Vilma Stone (née Felmingham), former Portlander.
  Graigwen, Pontypridd, Mid Glamorgan
Kaye and Trevor Stratton, Portland
Mr Andrew J. Straw, Portland
Mrs M. Tait, Portland
Alec V. Taylor, Symington, Scotland
Eric W. Taylor, Helensburgh, Scotland
David and Marian Thomas, Portland
Helen Thomas (former Portlander), Pontypridd,
  Mid Glamorgan
Mr Philip J. Thompson, Weymouth
Irene M. Thorne, Portland
Robert Tocher and Karen Landregan, Portland
Daren R. Tubbs, Burgess Hill, West Sussex
Steven P. Tubbs, Portland
John F.W. Walling, Newton Abbot, Devon
Mr Frederick John Wallis, Portland
Mr Michael J. Walsh
Reg Ward, Cove Cottages, Portland
Steve Ward, Portland
Andy G. Warner, Swindon
Chris C. Warner, Oxted
Grace L. Warner, Portland
Sylvia Way, Portland
Iris M. White, Portland
Margaret White, Portland
Mary White, Portland
Pam and John White, Birmingham
Mr Kenneth R. Whittle, Portland
K. Whittock, History Department. Royal Manor Arts
  College, Portland
Wayne Wilcocks, Portland
Mr David A. Williams, Portland
George Wills, Portland
Andrew Wills, Portland
Robert Edward Wills, Portland
Mr Paul Wilson, Portland
Winifred M. Wood, Fortuneswell, Portland
Mr T.C. Woodhouse, Portland
Michael Wright
YHA Portland
David J. Youngman, Portland

*There are now over 160 titles in the Community History Series. For a full listing of these and other Halsgrove publications, please visit www.halsgrove.com or telephone 01884 243 242*